Goals-Based Portfolio Theory

Franklin J. Parker, CFA

WILEY

Published by John Wiley & Sons, Inc., Hoboken, New Jersey.

Published simultaneously in Canada.

Library of Congress Cataloging-in-Publication Data:

Names: Parker, Franklin J., author.
Title: Goals-based portfolio theory / Franklin J. Parker, CFA.
Description: Hoboken, New Jersey : Wiley, [2023] | Includes bibliographical references and index.
Identifiers: LCCN 2022017468 (print) | LCCN 2022017469 (ebook) | ISBN 9781119906100 (cloth) | ISBN 9781119906117 (adobe pdf) | ISBN 9781119906124 (epub)
Subjects: LCSH: Portfolio management.
Classification: LCC HG4529.5 .P365 2023 (print) | LCC HG4529.5 (ebook) | DDC 332.6–dc23/eng/20220803
LC record available at https://lccn.loc.gov/2022017468
LC ebook record available at https://lccn.loc.gov/2022017469

Cover Design: Wiley
Cover Image: © NDogan/Shutterstock

SKY10036853_101722

To my clients, especially the early ones,
who trusted me to figure it out.
And to the ones I love,
who often pay the price for my intellectual obsessions.

Contents

Foreword

by Jean LP Brunel, CFA

"The Private Bank is a distribution channel!" How many times have professionals who attempted to serve the specific needs of individuals heard that comment, way back when? Wait, was it really so long ago? The evolution in the nature of private wealth and of asset management (in the US in particular) inevitably led to the epiphany: Individuals are different, and they need different services.

Yet, if one goes sufficiently far back, private wealth was often inherited and structured around various trusts. That wealth had been accustomed to receiving services that were not necessarily quite different from those provided to institutions, except for the associated fiduciary services trusts required. After all, while the amounts may have been less substantial (although that was surely not always the case), it was felt that family trusts were very much like pension funds: long-term horizon and in need of the higher returns associated with a substantial exposure to equities. Further, trust beneficiaries had been used to seeing equity market fluctuations and had seen that down legs were followed by up legs. The final element had to do with delegation: trust beneficiaries had no difficulty delegating the management duties; in reality, they were not even delegating them, as those duties belonged to trustees. Beneficiaries expected to be briefed on portfolio performance but had very limited, if any, expectations of being able to influence portfolio decisions.

Eventually, the long bull market that started in 1982 and the wave of mergers and acquisitions that began in 1981 brought an important change to private wealth. "New" wealth appeared: the "old inherited wealth" that had dominated was increasingly joined by "new wealth," which had been more recently made or at least monetized.

"New wealth" had a different perspective of financial markets. The financial sophistication of individuals related to running companies, in other words, managing an income statement subject to balance sheet constraints; not of managing a balance sheet subject to income constraints. Their experience with financial markets frequently was limited. They did not always distinguish between a company and a stock, failing to appreciate the crucial issue of whether they were price makers or price takers. Finally, generational and potentially philanthropic structures that would work for them and their families had to be built: there were choices to be made and priorities to be assessed. There was the total novelty of how to bring the next generation into the wealth: "From shirtsleeves to shirtsleeves in three generations" ring a bell to anyone? They needed a variety of advisors, no longer relying on the formerly ubiquitous private banker, investment manager, and trust and estate lawyer.

It may have taken a while, but a response from the wealth management industry was bound to come. And it did, based on the work of people like Daniel Kahneman, Richard Thaler, Terrence Odean, Hersh Shefrin, and Meir Statman, to name but a few. These introduced the notion that individuals come with a number of biases and preferences that cannot be ignored. They provided the basis on which one could build. The classical belief that an investment policy must be the basis for the management of assets morphed into the appreciation that the sustainability of the policy is critical: The investor's worst enemy is the "changing horses in the middle of the race" syndrome. Behavioral finance effectively indirectly promoted the idea that policy sustainability would be greatly helped if one could create a link between "my wealth" and "my goals." It led to the recognition that I do not have a single risk profile; I may well have a risk profile for each goal, noting that each goal may also have its own time horizon.

Early in the 2000s, a few individuals independently came to the view that identifying individual goals and specifying the portion of the wealth that should be dedicated to each was important.[1] The approach was originally named "goals-based wealth management." Unfortunately, the "s" of "goals"

---

[1]Jean L. P. Brunel, "How Sub-Optimal—If at All—Is Goal-Based Allocation?" *The Journal of Wealth Management* (Fall 2006): 19–34; Jean L. P. Brunel, "Revisiting the Asset Allocation Challenge through a Behavioral Finance Lens," *The Journal of Wealth Management* (Fall 2003): 10–20; Ashvin B. Chhabra, "Beyond Markowitz: A Comprehensive Wealth Allocation Framework for Individuals," *The Journal of Wealth Management* (Spring 2005): 8–34; Ashvin B. Chhabra, "Clarifications on 'Beyond Markowitz,'" The *Journal of Wealth Management* (Summer 2007): 54–59; Dan Nevins, "Goal-Based Investing: Integrating Traditional and Behavioral Finance," *The Journal of Wealth Management* (Spring 2004): 8–23; Michael M. Pompian and John B. Longo, "A New Paradigm for Practical Application of Behavioral Finance," *The Journal of Wealth Management* (Fall 2004): 9–15.

was briefly dropped, leading to the quip: "Is not goal-based wealth management very much like oxygen-based breathing"?

Four pioneers continued in their efforts and managed to convert a few people, but it took the seminal papers by Sanjiv Das, Harry Markowitz, Jonathan Scheid, and Meir Statman to truly open the path to the new discipline taking hold.[2] In fact, prior to the publication of these two papers, the published literature made an uneven use of "fancy mathematics" rather focusing their rationale on behavioral concepts. Their first paper, though, broke that mold using sophisticated mathematics to demonstrate with elegance that the so-called "bucket approach" was virtually equivalent to the classical efficient frontier process, provided one made a couple of minor changes: the main change was the redefinition of risk away from the volatility of returns to the required probability of success in achieving a goal.

This book follows on the most recent tradition offering quite a bit of quantitatively driven analysis and demonstration. In many ways, it is a welcome return to the basics of the challenge: How do we help individuals achieve their goals in a way such that they will minimize the risk of "changing horses in the middle of the race"? At the same time, Franklin substantially broadens the analysis relative to what predecessors did. In that, the book is a must read, a must have. Rather than simply focusing on the question of formulating an investment policy, its purpose is to craft an entire theory around the concept of goals-based wealth management. Thus, the author moves from the fundamental framework of strategic asset allocation to a review of all the kinds of decisions that individuals should make as they embark on the journey and remain on it.

Time allocation, portfolio rebalancing, tax efficiency, thematic investing, and goals-based reporting are but a few of the issues the book tackles with brio. The crucial point, to this reader, is that there is no discontinuity or incongruity between adopting a sharp focus on goals and staying "pure" in relation to most traditional finance concepts. In fact, Chapter 13 gets to that point, presenting goals-based portfolio theory as a bridge between traditional and behavioral finance, the former being normative while the latter is descriptive.

[2]D. Sanjiv, H. Markowitz, J. Scheid, and M. Statman, "Portfolio Optimization with Mental Accounts," *The Journal of Financial and Quantitative Analysis* 45, no. 2 (April 2010): 311–334; D. Sanjiv, H. Markowitz, J. Scheid, and M. Statman, "Portfolios for Investors Who Want to Reach Their Goals While Staying on the Mean-Variance Efficient Frontier," *The Journal of Wealth Management* (Fall 2011): 25–31.

Does this mean that we have reached the end of the road? The answer, in my opinion, is not a "simple no" but an "emphatic no." Goals-based wealth management opened the conceptual way to accept the reality that individuals can have multiple, and at times even superficially contradictory, goals. It proceeded naturally from the realization that wealth management was about a lot more than asset management. It all started with the notion that there were four stakeholders in "my wealth" and that individuals or advisors were particularly interested in three of them getting as much as they could while the fourth should be getting as little as possible. These four stakeholders were basic needs: the individual's personal needs, his or her family's and potential future dynasty's needs, his or her philanthropic needs or, eventually, those of his or her heirs and the needs to pay to the government taxes on income and transactions carried out in the taxable portions of the overall portfolio.

There is still quite a lot of potential work for those who want to extend Franklin Parker's portfolio theory to include the multiple asset location issues that can crop up. An example of such a strategy, which was timely at one point and may no longer be, were charitable lead trusts in a very-low-interest rate environment. They could facilitate efficient inter-generational transfers and accomplish charitable purposes as well. Their combined goals raised interesting investment and fiduciary issues, particularly as the assets had not terminally exited the family's ownership; only the part that went to charity had.

There are many other examples that one could point to, though the newest category seems to me to relate to the role of insurance products. Historically, investors have tended to eschew insurance, or at least eschew it as a part of a truly holistic wealth strategy. A common concern was that insurance comes with a cost. Some of that cost appeared to make sense, another part appeared too expensive, and individuals elected to self-insure. Yet, a broader evaluation of the issue may help see an intriguing analogy to the thought processes that at one point led advisors away from considering a single overall portfolio solution. Insurance companies must be paid for the risk they take; on the one hand, however, from their points of view, that risk is diversified across a large number of insured clients. On the other hand, from the point of view of each client, the outcome is often purely binary: I die, or I do not die; I live out my life expectancy or I do not, and many variants on the theme. Thus, the cost of purchasing the insurance (which should be determined here from the point of view of the solitary insured) is and should be dramatically different from the cost of selling insurance (which should be determined from the point of view of covering a diversified pool of insured). Is there not a potential arbitrage there?

Historically, insurance had been perceived primarily as a tool to manage potential future estate taxes. It was always seen as relevant in that context, although the increase in the taxation threshold had made the solution appealing only to a very small minority. Now, consider the goal of preserving the ability to live out my life without changing lifestyle as a goal. Any solution that rejects any form of annuity is effectively based on the assumption that I am taking on my own longevity risk. Indeed, what happens if I exceed the life expectancy I had assumed? Combine this with a potentially cyclically nasty investment environment within some years of the life expectancy assumption, and the situation could become quite stressful. Franklin's book lays down a few markers on this issue and, doing this, I believe it is the first to take the issue into consideration.

I am delighted to have had the opportunity to write this Foreword, as I feel quite confident that Franklin will be among those who take the idea to which I modestly contributed and carry it much further forward. I would not be surprised if another book by Franklin were to surface in 5 or 10 years with further expansion of this theory. The need to serve individuals is not going away. A couple of future directions might help plant one or two seeds. What about the visible differentiation that exists between "domestic money" (assets that are managed on behalf of an individual who resides in a country and trusts that country's government to "do the right thing") and "global money" (assets that are managed on behalf of individuals who want to keep some nest egg outside of their home country in order to ensure, in the words of a Filipino friend of mine 40 years ago, "that I or my children will never have to wash lavatories in San Francisco")? Experience suggests that these two types of investors have radically different views of the risk of equities and of the risk of foreign currencies. What about the needs of families who incorporate an increasingly multinational, multicultural, multireligious population? The various discrepancies in the tax regimes—and in the tax principles—of several of the main countries today is enough to drive anyone to argue: "Don't worry." But is that really the answer?

I certainly hope that you will enjoy the book as much as I did. It sets a new standard for our industry, one on which I hope Franklin and others will continue to build.

Preface

Goals-Based Investors and the Need for Better Theory

We all have goals. Sometimes those goals are financial.

Of course, many of our goals have little or nothing at all to do with finances, like respect from peers, raising children, being good people, or having a sense of purpose and accomplishment. Often, those goals are more important to us than our financial goals. They certainly occupy a larger percentage of our psychological capacity, day-to-day. Sometimes, we have goals we would like to achieve at some future date that could actually be accomplished using resources laid aside today. For those goals, some interaction with the ecosystem of financial institutions, markets, regulations, taxes, and people is warranted. When real people with real goals interact with this financial ecosystem, it is important that they have a reasonably effective map lest they find themselves wandering through the jungle that finance can so often be. This book is about using that ecosystem to accomplish financial goals—it is a better map (hopefully!).

But, to really understand how and why goals-based investing is different, we must first understand goals-based *investors*—that is, those real people who have real things they want to achieve in their very real lives. People do not enter this jungle for the fun of it, at least not usually. People enter this jungle hoping to come out the other side better off—to improve their lives and secure their future.

And it is here that traditional financial and economic theory has failed to provide even a reasonable map. I recently peer-reviewed a scholarly paper whose lead author was an academic I greatly respect. The paper claimed to be operating in a goals-based paradigm; that is to say, it was analyzing techniques that could be potentially used by goals-based investors. Yet, despite the claim, the paper carried the very common academic assumption that an investor could use *unlimited* and *costless* short-selling and leverage in an investment portfolio! I know of no real person who can borrow money in a portfolio and sell securities short without cost or limit. What an absurd assumption! Still, this assumption persists as the default for academics—largely because one must operate under the preferred paradigm of peer-reviewers, though it also simplifies the math considerably. Yet, this kind of silliness also generates a map for investors that is so inaccurate as to be entirely useless to real people interacting with real-world markets.

Building a proper map means we must first understand the people who are to use the map.

So, who are goals-based investors? A goals-based investor is, broadly speaking, any person or institution who has (a) specific funding requirements within (b) specified periods of time, and (c) some amount of wealth to dedicate to those objectives. Goals-based investors are your co-workers, your parents, aunts and uncles, friends, and your church. *You* are a goals-based investor.

Goals-based portfolio theory, then, is concerned with how to build an investment portfolio that delivers the maximum probability of attaining these real goals, given those inputs. If markets behaved as well as they do in theory (that is, if market returns were Gaussian), then most of those constraints would not matter. However, we know that markets are not so well-behaved, so these constraints *do* matter—and matter quite a bit! This fact was realized decades ago, and even Paul Samuelson (the first recipient of the Nobel Prize in Economics) acknowledged that higher moments of return distributions (skew and kurtosis) matter to investors.[1] Mistimed drawdowns, as we all know intuitively, can destroy our ability to accomplish our objectives.

There are other important considerations. I know of no one who can leverage a portfolio without cost and without bound. Similarly, short-selling is always limited in the real world—and not just by cost, but also by account type, regulation, and good, old-fashioned prudence. In contrast with traditional theory, goals-based investors are typically assumed to have no ability (or at least *almost* no ability) to short-sell and leverage a portfolio. Additionally, since markets are not well behaved and a mistimed market drawdown can completely wreck a financial plan, goals-based investors tend to be much more accepting of heuristics that can help protect a portfolio from the destruction that markets can bring upon the unsuspecting investor. And, as we shall see, this is not because investors do not like losses in the abstract; it is because goals-based investors intuitively understand that portfolio losses

---

[1] P. Samuelson, "The Fundamental Approximation Theorem of Portfolio Analysis in Term of Means, Variances, and Higher Moments," *Review of Economic Studies* 37 (1970): 537–542.

lower their probability of goal achievement. Losses generate less wealth and less time to regain those losses, and markets can only provide so much upside in a subsequent recovery.

Jean Brunel, the father of goals-based investing, enumerated another important distinction that is relevant here. When interacting with markets—whether public or private—very, very few individuals or institutions can be said to be price-setters; we must generally be content to be price-takers. And that distinction is important: price-setters have the luxury of conforming markets to their own need, to meet their own objectives. The rest of us, by contrast, must be content to take prices, to approach markets *as they are* and not as we wish they would be. This distinction is important, but is also not immediately obvious.

Another challenge for goals-based investors resides in the attitudes of those who fashion the tools and solutions. While our models of the world are very important, they also carry a danger. Much of academic theory, and even many practitioners, view markets as the equation on the page: *x* goes into the equation and *y* reliably comes out. But the real world is very messy, and we must account for that messiness, somehow. Goals-based practitioners, then, must view the equation as only an approximation of markets: *x* goes into the equation and maybe *y* comes out, but *z*, *m*, and *q* might happen, too, so we should be prepared! Markets are not the equation, and they certainly are not reliable in any real sense of the word. We, as goals-based investors and practitioners, must approach markets with a healthy respect. They can do much good, but they can also do much damage.

To put it as simply as possible: goals-based portfolio theory is about using financial markets to achieve human goals, *given real-world constraints. Markets as they actually are* is a real-world constraint. As we will see, goals-based investing is, in practice, not so simple. Unfortunately, real people and real-world constraints make the portfolio management problem more complex, not less, and we have to leave behind many of the tools with which we are comfortable. But, were *I* lost in the jungle, I would much prefer a map maker who erred on the side of too much detail, rather than too little.

A full understanding of goals-based investing begins with an understanding of the goals-based investor. More than any other point made in this book, I want to stress this one: *every investor is different.* If you, practitioner, are to do your job correctly, you absolutely must begin with a thorough understanding of your investor. We cannot treat each investor like all the rest. Each investor has her own panoply of goals, her own tax situation, her own career, her own levels of wealth. Each investor has her own moral constraints.

Traditionally, our business has focused on the investment aspect of our role, to the exclusion of pretty much all else. I recall how I was trained on financial planning early in my career. Rather than central to the process, financial plans were viewed as a sales tool. "Whoever owns the plan owns the client," "Use the planning process to uncover more assets," and "Plan for what they need, but close with what they want," were all common phrases. Talk about cynicism!

To be fair, this is how the business of wealth management saw the value they added: investing financial assets, not building and executing holistic financial plans. How could it be any different? In the end, the final investment decision was made by giving clients a risk-tolerance questionnaire, and the portfolio managed by some far-off investment committee. Risk tolerance is the only human input into the traditional portfolio optimization equation, anyway, and we cannot forget that it is a metric that regulators obsess over. Financial planning, though intuitively obvious, was superfluous in practice because the theory upon which portfolio theory was based made it superfluous.

This mistake in theory has been the foundation upon which wealth management was built. Wealth management firms tend to focus on the "big world," the world of markets and interest rates, politics, corporate cashflows, GPD growth, and so on. Firms, then, must differentiate themselves with different views of markets. Where some focus on value investing, others focus on a macro approach, others tend toward growth investing, and still others have an algorithm that was hewn in the fires of Mt. Quant by elves, each bearing the magic imparted by five PhDs.

Of course, this approach is woefully insufficient. Clients do not *really* care about differences in market views; they care about achieving their goals. Not to mention, clients are almost certainly unqualified to assess those differences, anyway (I am not sure that *I* am qualified). The business of wealth management, if it is to survive, must be about helping clients actually achieve their goals. Despite my apparent cynicism, I do believe that markets views are very important (like all of you, I have my own cherished view). Better market views do yield better outcomes. I simply want to stress that market views are not the beginning and end of what we do. Rather, goals-based investing sits at the intersection of the "big world"—the world of markets, interest rates, politics, earnings, P/E ratios, etc.—and *your* world—the world of your goals, your career, kids, taxes, moral constraints, and so on (as Figure I.1 illustrates). We cannot, *should not*, do our jobs without a proper understanding of *both*.

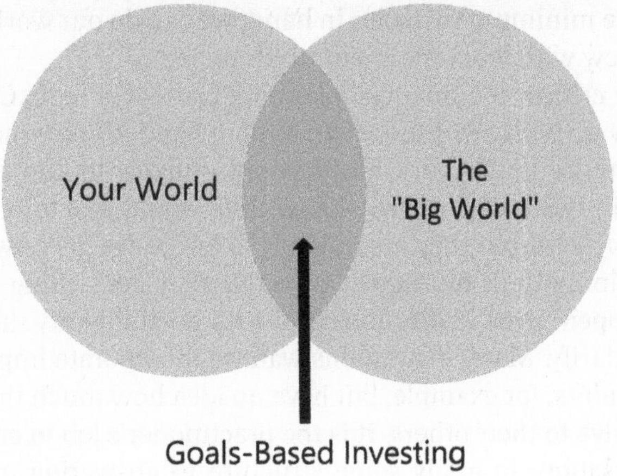

FIGURE I.1 Goals-Based Investing

This means, of course, we must have a framework for interacting and talking with clients about what makes them tick. More knowledge is better. Much of the value a good practitioner can add is from a deep connection and knowledge of her client's life. For example, I worked with a couple for many years before it came out that they were deeply concerned that their second child was a spendthrift. We wound up discussing how they might bequeath their assets such that their child could enjoy it, but not squander it. Had I not enjoyed the rapport and familiarity with them that I did, this concern might never have been addressed and the problem would have been left unsolved.

While more knowledge is better, we cannot be expected to only do business with our closest friends. At a minimum, then, we must understand:

- Financial goals, which are defined as
  - Future funding requirements
  - Time horizons
  - Their relative importance
  - Current wealth
- Our client's tax situation
- Any ethical constraints or mandates
- Our client's human capital
- Asset location (and potential restrictions thereto)
- Any other relevant constraints on the investment process

With these minimum variables in hand, we can do our work: interfacing our market view with what the client needs done.[2]

Note how critical the financial planning process is here. Clients do not typically show up with all of these variables in hand. Clients may well know they want to retire in 23 years, but they are unlikely to know exactly how much they will need. Clients may know they would like to buy a vacation home in seven years, but they are unlikely to know exactly how much probability of attaining their retirement objective they are willing to give up to make that happen. Even institutions deal with an ambiguity that practitioners can help clarify. Many institutions want to incorporate impact investing or ESG constraints, for example, but have no idea how much they value that objective relative to their others. It is the practitioner's job to engage her client in conversation, to apply some structure to answering questions like "How much do I need to retire?" or "How much return are you willing to give up to incorporate an ESG constraint?" In goals-based portfolio theory, financial planning is not a sales tool; it is foundational to the whole of portfolio management!

A full treatment of the financial planning process is beyond the scope of this book. There are numerous resources available to practitioners—many of them considerably better than I could ever hope to write. Thus, I will not dive any deeper into that topic here. However, I do hope it is clear that financial planning is the first step, and all else flows from first understanding our client. In subsequent chapters we will see just how important this step is. Unlike traditional portfolio theory, goals-based portfolio theory is chock full of human inputs. The better we understand those inputs, the better our solutions can be.

If it is not clear by now, let me be very explicit: This is not a book about market philosophy. This is not a book about how to outperform the S&P 500, how to build the next algorithm, or how to pick triple-bagger stocks. In fact, I have actively tried to avoid talking about my personal philosophy of markets. For one, I do not feel particularly qualified to do so—I have read plenty of books by practitioners who do it considerably better than I could (though I do have my own philosophy of markets, of course). More importantly, I want to stress that *any* philosophy of markets can fit within a goals-based framework. Convertible arbitrage, long/short options strategies, value investing, or buy-and-hold investing can all fit within the goals-based framework.

[2]And none of this to minimize the importance of estate planning, tax planning, business planning, and the various other responsibilities advisors will tend to take on!

This book is about organizing *your* market philosophy into a goals-based framework.

My motivation to write this book is twofold. First, I find it immensely rewarding to help individuals accomplish their financial goals. I have yet to meet someone who has a crass "I just want to get rich" attitude. The folks I have had the joy of serving have had real things they want to achieve in their lives, like sending their children to college, or funding philanthropic endeavors, or operating and growing a business. Those goals prompt them to save and invest. To be a guide through the jungle of finance, and helping those folks out the other side, is wonderfully meaningful to me. After more than a decade and a half searching, I deeply believe that goals-based portfolio theory is the best map through this jungle. It is the framework practitioners should be using in almost any circumstance.

Second—and this may be the most exciting aspect of goals-based portfolio theory—is the world these tools have the potential to build. Yes, goals-based portfolio theory generates portfolios that achieve financial goals more often than modern portfolio theory (or other tools in the literature). But it is also a tool to better understand people—a tool to better understand what it is they want, what they are willing to trade off to get it, and then to bring those desires to reality. As the industry begins to build and deliver the tools individuals need to fully express themselves in financial markets, then financial markets will better represent our society as a whole. Markets, in a world where people can express themselves through their investments more effectively, become considerably more *human*. This could be capitalism's greatest moment. This could be a time when we can look at financial markets, not as separate and distinct from our society, governed by rules and ethics of their own, but as a genuine mirror to our society. We may not always like what we see in the mirror, but we might finally agree that financial markets are an accurate reflection, nonetheless. This can only happen, however, if we as an industry do the necessary work to bring it about. What's more, I also believe it is how we continue to earn our fees. Capitalism works when value is exchanged for value. So much of our industry has become rent seeking, offering no real value other than clever marketing gimmicks. It is high time we start delivering real value.

This book is written to the searcher, to the sophisticated practitioner who is genuinely looking for the best way to serve her clients. There is plenty here for an academic, as well, but it is not my purpose to create an abstract document that is debated in the academy with no application to the real world. That said, I did allow myself one chapter to wax philosophical. For readers uninterested in how goals-based utility theory affects the broader conversation around behavioral and normative economics, Chapter 13 can be skipped with no real loss of narrative (I am clear about that point in the introduction to the chapter). I do not want to downplay my excitement about that potential bridge between the two branches of economics, but I also recognize that it is not readily applicable nor interesting to many practitioners. For those who so choose to go down that rabbit hole with me, I am delighted with your interest!

Other than that chapter, I would recommend reading the book from beginning to end. Each chapter builds on the previous. Since I find it easier to understand a concept if I understand its history, the narrative of its origin, I open with the story of the ideas that coalesced into goals-based portfolio theory. From there, I build out the foundation of the theory, and spend some time comparing it to the standard approach of modern portfolio theory. As we shall see, they are quite similar in some regards, but starkly different in others. Because the theoretical model carries some unique challenges in its implementation, we will explore some computational and practical solutions to these problems (though I do not claim they are the *best* solutions; they are simply my best effort).

The next few chapters build out the other points of goals-based investing, namely the "real-world constraints" part. I start by detailing a method for allocating wealth across multiple periods. While this seems superfluous, it is a common approach in the industry: A portfolio manager often has a multiperiod view, but most optimizers only span the coming period. Having a goals-native, multiperiod optimizer can add considerable value (assuming our capital market assumptions are reasonably accurate, of course). From there I explore how goals-based investors should view capital markets, generally, and I extend that discussion to how we might think of portfolio risk control, especially hedging. I find that investors should be willing to pay different costs to hedge a portfolio, and those costs are a function of an investor's goal variables. Derivative pricing is as dependent on the individual and her goal as it is on the portfolio manager's view of markets.

On a preliminary basis, I analyze how practitioners might view insurance through a goals-based lens. There is no shortage of clever insurance marketing schemes, and there is a critical shortage of research on the role of insurance in goals-based portfolios. It is clear, however, that insurance has a role in such portfolios—it is beneficial to goals-based investors to spend resources to offset various kinds of risks—and I hope this chapter offers both an approach for approaching the problem as well as a signpost for directing future research.

Building on the concepts of allocating wealth across goals, I next explore how goals-based portfolio theory informs impact investing. Impact, ethical, and ESG investing is very personal—each investor has a different view of what they want to do, the restraints they want to incorporate, and the impact they wish to leave. Thus, it is an excellent foil to demonstrate how the goals-based framework might be applied when goals compete for a limited pool of resources.

I take up taxes and rebalancing next. To me, taxes and rebalancing sounds like a boring chapter. Unfortunately, it is where the rubber meets the road. Taxes, like everything else in goals-based investing, is individualized, and, as we shall see, so is rebalancing. In that vein, we will also spend some time discussing the current state of client reporting and how the goals-based framework might inform the presentation and ongoing monitoring of investment portfolios. I also explore how portfolio managers might better align their performance metrics with the goals-based framework. As a first pass, I present two potential metrics that could better represent the value-add of a portfolio manager to a client than our existing stable of portfolio measurement metrics. I then present a fragility analysis of goals-based inputs. No matter how meticulous our forecasting efforts, we know that we are wrong to some degree. What amount of wrongness for which variables should keep us up at night? Given our limited man-hours, where should we spend the majority of our time and skill?

No goals-based discussion would be complete without a discussion of the human risks involved in private wealth management. While other authors have focused ad nauseum on cognitive biases as a source of risk, the purpose of my chapter on the subject is to identify the major nonfinancial risks present for the very wealthy. Those risks tend to be much more difficult to identify and are only tangentially related to the wide range of behavioral biases documented in the literature. Indeed, in my experience, managing financial risk is the easy part. Managing the human risks is considerably harder. Sadly, human risks are also the greatest threat to long-term wealth building and maintenance.

The final three chapters are experimental, and certainly more academic. An interesting outcome of goals-based portfolio theory is that it is, at times, perfectly rational to gamble. We don't call it *gambling*, of course—that would be too crude. In economic parlance, we would say that it is rational for individuals to be variance-affine or variance-seeking, as opposed to being always and everywhere variance-averse (I don't say "risk averse" because goals-based portfolio theory does not define risk as variance). This leaves practitioners with the question: How do we prudently manage a portfolio that is designed to *maximize* volatility, rather than minimize it? I do not claim any final answers here, hence the experimental nature of the chapter. Nonetheless, the conversation needs to be opened for practitioners, researchers, and even regulators, and my hope is that smarter people than me will take up the torch.

We then proceed to the more theoretical chapter, probably most interesting to academics. This is a project that excites me greatly. It is my belief that goals-based portfolio theory, by better modeling what it is individuals are actually trying to do in the world, might provide a bridge between normative economics (what we think of as traditional, rational economics) and behavioral economics. This chapter is my attempt at putting this particular stake in the ground. Again, I claim no final answers, only interesting preliminary outcomes of the theory. I am along for the ride, wherever those discussions go in the future.

To round out the meat of our discussion, I spend some time ruminating on what the future of wealth management and investment management might look like, especially if goals-based investing is more widely adopted. I find that the term *goals-based investing* has become quite popular, but it appears to be little more than marketing for many firms. Here is my take on how firms might implement the ideas at scale, and, by delivering more value to their clients, earn more revenue in the coming decades. I close with some thoughts, a recap of everything discussed, and some resources interested readers might visit for a deeper dive into the various subjects.

Finally, I would like to have a personal word with my fellow practitioners. I admit to carrying a certain amount of imposter syndrome writing a book such as this. After growing up in a small town in central Texas, I pursued an undergraduate degree in music. Other than my CFA charter, I have no formal training in finance or economics whatsoever—I am a country boy with a music degree. The year 2008 was intellectually formative for me, occurring within the first year of my entrée into wealth management, and I have spent the subsequent years testing the common advice that I parroted. This intellectual quest ultimately led me here, to goals-based portfolio theory, a practitioner-oriented theory that cuts out much of the mumbo-jumbo of academia and focuses on results. Needless to say, I felt that I had found my people. That said, it is entirely possible that I have "outkicked my coverage" and have gotten some (if not all) of this wrong. If that is so, I beg your forgiveness and humbly request that you publish some rebuttals—I do not want to hold nor advocate for incorrect views!

Given my background, I have a general disdain for discussions that are obviously more technical than they need to be. I have tried, as hard as possible, to present only the necessary and relevant bits, especially in areas that are particularly quantitative. I also have a deep disdain for matrix algebra. I typically roll my eyes when I see it presented in papers and books. Everywhere possible, I have tried to present the quantitative ideas in a way that a typical practitioner can decipher (read as: not in that form). That said, there are a few points where it simply could not be avoided. I ask your forgiveness and patience as you muscle through it (I had to muscle through when writing it!).

As a practitioner myself, I know the value of your time and attention. You have thousands of things pulling you in hundreds of directions. That you choose to spend your time with me and these ideas is a genuine honor. Thank you. I also want to be respectful of your time. This is not a book where I say something only to say it again in a different way and again in yet another. No. I try my best to communicate the ideas as concisely as possible, and when the idea has run its course, I will stop talking. Your time is too valuable for anything else. And since I tend to learn best through demonstration, I have included a few code examples for some of the more intricate topics for folks who would like to see it in action. All references to the book supplement can be found on the companion website: www.franklinparker.com/gbpt-book/

Clearly, these ideas are fairly new, and some are controversial, even to me. For those of us steeped in traditional portfolio theory, there are aspects of goals-based portfolio theory that will seem blasphemous. New and controversial ideas deserve extra scrutiny, and blasphemy even more so. Part of the purpose of this book is to open a wider due diligence on some ideas. I expect pushback, but I ask that we all keep open minds. More importantly, I expect that you will tell me where I am wrong. I have no desire to hold an idea that is incorrect, impractical, or even harmful to the people I have the privilege to serve. So, I humbly ask my fellow practitioners and researchers to point out my errors so that we may all learn and, through the ongoing conversation, grow this wonderful body of knowledge together.

With that, let us proceed.

Acknowledgments

My thinking on this topic has been influenced and informed by so many people, and I am grateful to all of them. First, I have to acknowledge my clients—especially the early ones—who went through some difficult markets with me, and whose questions and concerns set me on this ongoing intellectual quest. Ultimately, the ideas you hold in your hand were prompted by them.

I am grateful, in particular, to my friend Patrick Foster, who was an ongoing sounding board as I wrestled with these ideas. It was in conversation with him, in fact, that my central idea for allocating across goals found its genesis. In a similar vein, I am immensely indebted to Jean Brunel. My first submission to the *Journal of Wealth Management* was admittedly a mess, and I am grateful that he saw through its flaws to find the value in its core idea. Rather than rejecting that submission—and promptly ending my research career—he let me revise it until it was up to par. I am honored that he agreed to write the forward. In addition, Mr. Brunel has been an ongoing source of encouragement and ideas. This book would not be possible without him.

I am grateful to those who reviewed and commented on the early manuscript of this book, namely Sasha Lund, who offered helpful comments and early editing; Gregg Robins, for his comments and encouragement; Laurent Bernut, for his insights into publishing; Michael Finke, for his suggestions and direction on topics; and Sanjiv Das for his encouragement (and his own research into the topic).

Finally, I am grateful to those who saw value in the project: my editors at Wiley, Kevin Harreld and Susan Cerra, and my copyeditor, Cheryl Ferguson.

No doubt, I have missed some key people; you have my apologies!

I am genuinely excited about the ongoing research on this topic. I am excited to keep all of these conversations going, and I am excited to open new ones with new friends.

CHAPTER 1

The Story of the Idea

How Goals-Based Portfolio Theory Came to Be

"I've heard people compare knowledge of a topic to a tree.
If you don't fully get it, it's like a tree in your head with no trunk—
when you learn something new about the topic
there's nothing for it to hang onto, so it just falls away."

—Tim Urban

When presented a choice between multiple possibilities, which one should you choose? This simple question has perplexed many a human being. Modern economics found its beginning with an attempt to answer this basic question. The wealthy class of Europe had quite a bit of time on their hands, and, as it turned out, they enjoyed gambling on games of chance. The Renaissance had shifted the traditional view of these games—rather than simply accept randomness, some of these aristocrats began to analyze the games mathematically in an attempt to understand their randomness. It was not through any pure mathematical interest, of course, but rather an attempt to gain an edge over their fellow gamblers and thereby collect more winnings!

The thinking of the time coalesced around a central idea: expected value theory. Expected value theory stated that a gambler should expect to collect winnings according to the summed product of the gains or losses and the probabilities of those outcomes (i.e. $\sum_i p_i v_i$, where p is the probability of gaining/losing v, and i is the index of possible outcomes). If, for example, you win \$1 every time a six-sided die rolls an even number, and you lose \$1 when it rolls odd, then the expected value of the game is $1/2 \times \$1 + 1/2 \times (-\$1) = \$0$.

In 1738, Daniel Bernoulli challenged that idea. As a thought experiment he proposed a game: a player is given an initial pot of \$2, and a coin is flipped repeatedly. For every heads, the player doubles his money and the game continues until the coin lands on tails. When tails comes up, the player collects winnings of $\$2^n$, where n is the number of times the coin was flipped, and the game is over. Bernoulli's question is, how much should you pay to play this game?

Expected value theory fails us here because the payoff of the game is infinite![1] Clearly no one would pay an infinite amount of money to play the game, but why? Bernoulli's answer is our first glimpse of a marginal theory of utility—a theory that would come to support all modern economics:

> *Thus it becomes evident that no valid measurement of the value of a risk can be obtained without consideration being given to its utility, that is to say, the utility of whatever gain accrues to the individual or, conversely, how much profit is required to yield a given utility. However it hardly seems plausible to make any precise generalizations since the utility of an item may change with circumstances. Thus, though a poor man generally obtains more utility than does a rich man from an equal gain, it is nevertheless conceivable, for example, that a rich prisoner who possesses two thousand ducats but needs two thousand ducats more to repurchase his freedom, will place a higher value on a gain of two thousand ducats than does another man who has less money than he.*[2]

---

[1]On the first flip, the player has a $1/2$ chance of a heads, and the payoff of this flip is 2^1, leading to an expected payoff of $1/2 \times 2 = 1$. The player has a $1/2 \times 1/2 = 1/4$ chance of winning the second flip, and the payoff of this flip is $2^2 = 4$, so the expected payoff of the second flip is $1/4 \times 4 = 1$. When plugged into the expected value structure, we get $1/2 \times 2 + 1/4 \times 4 + 1/8 \times 8 + \cdots = 1 + 1 + 1 + \cdots$, hence the payoff of the game is infinite.

[2]D. Bernoulli, "Exposition on a New Theory on the Measurement of Risk," *Econometrica* 22, no. 1 (1954): 22–36.

The idea that humans do not value changes in wealth linearly, but rather find less value in the next ducat than they found in the first, launched the entirety of modern economics. Bernoulli went on to propose a logarithmic function for the utility of wealth—diminishing as the payoff grows. This, of course, solved the paradox. People are not willing to pay an infinite amount to play the game because they do not have infinite utility for that wealth. The value of each subsequent dollar is less than the previous one—that is the essence of marginal utility, and the foundation of modern economics.

Of more interest to this discussion, however, is that Bernoulli also gives a first glimpse of a goals-based theory of utility! Bernoulli points out that we must think of what it is the wealth *can do for us*, rather than the absolute value of that wealth. In other words, it is not the cash that we care about, but rather what that cash represents in the real world: freedom from prison in Bernoulli's Prisoner's case, and transportation, housing, leisure, food, and so on, for the rest of us. What you wish to do with the money is an important consideration to how much you would pay to play Bernoulli's game. This idea is echoed by Robert Shiller, winner of the 2013 Nobel Prize in Economics: "Finance is not merely about making money. It is about achieving our deep goals and protecting the fruits of our labor."[3] In short, investing is never done in the abstract! Investing is—and always has been—goals-based.

Bernoulli's central contribution to economics was the idea of marginal utility—an idea that would not come to full fruition for another two centuries. It would also be another two centuries before the theory underpinning rational choices was developed. John von Neumann and Oskar Morgenstern authored *The Theory of Games and Economic Behavior* in 1944, which has become the foundation upon which all theories of rational choice are built. In the next chapter, in fact, we will draw on their rational choice axioms to build a goals-based theory of rational choice, so I will save the deeper dive into their ideas for later. Von Neumann was a mathematician (and a brilliant one at that), so their additional contribution—beyond the actual foundational ideas—was to apply a mathematical rigor to the theory of human choice.

In 1948, Milton Friedman (later to win the 1976 Nobel prize in economics) and L. Savage explored the implications of von Neumann and Morgenstern's rational choice theory to an economic conundrum: why do people buy both insurance and lottery tickets? Rational choice theory would generally expect individuals to be variance-averse, so the fact that people

[3]"Q&A with Robert J. Shiller" from Princeton University Press, `https://press.princeton.edu/interviews/qa-9652`, retrieved April 22, 2019.

express preferences for both variance-aversion and variance-affinity in the same instance is troubling. This has since become known as the Friedman-Savage paradox, and their solution—saving the technical bits for a later chapter—was that the utility curve of individuals must not contain one curve, but many interlinked curves. That is, it must be "squiggly," shifting between concave and convex across the wealth/income spectrum—known as the double-inflection solution.[4] As it turns out, this is also a proto-goals-based solution, as the goals-based utility curve is also "squiggly," moving from concave to convex across the spectrum of wealth.

Even more than the method it contained, Markowitz's monumental 1952 paper "Portfolio Selection" was the first serious application of statistical techniques to investment management. Prior to Markowitz, investment management was a bottom-up affair: a portfolio was merely the aggregate result of many individual decisions about securities. Benjamin Graham's *The Intelligent Investor* is a characteristic example (though by no means the only approach at the time). Nowhere in his classic text is Graham concerned with how the various investments within a portfolio interact to create the whole. Rather, it is the job of the investor to simply identify attractive opportunities and add them to her portfolio, replacing ideas that have been played out. The portfolio, then, is the aggregate result of these many unrelated decisions.

By applying statistical techniques to the portfolio and suggesting investors evaluate individual investment opportunities within the context of the portfolio as a whole, Markowitz showed that (a) investors could get more done with the same amount of money, and (b) quantitative methods could have a significant role to play in investment management. Both of those breakthroughs hold to this day.

Markowitz was not the only voice in the debate, of course. In the same year Markowitz published his breakthrough paper, Roy published "Safety First and the Holding of Assets." Ironically, Roy's paper looks much more like what we have come to know as modern portfolio theory. Indeed, nowhere in Markowitz's original paper does the now-familiar efficient frontier appear, but Roy's has not only a proto-efficient frontier, but the capital market line, and an early version of the Sharpe ratio to boot! What's more, Roy's entire analysis is dedicated to the idea that individuals never have a "sense of security" in the real world. That is, never do people have all the information, nor

[4]When a utility curve is convex, individuals are variance-averse, and when concave, individuals are variance-affine. Friedman and Savage's solution is clever and was, in fact, reiterated by Markowitz's other 1952 paper "The Utility of Wealth."

are they always seeking to simply maximize profits. Rather, individuals are attempting to maximize profits *and* avoid the landmines that could well destroy their hard-won progress:

> *A valid objection to much economic theory is that it is set against a background of ease and safety. To dispel this artificial sense of security, theory should take account of the often close resemblance between economic life and navigation in poorly charted waters or maneuvers in a hostile jungle. Decisions taken in practice are less concerned with whether a little more of this or of that will yield the largest net increase in satisfaction than with avoiding known rocks of uncertain position or with deploying forces so that, if there is an ambush round the next corner, total disaster is avoided. If economic survival is always taken for granted, the rules of behavior applicable in an uncertain and ruthless world cannot be discovered.*

Roy is now known for his "safety-first" criterion, and although it is the term Roy himself used, I find it a bit misleading. Upon first hearing it, the implication is that investors operating under Roy's paradigm are unwilling to take much risk. That is not the case! Rather, Roy has an investor declare some return level that would be "disastrous" if the portfolio fell below. If the investor could estimate a portfolio's average distribution of returns and the variance of that distribution, then Roy argues that the investor should organize her investments in such a way as to minimize the probability of falling below that "disastrous" return. In addition to being the first instance of value-at-risk, Roy presents the first goals-based framework! Indeed, as we shall discuss in subsequent chapters, the goals-based framework has investors organize investments in such a way as to minimize the probability of falling below some threshold return. It does make one wonder how portfolio theory might have progressed if Roy, rather than Markowitz, had become the foundational thinker of the quantitative revolution. To be fair, Markowitz himself gives Roy substantial credit, "I am often called the father of modern portfolio theory, but Roy can claim an equal share of this honor."[5] Roy's central line of research, however, was not in portfolio theory, but other branches of economics.

[5]H. Markowitz, "The Early History of Portfolio Theory: 1600–1960." *Financial Analysts Journal* 55, no. 4 (1999): 5–16, DOI: `https://doi.org/10.2469/faj.v55.n4.2281`.

Markowitz's line of thinking also held considerable appeal to the well-funded pension schemes and insurance companies of the 1950s, 1960s, and 1970s. These institutions had the financial ability and interest to fund research that spoke to how they might better achieve the objectives of their pensioners and shareholders. Hence, portfolio theory developed with institutions—not individuals—in mind. For many years, it was assumed that the differences were so negligible as to be not worth exploring. After all, statistics is statistics whether the portfolio is worth $1 billion or $100,000.

Yet, as we now understand, there are *substantial* differences between a $1 billion pension fund and a $100,000 investment account. Surprisingly, it wasn't until 1993—three years after Markowitz collected his well-deserved Nobel prize—that Robert Jeffrey and Robert Arnott fired this first salvo at institutionally oriented portfolio theory. Their paper was titled "Is Your Alpha Big Enough to Cover Its Taxes?"[6] and it opens:

> *Much capital and intellectual energy has been invested over the years in seeking to make portfolio management more efficient. But most of this effort has been directed at* tax-exempt *investors such as pension funds, foundations, and endowments, even though taxes are a major consideration for owners of approximately two-thirds of the marketable portfolio assets in the United States. (emphasis is in the original)*

The authors go on to discuss how taxable investors can think about tax-drag as a central concern of their investment strategy, rather than as an afterthought. We will address taxes in a later chapter, but the relevant point in the historical development of goals-based portfolio theory is that their research was among the first to systematically redress a difference between individual investors and the investors for whom portfolio theory was developed, namely institutions. It was the first clue that, yes, portfolio results might legitimately be different for taxable investors, even if the statistical tools were the same.

Of course, by the early 1990s, the behavioral economics revolution was in full swing. A decade before, in 1979, Daniel Kahneman and Amos Tversky presented the results of their psychological research,[7] which had

---

[6]R. Jeffrey and R. Arnott, "Is Your Alpha Big Enough to Cover Its Taxes?" *Journal of Portfolio Management* 19, no. 3 (1993): 15–25, DOI: `https://doi.org/10.3905/jpm.1993.710867`.

[7]D. Kahneman and A. Tversky, "Prospect Theory: An Analysis of Decision Under Risk," *Econometrica* 47, no. 2 (1979): 263–292, DOI: `https://doi.org/10.2307/1914185`.

considerable bearing on economics. In short, they found that people feel the pain of financial loss more strongly than they feel the pleasure of financial gain, and when coupled with their further observation that people seem not to weight probabilities objectively, we have their full theory, known as cumulative prospect theory (CPT), for which Kahneman would later win the 2002 Nobel Prize in Economics.

Expanding their work, Richard Thaler (winner of the 2017 Nobel Prize in Economics) developed the concept of mental accounting. He proposed that people mentally subdivide their wealth into different "buckets," and each bucket carries a different risk tolerance. Mental accounting also resolved some behavioral conundrums, like the Friedman-Savage paradox. If people have some of their wealth mentally dedicated to survival objectives and some of their wealth dedicated to aspirational objectives, then these differing risk tolerances will yield people who buy both insurance and lottery tickets. Rather than one interlocking "squiggly" utility curve, mental accounting suggests that people have many separate utility curves.

Mental accounting was also a throwback to the ideas of psychologist Abraham Maslow.[8] People have multiple psychological and physical needs at any given moment: food, shelter, safety, a sense of belonging, self-esteem, and so on. While humans may have their physical needs met, they will still seek to fulfill more abstract psychological needs. Maslow proposed that these needs are fulfilled in a sort of hierarchy, with physiological needs being fulfilled first (food, water, shelter), and psychological needs fulfilled only after those physiological needs are met. This concept is usually presented as a pyramid, although Maslow was himself not so rigid, proposing that individuals will tend to prioritize these needs differently across the course of their life. Toward the end of our lives, for example, Maslow suggests we have a strong need for esteem and self-actualization, with more physiological needs a priority in earlier life. Although, if something happens that destroys an individual's sense of physiological safety, the higher objectives will collapse as the individual attempts to fulfill her base needs.

Mental accounting was foundational to goals-based investing because it was the first acknowledgment and theoretical treatment of investors who divvy their wealth across multiple objectives, reflective of Maslow's observation. Yet in Thaler's early treatment, mental accounting was

[8] A. H. Maslow, "A Theory of Human Motivation," *Psychological Review* 50, no. 4 (1943): 370–396, DOI: `https://doi.org/10.1037/h0054346`.

considered a cognitive bias and therefore irrational. It violated the basic premise that money is fungible—you can swap a dollar here for a dollar there—and as Markowitz showed, investors are best served by considering a portfolio of investments from the top down. Mental accounting, by contrast, was seen as a return to a bottom-up approach. So, though people may *behave* in a way that treats money differently depending on which mental account it is in, people *shouldn't* do that from the perspective of traditional economic theory. It was almost another two decades before Jean Brunel took up the question and demonstrated[9] that this subdivision of wealth across multiple accounts—mental or actual—is not necessarily irrational or suboptimal. Thanks to Brunel's work, there are now two uses of the term *mental accounting*. The first is the cognitive bias wherein people do not treat money as fungible. The second is the observation that people tend to dedicate their wealth toward different goals, and, in response to those differing objectives, they tend to pursue differing types of investments and strategies. While the former is irrational, the latter is not. Goals-based theory is concerned with the latter, as it expects money to be fungible, as we shall see.

The final idea that helped to coalesce the goals-based framework came in 2000 from Hersh Shefrin and Meir Statman, who developed behavioral portfolio theory (BPT).[10] BPT resurrects Roy's safety-first criterion and, in contrast to modern portfolio theory's risk-is-variance paradigm, BPT suggests that risk is the probability of failing to achieve some minimum required return. Said another way, BPT suggests that risk is the probability that you do not achieve your goal. When I think about my own life goals, this is *exactly* how I would define risk! In BPT, an investor builds a portfolio to balance expected return and the probability of failure, which is an analog to the mean-variance efficient frontier.

Despite its insight, BPT never gained mainstream acceptance. In 2010, however, Meir Statman teamed up with Sanjiv Das, Jonathan Scheid, and Harry Markowitz to merge the insights of behavioral portfolio theory with

---

[9]JLP Brunel, "How Suboptimal—If At All—Is Goal-Based Asset Allocation?" *Journal of Wealth Management* 9, no. 2 (2006): 19–34, DOI: `https://doi.org/10.3905/jwm.2006.644216`.

[10]H. Shefrin and M. Statman, "Behavioral Portfolio Theory," *Journal of Financial and Quantitative Analysis* 35, no. 2 (2000): 127–151, DOI: `https://doi.org/10.2307/2676187`.

the framework of modern portfolio theory.[11] They showed that the probability of failing to reach some threshold return is mathematically synonymous with mean-variance optimization, so long as short-selling and leverage were unconstrained (which is a common mean-variance assumption). In that context, an investor can simply declare the maximum probability of failure she is willing to accept for a given account, that metric can be "translated" into a risk-aversion parameter, and portfolio optimization can proceed in the traditional mean-variance way. Additionally, these authors showed, with considerable rigor, that the subdivision of wealth into multiple accounts is not necessarily irrational nor inefficient (an echo of Brunel's 2006 result).

My own entrée into the ideas of goals-based investing came in 2014 when, in the vertiginous years after 2008, I was left wondering whether the traditional methods of portfolio management were still relevant. Experience taught me—like it taught so many in 2008—that the math is simply different for individuals who have specific objectives to achieve within a specified period of time. I felt quite silly for waiving off previous client protestations of portfolio losses. They intuitively understood what I explained away with flawed theory. Insurance companies can wait five years for their risk to be rewarded, but individuals who plan to retire simply cannot, and those who are living off of portfolio withdrawals can even less afford to wait. After that experience, I had one central question: *How much can you lose in an investment portfolio before you've lost too much?* Markets, of course, come back—that was never my concern. My concern was whether they come back *in time* for my clients to achieve their goals. Again, I discovered what others had before me: portfolio theory for individuals is legitimately different than portfolio theory for institutions. After realizing that no one had an answer to my basic question, I developed my own answer, resulting in my first peer-reviewed publication.[12]

[11] S. Das, H. Markowitz, J. Scheid, and M. Statman, "Portfolio Optimization with Mental Accounts." *Journal of Financial and Quantitative Analysis* 45, no. 2 (2010): 311–334, DOI: `https://doi.org/10.1017/S0022109010000141`. For a more accessible, less quantitative version, I would direct readers to S. Das, H. Markowitz, J. Scheid, and M. Statman, "Portfolios for Investors Who Want to Reach Their Goals While Staying on the Mean-Variance Efficient Frontier." *Journal of Wealth Management* 14, no. 2 (2011): 25–31, DOI: `https://doi.org/10.3905/jwm.2011.14.2.025`.

[12] F. J. Parker, "Quantifying Downside Risk for Goals-Based Investors," *Journal of Wealth Management* 17, no. 3 (2014): 68–77, DOI: `https://doi.org/10.3905/jwm.2014.17.3.068`.

My basic question post-2008 is illustrative of another aspect of goals-based portfolio theory. While it is about optimizing portfolios in a way that maximizes the probability of goal achievement, the whole ethos is about more than that. At its core, goals-based portfolio theory is about organizing your resources to maximize the probability of achieving your goals *given real-world constraints*. It is the "real-world constraints" component that has been so often neglected by traditional portfolio theory. It would be nice if investors had access to unlimited leverage and short-selling, but they do not! It would be very nice if investment returns were Gaussian, but they are not. Pretending as though absurd assumptions are reality, then acting surprised when practice mismatches theory, is just plain silliness. While we must accept that theory is not reality, we can do better than a theory that could never be reality. More than anything, investors need a theory that is *useful*.

Recognizing this, Jean Brunel coalesced these various ideas into a whole in his book *Goals-Based Wealth Management*, which addresses how practitioners might tackle the problems of organizing resources for investors with goals to achieve. Having spent many decades at the beating heart of the financial system, serving real people with real goals to achieve, Brunel's work is uniquely positioned at the intersection of the "big world" and the client's world. How firms can systematize these ideas into scalable solutions is no small question (as we shall discuss in a later chapter), and his book addresses these practical challenges, as well.

Once the goals-based definition of risk gained wider acceptance, the next major question was how investors should allocate across their various mental accounts. The assumption for many years was that this allocation across goals was already done by the investor, so the practitioner's job was to organize the investments within each goal in the optimal way. However, to expect investors to rationally allocate wealth across goals is somewhat naïve. To be fair, there are currently several approaches in the literature. In this book, I will present my solution and briefly address my critiques of some of the other major approaches, but I do not want to sound as though this is a settled question. Other researchers may yet present a better solution than mine, and in that case I will yield the ground I claim here. Though solved to my mind, how investors should allocate across goals is still an open question.

And so, we are now up-to-date, more or less, on the current state of the theory. The next chapter details the theory of goals-based investing, as I see it, as well as how it differs from modern portfolio theory—the dominant approach in the industry. After covering the theory, we will discuss how to go about implementing it.

CHAPTER 2

A Theoretical Foundation

"There is nothing more practical than a good theory."

—Kurt Lewin

I think of theory like a map. A map is not reality, of course, but a good map can lead you to your destination much more readily than a bad one. In some cases, the map is accurate but not detailed. We call that a heuristic (or rule-of-thumb). A heuristic works because it is picking up some underlying truth, even though the justification for it may be wrong. Sometimes the map is mostly right, but is wrong in the details. We might be able to use it to get a sense of where we are going, but we may just as easily wind up lost. In other cases, the map is simply wrong, rendering it useless. In that case, we have to throw the map away, explore the unknown area, and draw a new map. As I have witnessed in my own practice, poor theory can lead to poor practical outcomes, but it is not enough to simply decry the map altogether. We must understand *why* the map is leading us astray. Is it *entirely* wrong? Or is it simply that the map is not detailed enough? Understanding where and why the map is wrong is an important component to drawing a new one! In my view, traditional portfolio theory is not an entirely useless map (though it is popular to paint it as such). Rather, it is a map that is mostly right some of the time, but often wrong in the details. I see current portfolio theory like one of those early post-Columbian maps showing that North America exists, but not in a way that helps you actually get to North America—the islands and dangerous shoals are not marked, and neither is the shoreline accurately reproduced. The purpose of this chapter is to fill in those details that help us actually get to where we want to be.

Like most models of choice, we must begin with John von Neumann and Oskar Morgenstern's axioms of rational choice.[1] In short, they find that any rational decisions must be consistent with four basic axioms:

A. **Complete.** For any choices, you must be indifferent to them or prefer one to the other. In other words, you must be able to *order* your preferences.
B. **Transitive.** For any choices, if you prefer A to B and you prefer B to C, then you must also prefer A to C.
C. **Continuous.** For any choices, there is some factor of your most-liked and most-disliked that you can incorporate to make you indifferent to the middle option. In other words, if you prefer A to B to C, then there exits some number, $0 \leq n \leq 1$, such that you are indifferent to getting nA and $(1-n)C$, or getting B by itself.
D. **Independent.** For any choices, adding some random third choice does not affect your preference. If you prefer A to B, you should still prefer getting A and C to B and C.

I do not think it is an exaggeration to say that von Neumann and Morgenstern's (hereafter I'll call them VNM) axioms of rational choice were responsible for sparking the behavioral economics revolution. Not even a decade after VNM's publication, Maurice Allais presented the results of an experiment[2] in which he showed that people tend to disregard the axiom of independence (Axiom D above). Allais's conclusion was that if reasonable people deciding between simple alternatives contradicted the axiom, then the axiom was a poor one. In his monumental 1959 book *Portfolio Selection*, Markowitz[3] retorted that "individuals choosing the 'wrong' alternative acted irrationally." And so, the normative-behavioral split was formed. Interestingly, because Allais relies on changes in probabilities, his experiment can also be

[1] O. Morgenstern and J. von Neumann, *The Theory of Games and Economic Behavior* (Princeton, NJ: Princeton University Press, 1944).
[2] M. Allais, "Le comportement de l'homme rationnel devant le risque: critique des postulats et axiomes de l'école Américaine," *Econometrica* 21, no. 4 (1953): 503–546.
[3] H. Markowitz, *Portfolio Selection: Efficient Diversification of Assets,* vol. 16 (New York: John Wiley & Sons, 1959).

solved if people do not perceive probabilities objectively. That is, if people feel the shift from, say, a 90% probability of success to a 95% probability of success more than they feel the shift from a 10% to a 15% probability of success, then Allais's results can be explained without the abandonment of the axiom of independence, but this, of course, creates a whole different set of problems with rationality.[4]

This is relevant because we must acknowledge what it is we are attempting to do when constructing our goals-based map. Behavioral finance is concerned with a *descriptive* theory of behavior—that is, how do people actually behave. Normative finance is concerned with a *prescriptive* theory of behavior—how people should behave. While I acknowledge the role of managing client (and our own!) irrationality, it is my objective to build a normative theory for goals-based investors. We want to know what the rational course of action is, even if we later decide to modify it to accommodate behavioral concerns. What's more—and this is the topic of a later chapter—when viewed through the lens of goals-based theory, it may be that individuals are not as irrational as normative finance makes it seem. Numerous behavioral-normative puzzles resolve themselves when we simply account for what it is individuals are attempting to do. In this way, goals-based portfolio theory may well provide a bridge across the chasm formed between normative and behavioral economics, and that is quite exciting to me!

Accepting that VNM's axioms are indeed a structure for making rational choices (and not just between lotteries as they originally indicated, but between any types of things), we will accept them and add one more: we will assume that individuals prefer a higher probability of achieving their goal than less. In the language of VNM:

E. **Attainment.** If you prefer having A to not having A, then you should prefer pA to $(1-p)A$ when $1 \geq p > 0.5$, you should be indifferent to pA or $(1-p)A$ when $p = 0.5$, and you should prefer $(1-p)A$ to pA when $0 \leq p < 0.5$.

[4]My instinct is that people do not weight probabilities objectively, though this would create problems for the existing framework of goals-based portfolio theory. If I had to venture a hypothesis, I would suggest that people have an exponential weighting of probabilities, so that the move from a 90% to 95% probability of success is felt much more strongly than a 10% to 15% probability of success. I do not see why this should be necessarily irrational—why is it rational to feel a 5% probability move equally no matter where it is in the 0 to 1 spectrum? Of course, this is just a hypothesis. Some work is needed to prove it, one way or another.

Thus, using these five simple axioms, we can build a theory for the rational allocation of wealth to investments (i.e. portfolio construction) and the allocation of wealth across goals.

Before we press forward, however, I want to clarify why starting from these basic axioms is important. Most people are well aware of the portfolio construction problem—how to allocate wealth across investments—as this has been widely discussed and practiced for decades. Constructing an investment portfolio is a question of allocating *within* goals. The allocation *across* goals, however, is a separate problem that has been given very little discussion in the literature. Until recently, it has been simply assumed that individuals have already allocated their wealth across their various goals appropriately. I would like to camp here for just a moment to clarify the problem so that the solution makes more sense.

People have more than one goal—this should be no big surprise. For example, suppose I want to retire in about 25 years. I also want to send my kids to college in eight years, and possibly buy a vacation home in five years. If I allocate some of my savings toward the vacation home, I necessarily reduce the probability of retiring and sending my kids to college. When I spend my limited resources on one goal, I reduce the probability of achieving my other goals. How, then, should I allocate my limited pool of wealth (existing savings as well as my future savings) in a rational manner? To date, the solution has been to engage in an iterative conversation with a financial planner. Effectively, we arrive at a proper allocation to goals by trial-and-error, presenting alternate probability of achievement scenarios for the various goals until the client says, "Yes, that is the right balance." Of course, I do not advocate for the abandonment of client conversation, but this iterative approach is demonstrative of the bigger problem: we have no theoretical basis for a solution. That is, we literally do not know how to rationally allocate across goals, we rely on a hedonic solution—on client feedback—and hope that it is rational enough. In this regard, surely *a* map is better than *no* map?

To be fair, the general solution in the literature has been to acknowledge a Maslowian hierarchy of goal allocation (Figure 2.1). In his book, Brunel[5] suggests that individuals will ensure they have funded their needs with a high probability of success, only then will they fund their wants and once those have been funded with a sufficiently high probability, investors will then seek to fund their wishes and dreams. This was also the perspective that

[5]J. Brunel, *Goals-Based Wealth Management* (Hoboken, NJ: John Wiley and Sons, 2015).

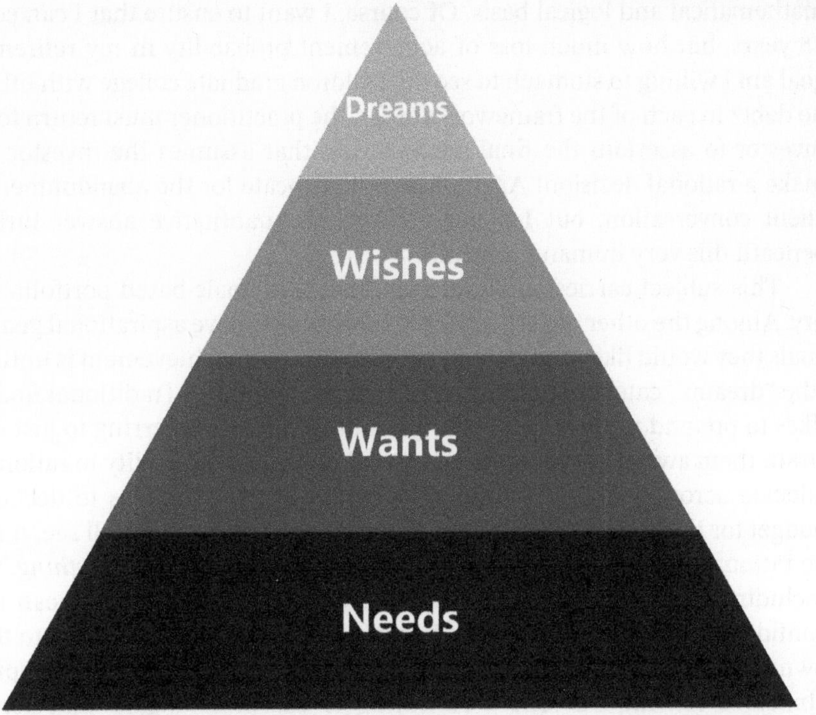

FIGURE 2.1 Maslow-Brunel Hierarchy of Goals

Chhabra[6] took in his seminal work, and Statman suggests a similar framework.[7] Deguest, Martellini, and Milhau,[8] building on the work of Chhabra, propose a more formalized idea: investors will allocate such that their essential goals are met for sure, and then divide wealth across goals that cannot be achieved for sure. While I agree with many of the elements from these frameworks, all of this is rather ad hoc, and none of the frameworks offer a complete and cohesive solution. More important to me is that none of these solutions can be properly called rational because they have no fundamental

[6]A. Chhabra, "Beyond Markowitz: A Comprehensive Wealth Allocation Framework for Individual Investors," *Journal of Wealth Management* 7, no. 4 (2005): 8–34, DOI: `https://doi.org/10.3905/jwm.2005.470606`.

[7]H. Statman, "The Diversification Puzzle," *Financial Analysts Journal* 60, no. 4 (2004): 44–53, DOI: `https://doi.org/10.2469/faj.v60.n4.2636`.

[8]R. Deguest, L. Martellini, and V. Milhau, *Goal-Based Investing: Theory and Practice* (World Scientific Publishing, 2021).

mathematical and logical basis. Of course, I want to ensure that I can eat in 25 years, but how much loss of achievement probability in my retirement goal am I willing to stomach to see my children graduate college with little to no debt? In each of the frameworks so far, the practitioner must return to the investor to ascertain the final answers, but that assumes the investor will make a rational decision! Again, I do not advocate for the abandonment of client conversation, but I believe there is a quantitative answer lurking beneath this very human problem.

This subject carries an additional nuance in goals-based portfolio theory. Among the other goals people set, most people have aspirational goals—goals they would like to achieve but realize that their achievement is unlikely (the "dreams" category in the Maslow-Brunel pyramid). Traditional finance likes to pretend these aspirational goals do not exist, preferring to just constrain them away.[9] Yet we know such goals exist, and an ability to rationally allocate across goals, including aspirational goals, allows us to declare a budget for these considerably more aggressive goals. As we shall see, it may be rational to gamble at times, but certainly not to gamble *everything*.[10] By including the allocation of wealth across goals in the theory, we can now confidently say when someone is behaving irrationally with respect to their own aspirations. We can also confidently say how much achievement probability of retiring our client is willing to sacrifice to gain that aspirational goal.

With these preliminaries now out of the way, let us press ahead with the technical details.

---

[9]In their book, *Modern Portfolio Theory and Investment Analysis*, for example, Edwin Elton, Martin Gruber, Stephen Brown, and William Goetzmann (Hoboken, NJ: John Wiley & Sons, 2009) add the constraint that a portfolio's required return must be less than the maximal return offered by the efficient frontier.

[10]That is not exactly true. In desperate times, it may well be rational to gamble everything; the model demonstrates this quite readily. However, I would expect that, for most practical applications, this is not the baseline case. Furthermore, and this is not a formal part of the model, goals are malleable and revokable, and goals tend to shift in response to both the opportunity set in the market as well as the resources available. Someone who loses 90% of their wealth is unlikely to maintain the same goals as before. More likely, this person's goals shift significantly (with considerable loss of utility), likely leading to a complete rewrite of their goals-space. This is a deficiency of the goals-based model as there is currently no way to account for the changing nature of individual goals. Goals, in this model, are simply taken as exogenous, and resources are reallocated when/if goals change, for whatever reason.

We assume that people set multiple goals, and that these goals compete for a "single" pool of wealth, which we will call ϖ. This pool of wealth is the sum of all financial assets plus the discounted value of all future savings (i.e. financial capital and human capital). Of course, in practice, this pool of wealth is going to have real-world frictions that matter to our model, but for now we will disregard those to be revisited later. We will refer to this set of goals as the goals-space, or $G:\{A, B, C, \ldots, N\} \in G$, where $A, B, C, \ldots$ are the N-number of goals in the goals-space.

The axiom of completeness means that we can rank-order the goals, so we will let A represent the most favored goal, B represent the second-most favored goal, and so on. For ease of mathematical discussion, let there be a value function of the goals, $v(\cdot)$, such that $v(A) > v(B)$ if A is preferred to B; $v(A) = v(B)$ if you are indifferent to A and B; and $v(A) < v(B)$ if you prefer B to A. Since all of this is a mathematical construct, let us simply say that A is always the most valued, B is always the second-most valued, and so on. The convenience of $v(A) > v(B)$ and the axiom of continuousness allows us to say that some number exists, $0 \leq p \leq 1$, such that $v(B) = v(A) \cdot p$.

Here we have reached an important point. That we can reduce the value of A sufficiently to make the choice equivalent to B means we can ascertain the value of B relative to A using a certainty equivalence method. This involves assigning an arbitrary number to $v(A)$. I like using $v(A) = 1$ (though any positive real number would do[11]). From there, we can ask whether you would prefer achieving B with certainty or achieving A with probability p. By varying p until you are indifferent to the choice, we can then infer that $v(B) = v(A) \cdot p$, or that B is only p as valuable as A.

Again, for convenience, let us create a new set of variables to hold these newly formed value ratios. As is my preference, $v(A) = 1$, so $a = 1$. $v(B)$, then, would be $v(B) = a \cdot p$. By repeating the certainty equivalence procedure across the goals-space, we can map these value ratios to the goals-space, $\{p, q, \ldots, n\} \rightarrow \{A, B, \ldots, N\}$, and the total value, then, of the goals-space is

$$v(G) = a + ap + apq + \cdots + apq \ldots n.$$

[11]A negative value would indicate negative utility (disutility) of achieving the goal—this may well be appropriate in some contexts, as Brunel discusses the avoidance of "nightmares, fears, worries, and concerns."

I think a "for instance" is appropriate here. Suppose an investor has four goals in her goals-space, which she has rank-ordered, $\{A, B, C, D\} \in G$. We now ask her the series of questions:

- Would you rather achieve goal B with certainty or goal A with probability p?
- Would you rather achieve goal C with certainty or goal B with probability q?
- Would you rather achieve goal D with certainty with certainty or goal C with probability z?

As mentioned, we vary p, q, and z until our investor is indifferent to the choices. Since we arbitrarily set $v(A) = a = 1$, we now have value ratios that correspond one-for-one to the goals-space: $\{a, p, q, z\} \to \{A, B, C, D\}$. It is important to remember that these value ratios are not the actual values that go into the model! There is one more step to get the goal values. The value of a goal is the product of the goal ratios that precede it in the ranked order. So,

$$v(A) = a = 1,$$

$$v(B) = a \cdot p,$$

$$v(C) = a \cdot p \cdot q,$$

$$v(D) = a \cdot p \cdot q \cdot z.$$

Of course, goals-based investors are investing because they do not currently have enough financial wealth to achieve all of their goals (if they did, then they would just apply the wealth to accomplish the goal). Furthermore, we assume there is some distribution of returns function that describes the investment portfolio (it need not be Gaussian!). If we let w, W, and t represent the initial wealth we dedicate to a goal, the final wealth amount that is required to achieve the goal, and the time horizon within which the goal is to be accomplished, respectively, then we can say that some cumulative distribution function exists that takes in these goal inputs and investment portfolio weights, and returns the probability of achieving the given goal: $\phi(w, W, t)$. We can alternately describe the initial wealth dedicated to a goal as some percentage of the total wealth pool owned by our investor. Let ϑ be the percentage of the total wealth our investor allocates to a given goal, and let us call our total wealth pool ϖ. Because $w = \vartheta\varpi$, our probability of goal achievement function now takes the form $\phi(\vartheta\varpi, W, t)$.

Lastly, we learn from Markowitz that the weighted-sum formulation of utility is a valid solution to VNM's axioms of choice:[12]

$$u = \sum_i v(i)p(i),$$

where the range of possible outcomes is indexed with i, $v(i)$ is the value of the ith outcome, and $p(i)$ is the probability the ith outcome. We can translate this solution into our context. As we have learned, each goal has its own value and its own probability of achievement based on the portfolio we choose and the relevant variables (time horizon, initial wealth, and required funding wealth). So, we can replace $p(\cdot)$ with our probability of achievement function, $\phi(\vartheta\varpi, W, t)$, and replace $v(\cdot)$ with the value of each goal in our goals-space.

By varying how much wealth we allocate to a particular goal (ϑ from above), and by controlling the weights of investments within each goal (let ω represent those weights), we can maximize our investor's well-being:

$$\max_{\vartheta,\omega} \sum_i^N v(i)\phi(\varpi\vartheta_i, W_i, t_i).$$

In this form, we have indexed the goals-space with i, so we are trying to maximize the sumproduct of the probability of achievement of goals A through N and the value of goals A through N. Notice how the allocation of the total wealth pool, the required funding level, and the time horizon are all indexed. That is because those variables are unique to each goal, and those variables are given by the client. The allocation to each goal (ϑ_i) and the weight of each investment (ω_j) are determined by an optimizer.

$\phi(\cdot)$ can be any function that takes the goal variables and portfolio weights as inputs and returns the probability of achieving the goal as its output. I say *any function* and choose not to be too specific here because the assumption of a Gaussian distribution of market returns is, by far, the most common in the literature, but it is also the least realistic. Practitioners should be concerned with a real-world model for asset returns because, I have said before and will say again, goals-based portfolio theory is about achieving goals *given real-world constraints*. It would be convenient if markets produced Gaussian distributions, but they do not. Therefore, in my view, non-Gaussian distributions

[12]Markowitz, p. 242.

are one of those real-world constraints. I will leave the rest of that discussion for a later chapter.

It is important to note that this model does not account for how people go about setting goals, it just assumes that they are set. This is a problem, and I believe that some model of goal creation is important and is likely to explain a lot. The goals-based utility model clearly shows that more goals yield more utility—up to a point. We can expect, based on the model, for individuals to fill their goals-space up to the point where the next goal would result in lowered utility. Since each goal requires some allocation of resources, if adding another goal would pull enough resources so as to lower the probability of achieving more important goals more than it would yield big enough probability gains to less important goals, then our investor will not add that goal to her goals-space. Consequently, windfalls, for example, would not necessarily be viewed through the lens of existing goals; rather, an investor will likely form new goals and dedicate the windfall to them (at least in part). Most laboratory economic studies that make offers of money to individuals, whether real or imaginary, are likely to be skewed by this *windfall effect* of goal formation. At the moment, we will have to accept this hole in the theory and hope that future research reveals a solution!

And that is pretty much the basic theory.

COMPARISON TO MODERN PORTFOLIO THEORY

While Markowitz's work in the 1950s is often cited as the foundation, modern portfolio theory (MPT) was built by numerous authors (many of whom won Nobel prizes) over the course of two decades. It seems to be a rite of passage for practitioners to level endless criticisms at MPT. However, and despite my own criticisms of the theory, I cannot stress enough how important the ideas of MPT have been to investors! More than anything, MPT gave investors a cohesive framework—a language—within which discussions of portfolio construction were possible. Prior to MPT, portfolio construction was an ad-hoc affair, the aggregate result of many small decisions. *The Intelligent Investor*, Benjamin Graham's magnum opus on value investing, for example, has no discussion of how securities should interact within a portfolio! MPT, then, even with all of its flaws, has been a boon to investors. By leveraging quantitative techniques, MPT offers investors a cohesive method for thinking about the management of a portfolio. We also have the benefit of piggybacking on the decades of research by some of the smartest minds in economics. We cannot forget that these original authors did not have such a benefit! Suffice it to say, the goals-based framework would not even exist without the work of these previous authors.

MPT is, rightly, now considered investment orthodoxy. Distilling 20 years and numerous authors down into a discussion that fits within a chapter is fraught with danger, so know that what follows will necessarily be an oversimplification. Even so, I feel it is important to understand where goals-based portfolio theory both connects to and breaks from the dominant framework in existence. If nothing else, we can better appreciate the goals-based framework when we view it in contrast to something—especially something as important as MPT. So, with those preliminaries out of the way, we shall barrel ahead.

While several utility functions exist under the MPT umbrella, the one that drives most portfolio optimization in MPT is the quadratic form of utility:

$$u = r - \gamma \frac{1}{2} \sigma^2,$$

where r is the expected return of the portfolio, σ^2 is the portfolio's variance, and γ is the investor's risk-aversion parameter. Given γ, and by varying the weights to a portfolio of investments, the optimal balance of portfolio return and variance can be found.

What is an investor's risk-aversion parameter? For many years, it was the purpose of risk-tolerance questionnaires to elicit this value. Of course, we immediately notice that this psychological evaluation has really nothing at all to do with what the investor *needs*; rather it is a measure of what the investor *wants*. In my mind, that is like going to the doctor and, after a battery of tests, learning that the doctor cannot treat you because the pain-tolerance questionnaire you filled out at intake is mismatched with the pain level of your treatment! No! We go to the doctor for diagnosis and treatment. The pain of a procedure is a factor in the discussion, but it is never the *only* factor. Similarly, clients approach financial professionals to get financial guidance and the execution of a financial plan. While psychological risk tolerance is a factor, it should not be the *only* factor.

Other researchers have noted that risk-tolerance questionnaires may, in fact, be entirely worthless! Michael Finke and Michael Guillemette, for example, showed that the reported risk tolerance of investors changes with gains and losses in the stock market.[13] As markets gain in value, people's

[13]M. Guillemette and M. Finke, "Do Large Swings in Equity Values Change Risk Tolerance?" *Journal of Financial Planning* 27, no. 6 (2014): 44–50.

reported risk-tolerance grows more aggressive. Conversely, as markets lose value, people's reported risk tolerance grows more conservative. Others have demonstrated similar effects. Since risk tolerance is the only human input to the MPT procedure, this may be reason enough to abandon traditional MPT—the foundational optimization equation is based on a very fragile measure![14] In the goals-based framework, risk-tolerance questionnaires are entirely superfluous—an interesting data point and worth discussing, but it is nowhere an input to the model.

Luckily, this critique was addressed by four authors in 2010 who adapted MPT to account for investor goals.[15] For a given goal, they have an investor declare the maximum probability of failure she is willing to accept. From there, a risk-aversion parameter can be inferred and the portfolio can be optimized in the traditional way. In effect, this adaptation is a "translation" mechanism—taking in the investor's goal variables and declared tolerance for risk (risk being goal failure) and outputting the best mean-variance optimal portfolio. It really is a clever solution!

Yet, this solution still does not offer guidance on the allocation of our total pool of wealth across the goals-space. Rather, this adapted MPT framework assumes that investors have already allocated their total pool of wealth across goals. At first blush, this seems to be no big deal. Though I tend to believe that people are more rational than we generally believe, even I struggle to defend the assumption that investors have, through sheer gut instinct, rationally allocated their wealth across goals! My experience lends credence to my skepticism as clients have regularly asked whether they can fund a short-term, lower-priority goal (like buying a vacation home). They ask because they intuit that funding this goal reduces the probability of achieving their more important and longer-term goals (like retirement). I have also regularly fielded questions about how future savings should be allocated. These are questions of how people value their goals relative to one another, hence neither of those questions can be answered within the MPT framework—even with its clever adaptations.

The adapted form of MPT has another flaw. As mentioned, it requires the investor to answer this question: "What is the maximum probability of

[14]C. H. Pan and M. Statman, "Questionnaires of Risk Tolerance, Regret, Overconfidence, and Other Investor Propensities" *Journal of Investment Consulting* 13, no. 1 (2012): 54–63.

[15]S. Das, H. Markowitz, J. Scheid, and M. Statman, "Portfolio Optimization with Mental Accounts," *Journal of Financial and Quantitative Analysis* 45, no. 2 (2010): 311–334, DOI: https://doi.org/10.1017/S0022109010000141.

failure you are willing to accept for this goal?" When asked such a question, is any response other than "0%" rational? Obviously, implicit in any given answer is the assumption that a lower failure probability would be preferable, if possible! Adapted MPT, then, violates our axiom of attainment. Under adapted MPT, we cannot account for this axiom, so when declaring this maximum probability of failure, the investor is getting a portfolio that yields that probability of failure—we must simply ignore that our investor would prefer a lower probability of failure, if it were possible to attain.

There is yet another, and considerably subtler, critique I level at adapted MPT. Declaring a maximum acceptable probability of failure is mathematically the same as declaring a minimum allocation of the investor's total wealth pool to the goal. Let me demonstrate this point, because it is not immediately obvious. Let the return required to achieve a goal be

$$R = \left(\frac{W}{\vartheta\varpi}\right)^{\frac{1}{t}} - 1.$$

Adapted MPT has the investor declare α, her maximum acceptable failure probability, so $\Pr[m \leq R] \leq \alpha$. The probability that our portfolio's return, m, is less than our required return, R, must be less than or equal to α. Using the logistic cumulative distribution function (for tractability), we can say that

$$\Pr[m \leq R] = \frac{1}{1 + \exp\left(-\frac{R - m}{s}\right)}.$$

Therefore, given our investor's declared failure probability, α, we can say that

$$\frac{1}{1 + \exp\left(-\frac{\left(\frac{W}{\vartheta\varpi}\right)^{\frac{1}{t}} - 1 - m}{s}\right)} \leq \alpha.$$

A rearrangement of this equation yields

$$\vartheta \geq \frac{W}{\varpi\left[1+m-s\ln\left(\frac{1}{\alpha}-1\right)\right]^{t}}.$$

Since ϑ is the percentage of wealth allocated to the goal, adapted MPT carries an inherent contradiction when the investor's declared α mismatches what they have actually allocated to the goal!

This contradiction was deftly handled by Jean Brunel,[16] who, rather than see it as a deficiency to overcome, used it as a tool. In essence, Brunel converted the inequality above to a strict equality and then used it as a way to allocate across goals. In other words, if an investor declares a maximum acceptable failure probability, Brunel uses the above relationship to convert the investor's declaration into an allocation to that goal. It is a solution to the problem of allocating wealth across goals. I admit, I was a bit starstruck by his cleverness! Unfortunately, though Brunel's solution does mostly solve the problem of across-goal allocation within MPT, it does not get us all the way there. After the initial allocation across goals is done, our client is likely to either have wealth left over or—and this is more likely in my experience—not enough wealth to go around.[17] What are we to do then? How do we rationally allocate any excess wealth, or rationally recall wealth from goals when there is not enough? We find ourselves back at square one.

A peer-reviewer of the paper I published describing this problem questioned why this was even relevant. So what if we cannot allocate the *exact* amount of wealth in the wealth pool without client input and feedback? It is a fair question, especially in light of Brunel's solution. The answer is quite simple: Having an endogenous framework, a framework that does not require *ongoing* client input and feedback once the initial variables are ascertained, is critical to automating the solution and allowing for scale at the level of a wealth management firm. As will become extremely clear in later chapters, goals-based solutions are hyper-customized and hyper-individualized. The only way to scale the delivery of those solutions, at the level of the firm, is to use the lever of technology. In short, everyday folks would never have access to the benefits of goals-based solutions without a

[16] J. Brunel, *Goals-Based Wealth Management* (Hoboken, NJ: John Wiley and Sons, 2015).

[17] For example, suppose our investor has $1,450,000 to allocate across three goals. Using Brunel's method, we allocate $723,000 to goal A, $389,000 to goal B, and $124,000 to goal C. But that still leaves another $214,000 unallocated. How do we allocate that sum?

fully endogenous model, like the one I am presenting here. But more on that in later chapters.

The whole problem is further compounded by another basic assumption of MPT: unlimited leverage and short-selling. Because investors are assumed to have no limit in their ability to borrow and sell short, MPT assumes there is no endpoint to the efficient frontier. However, all of us know that this is a silly assumption. Not only are investors constrained in their ability to borrow, but very often the mere costs of portfolio margin are prohibitive enough to eliminate any benefits. Shorting is outright prohibited in some account types. Not to mention, levering a client portfolio because MPT told us to is a sure way to have a regulator put you out of business! No matter how we slice it, there *is* an endpoint to the efficient frontier, and that presents a whole new set of problems.

When the investor's required return is less than the maximum return we can get on the efficient frontier, then goals-based optimization is mathematically the same as mean-variance optimization. If you agree with MPT and assume no endpoint to the mean-variance efficient frontier, then this conversation is over—you can put this book down and move on to something more productive. However, when we do have an endpoint to the frontier, we find that, sometimes, an investor's required return is greater than the return offered by the efficient fronter. In that case, an investor maximizes the probability of achieving a goal by *increasing* variance, rather than minimizing it! This, of course, pushes portfolios off of the efficient frontier. Since I realize that this is economic blasphemy, allow me to demonstrate the point a bit more formally.

For tractability, let the probability of failure be defined by the logistic cumulative distribution function, so

$$\Phi(r; m, s) = \frac{1}{1+\exp\left(-\frac{r-m}{s}\right)},$$

where $r = (W/w)^{1/t} - 1$ is the return required to achieve the goal, m is the expected return of the portfolio, and s is the scale parameter (the logistic distribution's version of standard deviation). Let $r - m = a$, and we are concerned with the truthiness of $\Phi(r; m, s_1) > \Phi(r; m, s_2)$:

$$\frac{1}{1+\exp\left(-\frac{a}{s_1}\right)} > \frac{1}{1+\exp\left(-\frac{a}{s_2}\right)},$$

simplifying to

$$-\frac{a}{s_1} < -\frac{a}{s_2}.$$

We are concerned with when $r > m$, so $a > 0$. Simplifying further yields

$$s_1 < s_2.$$

Recalling our original question of how the properties of s affect the lowest probability of failure, $\Phi(r; m, s_1) > \Phi(r; m, s_2)$, it is now clear that the probability of failure is minimized when we choose the bigger s! We get the opposite conclusion when $r < m$, yielding $a < 0$. Simplifying with that difference yields

$$s_1 > s_2.$$

Hence, when the required return is less than the expected return, we minimize failure probability by minimizing variance—which is the mean-variance paradigm. When our required return is greater than the expected return at the endpoint of the frontier, we minimize failure probability by increasing variance.

As the quadratic utility of MPT demonstrates, mean-variance investors will *never* prefer a higher variance (because of the $-\gamma\sigma^2/2$ part) of the equation. Thus, adapted MPT has a whole class of portfolio solutions that are infeasible. That is, they return no result. More traditional MPT simply constrains-away this problem by setting an additional optimization constraint that the portfolio's required return must be less than the endpoint of the efficient frontier.

This simple demonstration shows that goals-based portfolio optimization results in portfolios that are *usually* the same as mean-variance optimized portfolios—that is, when $r < m$. However, goals-based portfolio optimization yields *some* portfolios that deliver a higher probability of achievement than mean-variance optimized portfolios—that is, when $r > m$. Therefore, goals-based portfolio optimization first-order stochastically dominates mean-variance optimization—a fancy way of saying that the results are the same, except in at least one case where the goals-based approach yields a better result (see Figure 2.2). The traditional decision rules of economics demand we choose the stochastically dominant option.[18] Furthermore,

[18]See, for example, J. Hadar and W. Russell, "Rules for Ordering Uncertain Prospects," *American Economic Review* 59, no. 1 (1969): 25–34.

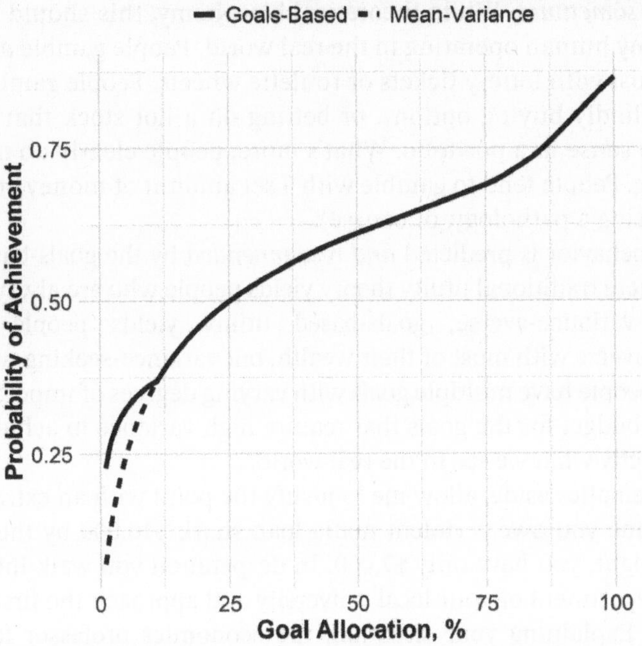

FIGURE 2.2 Stochastic Dominance of Goals-Based Portfolio Optimization

goals-based portfolio optimization also yields results even when the results of adapted MPT are infeasible.

When is an investor's required return greater than what is offered by the efficient frontier? Quite simply, it is when the goal is at the top of the Maslow-Brunel pyramid. We colloquially call these goals dreams, aspirations, or even fantasies. Using the theoretical language we have put together, we can more technically say that these are goals that are not valued highly enough relative to other goals in the goals-space to warrant a high enough allocation of the wealth pool to keep it on the efficient frontier.

That anyone is surprised such goals exist is a mystery to me. *Obviously*, we all have dreams and aspirational objectives. We all have goals we dream of achieving but would be just fine if we did not. We are willing to accept a much lower probability of achievement for these goals than we would for a goal lower on the pyramid, and, therefore, we allocate relatively few resources to them. More foundational goals, goals more central to our survival, carry more weight in our hierarchy, so they will naturally pull the majority of our resources. What is left over is usually dedicated to these less important, but more fulfilling, goals.

Before you simply accept what I am saying here, dear reader, let me say it a bit clearer. Sometimes it is *rational* to gamble! Yes, rational to gamble—*sometimes*. While theoretical blasphemy, this should be no surprise to any human operating in the real world. People gamble *all the time*, and not just with lottery tickets or roulette wheels. People gamble in markets by blindly buying options, or betting on a hot stock that otherwise makes no sense in a portfolio. What's more, people clearly do not gamble *everything*. People tend to gamble with a set amount of money and then let it go (barring a pathology, of course).

This behavior is predicted *and recommended* by the goals-based framework! Where traditional utility theory yields people who are always and everywhere variance-averse, goals-based utility yields people who are variance-averse with most of their wealth, but variance-seeking with a little. Because people have multiple goals with varying degrees of importance, they will set a budget for the goals that require high variance to achieve. Again, this is exactly what we see in the real world.

Mathematics aside, allow me to justify the point with an extreme example. Imagine you owe a violent mafia loan shark $10,000 by the morning. Sadly, tonight, you have only $7,000. In desperation you walk into the economics department of your local university and approach the first professor you find. Explaining your situation, the economics professor follows the rational course: she administers a risk-tolerance questionnaire and optimizes a portfolio using the mean-variance method. "I'm sorry," she reports, "there just isn't enough time for a 70% stock/30% bond portfolio to return 43% by tomorrow morning." Do you leave, distraught, certain of your hospital visit tomorrow morning? No! The only *rational* answer is to go to a casino—how else would you avoid a hospital visit in the morning? You enter the casino and gamble until you have gained the required $3,000 or lost all of your bankroll.

To be fair, "go to a casino" is not entirely foreign to traditional utility theory. Traditional utility theory would expect some people to be variance-seeking. The trouble is that, once proven variance-affine, the "rational" course, according to traditional economics, is to gamble until all of your wealth is gone—there is no point of satiation. But that *certainly* isn't rational! No, in this extreme example, you would gamble until you had $10,000 (or $0), then you would leave the casino because you would have accomplished (or failed to accomplish) your goal.

In the final analysis, given all of the problems with using MPT in a goals-based setting, it seems so much more sensible to adopt a framework that is designed for the intended setting. When the best theoretical map we have is tattered, hand-corrected, and full of "beware of that," "remember this," and "thar be dragons," we use what we have to get us where we are going. But no navigator keeps this map as primary when a more accurate one is available. Goals-based portfolio theory is, at least in my view, a more accurate theoretical map. It yields feasible solutions when adapted MPT yields infeasible ones. Goals-based optimization stochastically dominates MPT optimization when real world constraints are included (like limited short-sells and limited leverage)—that is, it yields higher probabilities of goal achievement than MPT. Where traditional MPT has only a variance-aversion parameter, goals-based portfolio optimization accounts for all the variables that makes a goal a goal. Adapted MPT, though a better accounting of goals than traditional MPT, violates our axiom of attainment. And, the goals-based framework provides a mechanism to allocate wealth both within and across goals, which is offered by neither traditional nor adapted MPT.

While MPT has served an important role in finance and economics, a role that goals-based theory builds on, it is a less-refined tool than goals-based portfolio theory. This fact is evidenced by the myriad ad hoc heuristics designed to compensate for its flaws in the real world. People want to minimize the probability of failing to achieve goals, not minimize variance per se. People want to allocate to low-value, low-probability goals, and that requires leaving the efficient frontier in search of high-variance, lottery-like investments. People are constrained in their ability to borrow and sell short. It seems to me that investors and practitioners would both be better served by a model that is constructed with them and the real world in mind from the start, which is exactly how goals-based portfolio theory has been built.

With the theoretical foundation now complete, let us address the practical questions of implementation. Because the foundation is different, the techniques will be somewhat unfamiliar. I will ask you to be patient as we explore these methods together, and I also humbly ask that you be open to finding your own, better, solutions. When you do, please share them! Research on this topic is an ongoing conversation, heavily informed by those of us who are in the trenches together.

CHAPTER 3

Allocating Wealth Across Goals and Across Investments

"If you want to live a happy life, tie it to a goal. Not to people or things."

—Albert Einstein

I admit it seems odd to write a whole book on a theory that can be expressed in a page and a half. Yet, though the presentation of the theory is relatively simple, it is not so simple to put into practice! Most notably, the optimal allocation of wealth to a particular goal depends on the allocation to investments within that goal, and the optimal allocation of investments within a goal also depends on the allocation of wealth to that goal. This recursivity, coupled with the unfamiliar optimization approach, make it worthwhile to spend time solving these problems from the perspective of a practitioner. There are other practical problems, like eliciting the relative goal values from clients. The model takes these points as a given, but they are, in practice, not so straightforward to solicit. This discussion will be about how a practitioner might go about solving these problems, though I will not claim a monopoly on these solutions—others could likely do better! Even so, we shall press ahead, and let us start with the simpler problem first.

How can we ascertain the relative value of goals in an investor's goals-space? How can we know how much an individual values retirement relative to sending her kids to college, for example, or how much she values funding an estate goal versus buying a vacation home? In the previous chapter, I suggested asking a series of questions: *Would you rather send your kids to college with certainty, or retire with a probability of p?* We vary p until our investor is ambivalent to the choice. We might think of this as the goals-based analog of a risk-tolerance questionnaire. An annoying part of the process, to be sure, but a necessary one.

That said, I feel I must acknowledge my doubts about whether clients have the patience to give feedback at any serious level of granularity. It would be considerably more convenient to have a reasonable approximation of these figures. Practitioners could assume that all "need" goals have a value of 1.00, and perhaps "want" goals have a valuation of 0.75. Or, at the very least, practitioners could use that baseline as a starting point to begin the conversation, calibrating more accurate valuations based on feedback from the client. I genuinely hope the literature on this topic will evolve because I do not feel that my method is particularly client friendly. Though, since I have no better solution, we will have to table the practical problems involved with eliciting goal values, and let us turn to the bigger problem of model recursivity.

The model is recursive because we have to find both the optimal across-goal allocation (how much wealth we dedicate to each goal) *and* we have to find the optimal mix of investments within each goal. Both of those allocation levels are in play simultaneously, creating a decided nonlinear problem.[1] I find it easiest to work from the bottom up. First, we find the optimal investment allocation within each goal for each potential level of across-goal wealth allocation. That is to say, we find and log the optimal investment mix when we allocate 1%, 2%, 3%, ..., 97%, 98%, 99%, of our total wealth to the goal.

Granularity is an obvious question at this stage—more granularity is better, but we can quickly run into unreasonable computation times and memory needs. If ϱ is our level of resolution ($\varrho = 100$ for 1% intervals, $\varrho = 20$ for 5% intervals, $\varrho = 10$ for 10% intervals, etc.) and N is the number of goals, then we must calculate and hold in memory $\varrho \times N$ portfolios. Five goals run with a resolution of 100 yields $5 \times 100 = 500$ portfolio calculations that must be made and held in memory. In the end, the practitioner has to make this

---

[1]Modern portfolio theory has well-known closed form solutions for finding the optimal investment mix of a portfolio. The goals-based problem is considerably more complex since it has two layers of optimization occurring simultaneously. If there is a closed-form solution, it is well beyond my mathematical ability to derive it.

decision based on the application at hand and the computational resources available. It may well be that a resolution of 20 or 10 is sufficient for a particular application. I do not believe there is one right answer here.

Once we have generated optimal portfolios for each goal given each potential level of wealth, we use the results of these optimal investment allocations to inform the optimal across-goal allocation. Because of the discrete nature of our portfolio allocation results, I recommend using a Monte Carlo engine to simulate various across-goal allocations and their effects on total utility. Obviously, we are trying to find the across-goal allocation that yields the highest utility. For each simulation of across-goal allocation, we match the optimal portfolio for that level of across-goal allocation and return a probability of achievement. That probability is the input used in the utility function.

Finally, we match the optimal across-goal allocation with the optimal within-goal portfolio weights and return the optimal aggregate portfolio (or keep them separate, whichever the implementation strategy demands).

That is the procedure summary. Now, let's tackle the first-stage optimization algorithm.

Define:
investment universe of k-number of potential investments.
necessary level of resolution, log this as ϱ.[2]
N-number of empty $\varrho \times k$ matrices, log these as $\Omega_1^{\varrho \times k}, \Omega_2^{\varrho \times k}, \ldots, \Omega_N^{\varrho \times k}$.[3]

$\pi(\boldsymbol{\omega})$ returns the parameters of our chosen cdf, given portfolio weights, $\boldsymbol{\omega}$.[4]

$\Phi\left(\left(\frac{W}{\vartheta \varpi}\right)^{1/t} - 1; \pi(\boldsymbol{\omega})\right)$ is the lower-tail cdf with our required return and parameters

[2] ϱ is the number of optimal portfolios to calculate, and since possible allocations run from 0 to 1, we know that our intervals, I, are defined as $1/\varrho = I$. So, $\varrho = 5$ yields optimal portfolios for every 20% of allocation to the goal. $\varrho = 100$ yields optimal portfolios for every 1% of allocation to the goal, and so on.

[3] There will be a different matrix for each goal: each row in the matrix represents a potential across-goal allocation of wealth (rows represent values of ϱ), and each column will represent the weight of an investment (columns represent $\boldsymbol{\omega}$).

[4] For example, mean and variance for a Gaussian distribution, location and scale for a logistic distribution, alpha, beta, gamma, sigma for an alpha-stable distribution, and so on.

the objective function as

$$f(\varpi\vartheta, W, t, \omega) = \Phi\left(\frac{W}{\vartheta\varpi}^{\frac{1}{t}} - 1; \pi(\omega)\right) + 100 \cdot (1 - \mathbf{1}'\omega)^2,$$

$$\text{s.t.}\, \omega \in [0,1].$$

For $j = 1$ to $j = N$:

For $i = 1$ to $i = \varrho$:

$$\vartheta_i = \frac{i}{\varrho}$$

Find ω_{optim} that satisfies: $\min_{\omega} f(\varpi\vartheta_i, W_j, t_j, \omega)$

Log $\boldsymbol{\Omega}_j^{i,1:k} = \omega_{\text{optim}}$

And we are left with a matrix of optimal investment allocations, $\boldsymbol{\Omega}$, with each row of the matrix corresponding to a potential across-goal allocation and each column representing a different investment in our investment universe. Notice how our target function—the function we are minimizing—includes the constraints that the investment weights must sum to 1, and that the investment weights cannot be greater than 1 nor less than 0. The latter is the no-short-sell/no-leverage constraint. These constraints could, of course, be removed or modified by adjusting or eliminating the constraint applied to the investment weights in the optimization function, but I prefer to include them as I know of very few goals-based investors who would accept leverage and short sales as a matter of core policy.

This algorithm is pretty straightforward in practice. We are trying to build a matrix where the rows correspond directly to each possible across-goal allocation and each column corresponds to the weight of an investment in our investment universe. If we have 99 potential across-goal allocations and, say, 10 potential investments to choose from, then $\boldsymbol{\Omega}$, our matrix, would have 99 rows and 10 columns. From there, we simply iterate through each potential level of across-goal allocation and record the investment weights that give us the least chance of failure, given the goal specifics. Of course, we do this for each goal, and each goal will have its own matrix of results.

Our second stage of optimization is to combine the across-goal allocations in such a way as to deliver the highest utility. Obviously, our previous optimization was not continuous—that is, we had to choose some level of resolution and optimize over each of those specific values. So, our second stage algorithm cannot be continuous, either. Given discrete optimization, there is no guarantee that we have found the solution that is *exactly* correct. I lose no sleep over this. The practitioner will need to find the level of resolution that best balances computing time and estimation accuracy for the project at hand, but there is no sense in "being wrong to several decimal points," as Jean Brunel has cautioned.

One more note before moving forward. Whereas more traditional non-linear optimizers can be deployed on the target function in the first optimization algorithm, I employ a Monte Carlo technique in the second stage. I find it is simple, effective, and takes minimal computing time. Again, I will leave it to the practitioner to find the right balance for her own application. Keeping the notation from our first algorithm going, the second stage of optimization is as follows.

Define:

the number of simulation trials as τ

ϑ as the vector of N-number of simulated across-goal allocations, subject to

$$\mathbf{1}'\vartheta = 1,$$

$$\vartheta \in (0,1)$$

the objective function[5] is

$$g\left(\vartheta, \Omega_{1:N}\right) = \sum_{j=1}^{j=N} v_j \times \left[1 - \Phi\left(\frac{W_j}{\vartheta_j \varpi}^{\frac{1}{t_j}} - 1; \pi\left(\Omega_j^{\varrho\vartheta^j, 1:k}\right)\right)\right]$$

For $i = 1$ to $i = \tau$:

[5]There is a lot going on in this objective function. Effectively, we are just applying the goals-based utility function: taking the sumproduct of the value of a goal v_j and its probability of achievement. Our parameter function is now taking a row-vector from our Ω matrix (columns 1 through k), since the matrix holds optimal investment weights for various across-goal allocations. We can find the needed row number of the matrix by multiplying our chosen resolution, ϱ, by the simulated across-goal weight, ϑ^i.

if $g(\vartheta^i, \Omega_{1:N}) > g(\vartheta^{i-1}, \Omega_{1:N})$

then $\vartheta_{\text{optimum}} = \vartheta^i$

else next

Return:

$$\vartheta_{\text{optimum}}$$

$$\Omega_{j:N}^{\varrho\vartheta_{\text{optimum}}^{j:N},1:k}$$

In summary, we are simulating many possible allocations of wealth to each goal until we find the mix that delivers the maximal balance of achievement probabilities and goal values. We simulate some number of potential across-goal allocations, One simulated value at a time is plugged in for ϑ in the optimization function above. From the goal's matrix (Ω_j) we pull the row of investment weights that matches the across-goal allocation we are testing, written as $\Omega_j^{\varrho\vartheta^j,1:k}$ (the matrix for goal j, row number defined as $\varrho\vartheta^j$, and columns 1 through k) and we log the mix of those across-goal allocations that delivers the maximal utility across all simulations. Finally, we return the optimal across-goal wealth allocation and the optimal investment weights for each goal. When implementing, then, we can either keep the accounts separate or aggregate the optimal weights into a single portfolio, whichever is preferred.

CASE STUDY

Let's consider a case study together to help illustrate the procedure. For interested readers, I have included the relevant R code script as part of the book supplement. Again, I want to stress that the actual procedure may not be optimal from a computational perspective—I would encourage other practitioners and researchers to develop their own approach—but it suffices for my purposes.

A client joins our firm. Our first step as advisors is to spend ample time in conversation. We need to fully understand her goals, her tax situation, her ethical constraints (more on that later), and so on. We must also ensure that she has reasonable expectations, both of herself and us. We should never take on a client with unreasonable expectations or a client mandate that is not within our ability. This conversation is, then, a two-way street, determining whether this client will fit within our process as well as for the client to get a handle on her financial goals and financial picture.

Another objective at this stage is to help the client dream a little. I have found that, very often, clients do not have a clear picture of their goals. One of an advisor's jobs is to help the client crystalize her objectives. They are changeable, of course, and communicating that point is important, as well; clients will have a harder time committing to 30-year objectives that they feel can never be updated. This involves plenty of listening as clients talk themselves through their needs, wants, wishes, and dreams. We need to spend time forecasting our client's psychological state ("how would you feel if. . ."), as well as forecasting their financial state ("what is your pattern of raises. . ."). Client homework is not uncommon after the first meeting or two.

After ample conversation, we determine that our new client has the following goals in her goals-space:

- She wants to leave an estate to her children of $5,000,000, planned in 30 years from now.
- She needs to maintain her lifestyle expenses starting in 10 years, and we estimate that she will need $5,157,000 to do that.
- Our client would like to purchase a vacation home in 4 years, and her estimated price is $713,500.
- If possible, our client would like to donate $8,812,000 to her alma mater sometime around 18 years from now. This donation carries naming rights to a building on campus.
- Currently, our client has $4,654,400 in wealth from which to draw to fund her goals.

And with her goals fleshed out, we must now determine their value relative to one another. First, we have our client rank-order her goals from most important to least important. Here are the results of her goal ranking:

A. Living expenses
B. Children's estate
C. Vacation home
D. Naming rights

We now ask our client a series of questions and log the results:

- Would you rather achieve your children's estate goal with certainty or your living expenses goal with probability *p*?
- Would you rather buy your vacation home with certainty or achieve your children's estate goal with probability *p*?
- Would you rather fund your alma-mater with certainty or buy your vacation home with probability *p*?

At each stage, we vary *p* until she is indifferent to the choice. In our case study, our client has responded, and we have logged the value ratios as:

- 1.00 for her living expenses goal
- 0.45 for her estate goal
- 0.50 for her vacation home goal
- 0.58 for her naming rights goal

Recall, there are two steps to determining a goal's value. The first is the value ratio of each goal—the raw results we just elicited from our client. To determine the actual value of each goal, however, we have to take the cumulative product of the value ratios, from the most important up to the goal we are considering. So, our living expenses goal gets an automatically assigned value of 1.00. Our client's estate goal gets a value of $1.00 \times 0.45 = 0.45$, which is the value of the living expenses goal times the value ratio of her estate goal. The vacation home goal gets a value of $1.00 \times 0.45 \times 0.50 = 0.225$, which is the product of the value ratios for the living expenses goal (1.00), the estate goal (0.45), and the vacation home goal (0.50). Her naming rights goal gets a value of $1.00 \times 0.45 \times 0.50 \times 0.58 = 0.1305$. Hence, the rank-ordered goals have declining values, as we would expect: $\{1.00, 0.45, 0.225, 0.131\}$.[6]

With the details of her goals fleshed out, we can couple our client's goal details with our firm's capital market expectations and run our

[6]We could run a quick check of preference consistency here and ask another question: *would you rather achieve your naming rights goal with certainty or your living expenses goal with probability p?* Clearly, we expect the *p* to equal something close to 0.131. If it does not, then our client's preferences are not transitive (which is one of our axiomatic assumptions), and we have a problem. It would be worth a research study to measure the consistency of these types of preferences.

TABLE 3.1 Sample Capital Market Expectations

	E (return)	E (volatility)
Equity		
Large Cap	0.09	0.15
Mid Cap	0.11	0.16
Small Cap	0.12	0.17
Int'l Developed	0.07	0.15
Emerging Markets	0.09	0.17
Fixed Income		
US Agg Bond	0.04	0.05
US High Yield	0.06	0.09
US Treasury	0.03	0.03
Corporate	0.05	0.07
Alternatives		
Gold	0.06	0.19
Oil	0.04	0.32
Lottery-Like		
Private Equity	0.15	0.28
Venture Capital	0.16	0.30
Angel Venture	-0.01	0.82
Cash	0.01	0.001

optimization procedure. Obviously, capital market expectations are a critical step. Better forecasts yield better outcomes. It is not my intent to write a book about building a better investment philosophy—there are plenty of those in the world written by practitioners with much more skill than I have! It is here, however, that investment teams infuse their own belief about markets, and that can add considerable value when done well. For the sake of our illustration, let us suppose our capital market expectations are those listed in Table 3.1.

Here is where we employ the optimization algorithm from above. As mentioned, we first find every optimal portfolio for possible allocations of wealth to each goal (ϑ, in our equations), subject to some level of

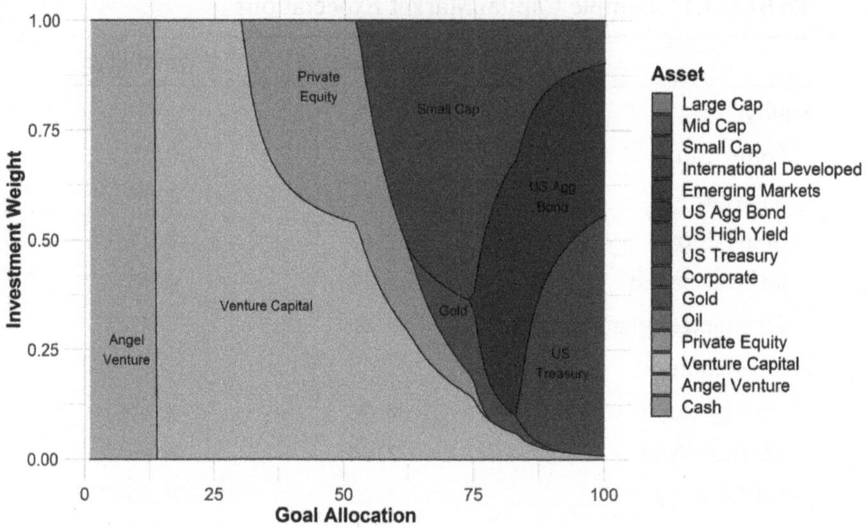

FIGURE 3.1 Optimal Portfolios for Various Levels of Wealth Allocation

resolution, ϱ. In the plot, I have demonstrated the optimal investment weights ($\boldsymbol{\omega}$, in our equations) for each possible allocation of wealth to our client's living expenses goal, and this was done at a resolution of 100. Meaning, an optimal portfolio was built for a 1% goal allocation, 2% goal allocation, 3% goal allocation, all the way up to a 100% goal allocation, moving in increments of 1% point. Figure 3.1, then, is a visual representation of a goal's allocation matrix, $\boldsymbol{\Omega}$.

Note that there is no 0% goal allocation. The theoretical model insists that *some* level of resources be dedicated to a goal, no matter how small. If there are no resources dedicated to the goal, then we cannot properly call it a goal. There is a philosophical discussion to be had here, no doubt, but I will spare us all. Suffice it to say, if there are objectives you want to achieve in life, you have to do *something* in the real world, no matter how small, to move toward their accomplishment. Otherwise they are not goals at all—and that is a mathematical fact.

From here, we go about optimizing the across-goal allocation of wealth. I use a Monte Carlo simulation at this stage because, as mentioned above, I find it easiest to marry the discrete nature of each within-goal portfolio with possible across-goal allocations. In that case, we simulate some large number of potential across-goal allocations, each of them rounded to match our chosen level of resolution—we will not be able to match a simulated 41.255%

goal allocation if our level of resolution is in increments of 10%, so we would have to round 41.255% to 40% before proceeding. For each of those simulations, we pull the probability of achieving each goal with their respective levels of across-goal allocations, then plug the results in to our utility model. Obviously, we are trying to find the across-goal allocation mix that yields the highest utility.

Table 3.2 shows the results of the allocation procedure. Our highest valued goal, the living expenses goal, receives 81% of the wealth pool, giving our client a 72% chance of success for that goal. Somewhat surprisingly, the children's estate goal receives only 3% of the wealth pool. Yet, because of the time horizon, the size of the wealth pool, and our capital market expectations, our client has a 55% probability of attaining that goal.[7] The vacation home goal receives 15% of the wealth pool, meaning it can be funded today. Note that the allocation engine returns an all-cash allocation for a fully funded goal; this is a hard-coded preference of mine but need not always be the case (in many cases, it would not be appropriate). Our aspirational naming-rights goal garners a 2% allocation of the wealth pool. Because it is valued so low compared to the other goals, and because its achievement is very improbable, anyway, the goal is reliant on the lottery-like angel venture investment. Even still, it carries a 36% probability of achievement.[8]

These results quite clearly illustrate the benefits of the goals-based framework. To begin with, the academic literature has offered no mechanism for allocating wealth across goals. Up to now, the assumption has been that investors have already allocated wealth across their goals, which is an odd assumption, especially considering that so much of the literature assumes investors are not rational. Assuming that investors have *already rationally allocated* wealth across goals seems silly, at least to me.

What's more, these results can be somewhat counter to our initial intuition. We are fully funding the vacation home, for example, but there is only a 72% chance of maintaining lifestyle expenses. If we directed all resources to this lifestyle funding objective, our client would have an 87% probability of achieving it. But, for 14% points of achievement probability, our

---

[7]This does not include the value of the vacation home, which would be ultimately included in our client's estate goal.

[8]This is a cartoon example of course, as the angel venture investment was assumed to have a Gaussian distribution, which it certainly would not. I address non-Gaussian distributions in a later chapter, but it is worth noting that the practitioner can (and should) model investments like this with a more appropriate distribution.

TABLE 3.2 Resultant Optimal Allocation of Wealth, Within and Across Goals

Not all percentages add to 1 due to rounding.

	Aggregate Portfolio	Living Expenses	Children's Estate	Vacation Home	Naming Rights
Goal Allocation		**81%**	**3%**	**15%**	**2%**
Equity					
Large Cap	–	–	–	–	–
Mid Cap	–	–	–	–	–
Small Cap	**29%**	36%	–	–	–
Int'l Developed	**–**	–	–	–	–
Emerging Markets	**–**	–	–	–	–
Fixed Income					
US Agg Bond	**42%**	52%	–	–	–
US High Yield	**–**	–	–	–	–
US Treasury	**–**	–	–	–	–
Corporate	**–**	–	–	–	–
Alternatives					
Gold	**4%**	5%	–	–	–
Oil	**–**	–	–	–	–
Lottery-Like					
Private Equity	**1%**	–	25%	–	–
Venture Capital	**7%**	7%	75%	–	–
Angel Venture	**2%**	–	–	–	100%
Cash	**15%**	–	–	100%	–

client can buy a vacation home today and fund, with reasonable confidence, her other goals. Again, the goals-based framework is a tool to rationally trade the achievement of one goal for another, a tool that has been largely absent in the literature to date.

Modern portfolio theory would also entirely eliminate lottery-like investments from consideration, and, therefore, our naming-rights goal would be considered an infeasible goal—it would return an error, in other words, and we would have to change something about the goal's variables or our expectations. We could adapt the goals-based method to always be consistent with MPT. To do this, we simply maintain exposure to the last portfolio on the efficient frontier, even if the return required by the goal is greater than the return offered by that last portfolio. Doing so would allow us to allocate across our goals, and it would keep all portfolios on the efficient frontier, but it comes at the cost of lower probability of achievement for aspirational goals. For practitioners who are mean-variance constrained, or for those of us who are reluctant to allocate to lottery-like investments in a professional setting (it is a brand-new idea, after all), adapted MPT carries some appeal. I have included the procedure for adapting MPT in the code scripts attached to this chapter.

At any rate, this is a method for solving some of the challenges of allocating wealth in the goals-based framework. It is, unfortunately, more complicated than the traditional method, carrying an inherent recursivity. Fortunately, that extra complication is easily handled by modern computing power. For investors who choose to remain mean-variance constrained, the goals-based framework can be adapted to keep all portfolios on the efficient frontier. The practitioner need only add an instruction in the algorithm to check if the goal's required return is greater than the return offered by the last portfolio on the frontier. If yes, then maintain exposure to the endpoint portfolio.

With our two-layer allocation problem now solved, I turn to another complex problem which the goals-based framework allows us to solve: allocating wealth when a portfolio manager has a market view that spans more than one period.

CHAPTER 4

Allocating Wealth Through Time

". . .the present is short, the future is doubtful, the past is certain."

—Seneca

I remember, after 2008, when I had finally cobbled together my "recession dashboard," I excitedly put my capital market expectations into a typical mean-variance optimizer. I expected to uncover some secret, that this optimizer would suddenly "see" what I saw—that a probable recession warrants a defensive portfolio posture. The output was extremely disappointing. Rather than suggest a defensive allocation of cash and bonds, as I may have expected, the optimizer had only slightly reduced holdings of stocks and increased holdings of gold. I did the same for my goals-based optimizer (which maximized the probability of attaining a required return). The results there were even sillier. Again, rather than suggest a defensive allocation, the goals-based optimizer suggested an all-gold allocation. Sigh. What was I doing wrong?

Quite simply, it is not accurate to allocate wealth in the context of the coming period only. We intuitively understand this, which was the entire motivation for me to develop my own recession dashboard. Intuitively, we know that a defensive posture ahead of a potential market selloff gives us cash to buy when prices are lower, thereby pushing our wealth significantly closer to our goal when prices recover. In the face of a probable recession, for example, our market return expectations might be significantly lowered and variances significantly raised, but a single-period optimization based on those capital market expectations alone is going to yield silly results, like an all-gold allocation. How could it do anything else? While *we* can see the recession followed by a recovery, the optimizer cannot. How could it? Those inputs are not included!

All of this is an indication to me that our tools are not as accurate as they need to be. While we may be using single-period tools, we are actually running multiperiod models in our head. That is why, when an optimizer suggests an all-gold allocation leading into a recession, we chuckle and "fix" it to be heavy cash/bonds/gold, rather than simply accept the original output. Rather than pretend that problem does not exist and come up with some ad-hoc corrections, this chapter is an attempt to solve it head on. As always, my objective here is not to curtail thinking critically about an optimizer's output! Rather, I assume that finer tools in the hands of craftsman yield finer products.

In the literature, the most practical solution to the problem of allocating through time, especially in light of varying capital market expectations, is sketched out in a forthcoming paper from Sanjiv Das et al.[1] Their approach leans on Bellman's dynamic programming technique, and the approach is quite useful for practitioners. However, I have several critiques that drive me to present my own solution. First, in their framework, they maintain the unlimited short-sale and leverage assumption. While this is defensible from a theoretical perspective, in practice this is neither simple nor recommended. For one, leverage and short-sale costs alone are likely to remove the benefits of such an allocation, but more pressing: for most goals-based investors, leverage and short-sales are constrained or eliminated in real life.

Second, their solution relies on a "model portfolio" approach—representative portfolios are formed along the efficient frontier for each type of market (good, bad, or good/bad mix). Then, dynamic programming is

[1]S. Das, D. Ostrov, A. Casanova, A. Radhakrishnan, and D. Srivastav, "Optimal Goals-Based Investment Strategies for Switching Between Bull and Bear Markets," *Journal of Wealth Management* 24, no. 4 (2022): 8–36, DOI: https://doi.org/10.3905/jwm.2021.1.161.

There are other approaches that are not based on the goals-based methodology. I do not address them here since they are even more entrenched in the mean-variance paradigm and not particularly helpful to the goals-based practitioner.

used to select which model portfolios should be selected for the coming period (informed by the probability of a good or bad year). This is a very reasonable and clever approach, given the way our business currently operates. However, I see a move away from model portfolios in the future, as we will discuss in Chapter 14. A tool that can make use of any weight combination to any investments would be valuable.[2]

What I did find very informative in their work was their treatment of how right we need to be when building multiperiod capital market expectations. There is always the risk that we allocate a portfolio to prepare for a bad market and we get a good market instead, or vice versa. How right we need to be is a critical question to answer before we embark on a total portfolio overhaul, incurring the risk of incorrect allocations and, worse yet, the costs of taxable gains. Using a simple buy-and-hold-through-all-market-environments strategy as a baseline, the authors found that we need to be about 80% sure that a bad market environment is about to happen to justify reallocating the portfolio. That is, of course, before the costs of taxes and fees are assessed. This is a very important lesson to practitioners: we need reliable models *and* high levels of conviction before moving away from a buy-and-hold strategy! Of course we kind of knew that already, but having a specific "certainty threshold" is worth quite a lot.

This approach differs from the dynamic programming one in a couple of ways. It can account for either mean-variance efficient portfolios or real-world constrained portfolios. Investment weights are allowed to be continuous, to vary by any degree—that is, we can use an optimizer to generate any combination of investments to find the optimal outcome, rather than rely on discrete and predetermined portfolios in each period. In essence, the method herein is a way to combine probability distributions that are independent of one another. Given the differences, and given the method for combining otherwise uncombinable distributions, I figure it never hurts to have a couple of solutions in the marketplace of ideas. Practitioners, then, can draw from the one that makes the most sense given the application.

---

[2] I should note that one could apply their approach to build unique "model portfolios" for each account; one would not need to rely on a firm-level model. However, I still find the discrete nature of the approach (i.e. building specific portfolios ahead of time) somewhat "clunky," motivating me to generate an alternate solution. All of this said, their approach has the distinct advantage of computational efficiency, which, given the application, may be the overriding concern.

To attempt to solve this problem, we need to first locate its source. We know that goals-based investors are attempting to attain some minimum wealth level, W, within some period of time, t. Given their starting wealth, w, we can invoke the time-value of money, so our expected future wealth is a function of existing wealth, time, and expected return: $W = w(1+r)^t$. A simple rearrangement yields the average annual return required to attain the goal: $r = (W / w)^{1/t} - 1$. When coupled with our capital market expectations, our optimizer attempts to find the portfolio that delivers the maximum probability of attaining r. As we have discussed, however, if our capital market expectations result in no possible portfolio that can attain r, then it will seek to maximize variance because that is how we maximize our probability of achievement in that scenario—hence the silly results like an all-gold allocation. The problem here is that our optimizer is maximizing variance in a moment when we probably should be doing the opposite.

The clue to our solution is in the implicit assumption contained within r. This is the *average* annual return we need to achieve our goal across t years, *not the exact return that must be had in every single year*. If we needed $r = 7\%$ over three years, for example, we could achieve our goal using a portfolio that delivered a 7% return in each of the three years, or a portfolio that delivered a 1% return in years one and two followed by a 20% return in year three, or a portfolio that delivered -3%, 15%, then 10%, or any combination that turned \$1 into \$1.23 across those three years. The point is, we are indifferent to the specific returns in any *given* year, so long as they *average* into what we need over the whole period.

The source of our problem, then, is twofold. First, our optimizer is assuming that our capital market expectations apply across all periods in the future rather than just the period immediately in front of us. Second, our optimizer assumes we are inflexible in our achievement of r for every single year, rather than our willingness to be flexible as to returns in any single year, but inflexible in the average of those years.

We shouldn't be too surprised by this deficiency. No model can be accurate with respect to inputs it does not have. Nowhere in a single-period model do we input our capital market expectations for subsequent periods. How, then, could it "know" the optimal allocation across those periods? This is good news! It means that we can simply update our model so that it can intake our multiperiod capital market expectations, our flexibility in r in any given year (though not in its average), and output an optimal mix of investments for each of those periods.

Did I say “simple”? I misspoke. Indeed, intertemporal optimization was an early project of some of the brightest minds in economics and mathematics.[3] Stated politely, these solutions are quite intricate. Not to mention, save for possibly Bellman’s and Samuelson’s (who draws on Bellman’s) solutions, they do not reflect how practitioners actually go about their work. Contrary to these authors’ assumptions, practitioners do not develop continuous-time capital market expectations. I, like most of my colleagues, develop capital market expectations in discrete time (that is, for coming *years* or *quarters*). Second, these solutions are not really intended to be portfolio allocation tools anyway—they were developed to answer different economic questions altogether. The deciding factor for me, however, is that these solutions all carry deeply rooted mean-variance assumptions. Namely, that leverage and short-sells are unconstrained, and that investors have a constant risk-aversion parameter. Since neither of those are true in practice, and given the other problems mentioned, I think investors are better served with a goals-native, updated theory that matches what they are trying to do.

Since I learn the details better when I understand the how they fit in the bigger picture, let me begin by summarizing the concepts involved. The time horizon of a goal can be subdivided into any number of subperiods. A three-year time horizon, for example, can be subdivided into three one-year subperiods. We then develop capital market expectations for each of those subperiods. Of course, our choice of investment weights in each period will tell us what return distribution to expect for the portfolio in each subperiod. This is, so far, straightforward.

Here comes the intricate part: We are going to take samples from each subperiod’s distribution and log the possible returns and the probability of the portfolio delivering each of those returns. Each of these sample points becomes a “path” that our portfolio could travel over those periods. Because we are concerned with the aggregate return of each path, we take these samples and subject them to a geometric return process. Obviously, each possible path will yield its own outcome, and it is these collections of outcomes that will define the distribution of possible aggregate returns with which we are concerned.

[3]R. Bellman, “On the Theory of Dynamic Programming,” *Proceedings of the National Academy of Sciences* 38, no. 8 (1952): 716–719; P. Samuelson, “Lifetime Portfolio Selection by Dynamic Stochastic Programming,” *The Review of Economics and Statistics* 51, no. 3 (1969): 239–246; R. Merton, “Lifetime Portfolio Selection under Uncertainty: The Continuous-Time Case,” *The Review of Economics and Statistics* 51, no. 3 (1989): 247–257; J.C. Cox and Chi-fu Huang, “Optimal Consumption and Portfolio Policies When Asset Prices Follow a Diffusion Process,” *Journal of Economic Theory* 49, no. 1 (1989): 33–83.

Probabilities, however, process across periods differently than returns. While a geometric process defines aggregated returns across periods, the probability of a particular path of returns is governed by the rule of independent probabilities. The probability of a given path is the probability of hitting a specific return in the first subperiod times the probability of hitting a specific return in the second subperiod, and so on (and iterated across all possible paths!). Obviously, it is important to keep the resultant return of each possible path separate but aligned with the probability of each possible path. And this sampled approach—the combination of aggregate returns and the probability of each of those returns—can be used to generate a final distribution of aggregate return possibilities. That distribution, of course, tells us the probability of failing to achieve our desired average return over the entire period.

Let's get to the specifics of the method. We need to adjust the vector of portfolio weights, $\boldsymbol{\omega}$, in each subperiod, $t, t+1, t+2, \ldots, T$, to maximize the probability of achieving our average annual return, $\mathcal{R}$. Let's keep this separate from the return *distribution* of each period, which we will call $\tilde{R}$. In each subperiod, then, we will have a potential distribution of returns that are defined by our choice of portfolio weights and capital market expectations for that period, the combination of which yield the parameters of $\tilde{R}$'s distribution, which we will house in the vector $\boldsymbol{\pi}$: $\tilde{R}_t(r, \boldsymbol{\pi}), \tilde{R}_{t+1}(r, \boldsymbol{\pi}), \tilde{R}_{t+2}(r, \boldsymbol{\pi}), \ldots, \tilde{R}_T(r, \boldsymbol{\pi})$. Note that these return distributions need not be Gaussian—they can be any distribution whatsoever, so long as the distribution is parametric (i.e. can be written down and generates specific results) and so long as the distribution has a cumulative distribution function.

Since we are going to take samples of each period's return distribution, we need to define a minimum and maximum as our sample space to operate within (we cannot choose $-\infty$ to ∞ since this is not a closed-form solution), so let us use $[r_{min}, r_{max}]$. Obviously, this minimum and maximum should be chosen so as to encompass as much of the return distributions as possible. If N is the number of samples we wish to take (meaning N must be a positive integer), then $\Delta r = (r_{max} - r_{min})/N$ is the distance between the sample points we are going to take. We can also think of Δr as the resolution of our point estimates. Clearly, N needs to be sufficiently large to deliver meaningful results (Δr needs to be sufficiently small), but that must be balanced against computational considerations (more on this later).

Now that we have divided our return distributions into N sample regions ranging from r_{min} to r_{max}, we can create a vector of return point estimates by averaging the return of each region of the distribution. We build this vector by starting at $n = 1$ and progressing to $n = N$ for each time period and according to the following rule:

$$\mathbf{r}_t = \langle \frac{1}{2}[(r_{\min} + n\Delta r) + (r_{\min} + (n-1)\Delta r)] \rangle_{n=1}^{n=N}.$$

Using our preferred cumulative distribution function ($\tilde{R}(r,\pi)$, in our example), we create a vector of probability estimates. The probability of any given return occurring is estimated as the probability of the return at the right edge of a given region minus the probability of return at the left edge of the region. We build the vector from $n=1$ to $n=N$ according to the following rule:

$$\mathbf{p}_t = \langle \tilde{R}(r_{\min} + n\Delta r, \pi) - \tilde{R}(r_{\min} + (n-1)\Delta r, \pi) \rangle_{n=1}^{n=N}.$$

Now, we apply our choice of return process. That is, since it is our objective to maximize the probability of attaining our required return on average, across all of the period's return distributions, we have to decide how it is we would like to define our *average* return. I prefer a geometric average as it is more accurate with respect to volatility, but an arithmetic average could also work. The other key at this stage in the algorithm is that every point estimate of return must process through every other point estimate of the return distributions that come after it. That is to say, all of the potential returns in the first time period must be subjected to all potential returns in the second time period, which must then be subjected to all potential returns in the third time period, and so on.

Choosing a geometric average yields a final return vector of

$$\mathbf{r}_F = [(\mathbf{1} + \mathbf{r}_t) \otimes (\mathbf{1} + \mathbf{r}_{t+1}) \otimes \cdots \otimes (\mathbf{1} + \mathbf{r}_T)]^{\frac{1}{T}} - \mathbf{1},$$

where $\otimes$ represents the Kronecker product.[4] The arithmetic average would be

$$\mathbf{r}_F = \frac{\mathbf{r}_t \oplus \mathbf{r}_{t+1} \oplus \cdots \oplus \mathbf{r}_T}{T},$$

[4]A Kronecker product takes every element of the first vector and multiplies it by every element of the second vector to create a third vector. So, if we have $(a, b, c) \otimes (x, y, z)$ we get a resulting vector of $(ax, ay, az, bx, by, bz, cx, cy, cz)$. Similarly, a Kronecker sum creates a new vector by summing every element of the first vector with every element of the second: $(a, b, c) \oplus (x, y, z) = (a + x, a + y, a + z, b + x, b + y, b + z, c + x, c + y, c + z)$. I am as annoyed as you by all of this.

where $\oplus$ represents the Kronecker sum. Assuming no correlation between the return distributions from one period to the next, the probability of any given return is independent of the previous, allowing us to lean on the multiplicative rule of probabilities. Our final vector of probability estimates, then, is

$$\mathbf{p}_F = \mathbf{p}_t \otimes \mathbf{p}_{t+1} \otimes \cdots \otimes \mathbf{p}_T.$$

A quick note of orientation here. $\mathbf{r}_F$ is the vector of final returns. $\mathbf{p}_F$ is the vector holding the probabilities of each of the returns in $\mathbf{r}_F$. We have kept them separate up to now because returns and the probability of those returns are governed by different processes. Returns are processed through each distribution according to the rules of our chosen return processes (i.e. either arithmetic or geometric). The probability of those returns is processed according to the rules of independent probabilities. Because the elements of $\mathbf{r}_F$ and $\mathbf{p}_F$ carry a one-to-one correspondence (the first element of $\mathbf{r}_F$ corresponds to the first element of $\mathbf{p}_F$, the second element of $\mathbf{r}_F$ corresponds to the second element of $\mathbf{p}_F$, and so on), we can arrange them into a matrix. We are, of course, interested in the probability of attaining our required return across these multiple periods, so we will also row-order the matrix from the lowest value to the highest value with the first column (which holds our return vector) as the argument. Note that the whole row is rearranged so that the probability information keeps its correspondence with the returns information.

Let $\langle\cdot,\cdot\rangle^{\downarrow}$ be a min-to-max row-ordered matrix with the first column as the argument. To get our final probability estimate, we note which row number of the first column is just less than or equal to our required return. This is indicated as $\lfloor \mathbf{r}_i \rfloor = \mathcal{R}$ in the summation. Then, we sum the second column from the first row to the row we just noted:

$$\widehat{\Phi}(\mathcal{R}) \approx \sum_{i=1}^{\lfloor \mathbf{r}_i \rfloor = \mathcal{R}} \langle \mathbf{r}_F, \mathbf{p}_F \rangle^{\downarrow}.$$

And we now have an estimate of the probability of failing to achieve the minimum required return over the course of multiple periods.

I work better with specific examples, so now that we have detailed the theory, let's apply it to a for-instance. Suppose we believe that portfolio returns are logistic rather than Gaussian. We define our return distributions, then, as

$$\tilde{R}(r) = \frac{1}{1+\exp\left(-\frac{r-\mathbf{m}'\boldsymbol{\omega}}{ç\sqrt{\boldsymbol{\omega}'\boldsymbol{\Sigma}\boldsymbol{\omega}}}\right)},$$

where $\mathbf{m}$ is the vector of expected asset returns, $\boldsymbol{\Sigma}$ is the covariance matrix, and $ç = 0.60$ is the Gaussian-to-logistic volatility conversion factor. Let me pause here for a second. There are, in fact, few practical tools for combining the portfolios of non-Gaussian assets. In this example, we are assuming the investments themselves are Gaussian so that we may lean on familiar tools: correlation, volatility, and average returns. We then "convert" that Gaussian portfolio into a logistic distribution to capture the nature of a real-life portfolio, namely the fatter tails. Since both Gaussian and logistic distributions are symmetrical, the location parameters (the average of the distribution) sync up automatically (this would not be so if we were incorporating the higher moments of skew and kurtosis).

Unlike the location parameter, the scale parameter of a Gaussian distribution is not the same as the scale parameter of a logistic distribution, hence the conversion factor, $ç$. Of course, exactly what value $ç$ should take is an empirical question. I have chosen $ç = 0.60$ as it keeps the distribution similar enough without compromising the fat-tailed nature of the logistic distribution. This is all a heuristic, but I want to illustrate how the intertemporal optimization method of this chapter can apply to any return distribution so that practitioners might implement it as they wish.

Using our logistic-ish distribution, the capital market expectations from Table 4.1, and supposing we have a three-year time horizon, we can influence the cumulative distribution function of each year by adjusting the investment weights in each period. Let us set $r_{\min} = -1.0$ and $r_{\max} = 1.0$, with $N = 4$, so $\Delta r = (1 - -1)/4 = 0.50$. Clearly, four sample points ($N = 4$) is far too low a resolution to derive meaningful answers, but I want to first illustrate how to do this "by hand." Then we can look at the results with higher levels of resolution. Our first step is to build point estimates for $t = 1, t = 2$, and $t = 3$, and to keep things simple, we will keep our weights constant in each period: $\boldsymbol{\omega} = (0.50, 0.25, 0.125, 0.125)$.

TABLE 4.1 Example Multiperiod Capital Market Expectations

Year 1: Average Year					
		Covariance (Correlation$_{row,column}$ × Volatility$_{row}$ × Volatility$_{column}$)			
	Expected Return	Stocks	Bonds	Alternatives	Cash
Stocks	10%	1.00(0.16)(0.16)	0.20(0.16)(0.03)	0.10(0.16)(0.18)	0.01(0.16)(0.001)
Bonds	3%	0.20(0.03)(0.16)	1.00(0.03)(0.03)	0.20(0.03)(0.18)	0.01(0.03)(0.001)
Alternatives	4%	0.10(0.18)(0.16)	0.20(0.18)(0.03)	1.00(0.18)(0.18)	0.01(0.18)(0.001)
Cash	1%	0.01(0.001)(0.16)	0.01(0.001)(0.03)	0.01(0.001)(0.18)	1.00(0.001)(0.001)

Year 2: Recessionary Year					
		Covariance (Correlation$_{row,column}$ × Volatility$_{row}$ × Volatility$_{column}$)			
	Expected Return	Stocks	Bonds	Alternatives	Cash
Stocks	−10%	1.00(0.22)(0.00)	0.40(0.22)(0.06)	0.20(0.22)(0.20)	0.01(0.22)(0.001)
Bonds	6%	0.40(0.06)(0.22)	1.00(0.06)(0.06)	0.40(0.06)(0.20)	0.01(0.06)(0.001)
Alternatives	3%	0.20(0.20)(0.22)	0.40(0.20)(0.06)	1.00(0.20)(0.20)	0.01(0.20)(0.001)
Cash	1%	0.01(0.001)(0.22)	0.01(0.001)(0.06)	0.01(0.001)(0.20)	1.00(0.001)(0.001)

Year 3: Recovery Year					
		Covariance (Correlation$_{row,column}$ × Volatility$_{row}$ × Volatility$_{column}$)			
	Expected Return	Stocks	Bonds	Alternatives	Cash
Stocks	12%	1.00(0.12)(0.12)	0.20(0.12)(0.03)	0.10(0.12)(0.18)	0.01(0.12)(0.001)
Bonds	3%	0.20(0.03)(0.12)	1.00(0.03)(0.03)	0.20(0.03)(0.18)	0.01(0.03)(0.001)
Alternatives	5%	0.10(0.18)(0.12)	0.20(0.18)(0.03)	1.00(0.18)(0.18)	0.01(0.18)(0.001)
Cash	1%	0.01(0.001)(0.12)	0.01(0.001)(0.03)	0.01(0.001)(0.18)	1.00(0.001)(0.001)

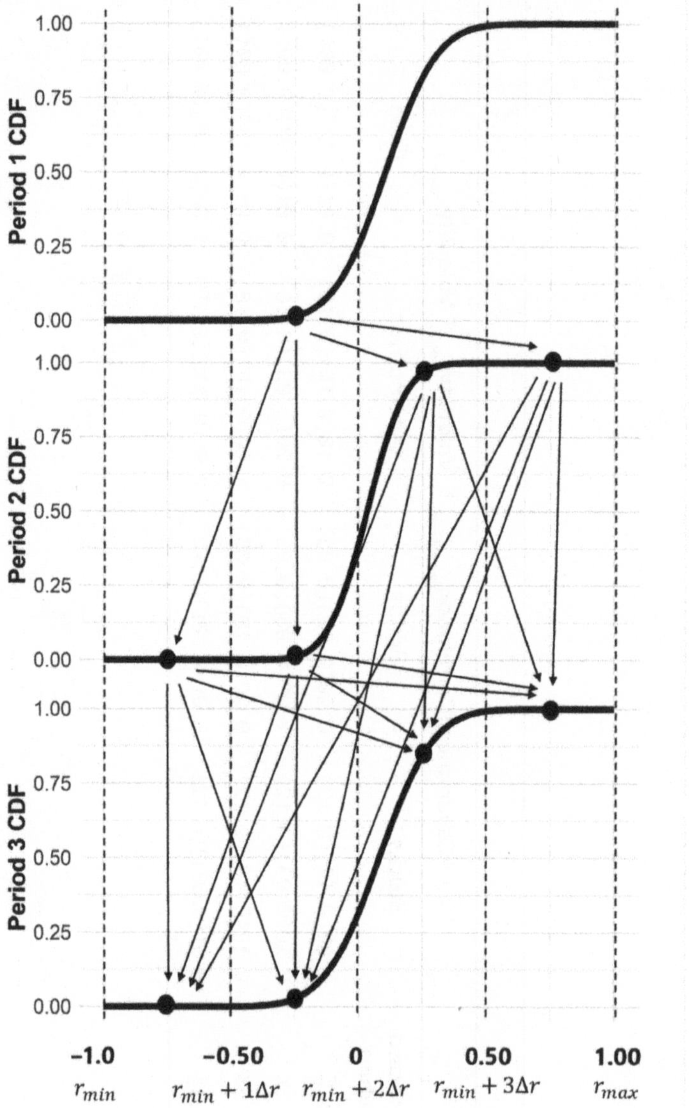

FIGURE 4.1 CDF of Returns for Each Period

With these distributions in hand, each point estimate must process through the point estimates in the subsequent distribution, as illustrated in Figure 4.1. Doing the actual calculations, we have:

$$\mathbf{r}_1 = \begin{pmatrix} \frac{1}{2}[(-1+(1)(0.5))+(-1+(1-1)(0.5))], \\ \frac{1}{2}[(-1+(2)(0.5))+(-1+(2-1)(0.5))], \\ \frac{1}{2}[(-1+(3)(0.5))+(-1+(3-1)(0.5))], \\ \frac{1}{2}[(-1+(4)(0.5))+(-1+(4-1)(0.5))] \end{pmatrix},$$

reducing to $\mathbf{r}_1 = (-0.75, -0.250, 0.25, 0.75)$. Doing the same for periods two and three we get the same vectors:

$$\mathbf{r}_2 = (-0.75, -0.25, 0.25, 0.75),$$

$$\mathbf{r}_3 = (-0.75, -0.25, 0.25, 0.75).$$

Addressing the probabilities from each period:

$$\mathbf{p}_1 = \begin{pmatrix} \tilde{R}(-1+(1)(0.5)) - \tilde{R}(-1+(1-1)(0.5)), \\ \tilde{R}(-1+(2)(0.5)) - \tilde{R}(-1+(2-1)(0.5)), \\ \tilde{R}(-1+(3)(0.5)) - \tilde{R}(-1+(3-1)(0.5)), \\ \tilde{R}(-1+(4)(0.5)) - \tilde{R}(-1+(4-1)(0.5)) \end{pmatrix},$$

reducing to $\mathbf{p}_1 = (0.00, 0.23, 0.77, 0.00)$. Calculating the second and third periods in the same way, we derive

$$\mathbf{p}_2 = (0.00, 0.60, 0.40, 0.00),$$

$$\mathbf{p}_3 = (0.00, 0.14, 0.86, 0.00).$$

Next, we apply our geometric returns process and our probabilities process to yield the final return vector and probability vector. Recall, every point in $\mathbf{r}_1$ must process through every point in $\mathbf{r}_2$, which must then process through every point in $\mathbf{r}_3$, and this process follows the geometric or arithmetic formula from above. This means that our final return vector will be

$4^3 = 64$ elements long. I won't bore you by delineating the actual calculation, but the final vector of returns looks like this (read left-to-right, top-to-bottom):

```
-0.750 -0.639 -0.573 -0.573 -0.639 -0.480 -0.383 -0.383 -0.573 -0.383
-0.269 -0.269 -0.573 -0.383 -0.269 -0.269 -0.639 -0.480 -0.383 -0.383
-0.480 -0.250 -0.111 -0.111 -0.383 -0.111  0.054  0.054 -0.383 -0.111
 0.054  0.054 -0.573 -0.383 -0.269 -0.269 -0.383 -0.111  0.054  0.054
-0.269  0.054  0.250  0.250 -0.269  0.054  0.250  0.250 -0.573 -0.383
-0.269 -0.269 -0.383 -0.111  0.054  0.054 -0.269  0.054  0.250  0.250
-0.269  0.054  0.250  0.250
```

Using our method above, we also build our vector of probabilities. Remember, this vector is our estimate for the probability each of those return outcomes occurring. Again, since each element in the first period's probability vector must pass through each point in the second and third period's elements, I won't bore you with the extended calculation. Our final vector of probability estimates look like this:

```
0.00000 0.00000 0.00000 0.00000 0.00000 0.00000 0.00001 0.00000 0.00000
0.00000 0.00001 0.00000 0.00000 0.00000 0.00000 0.00000 0.00000 0.00006
0.00038 0.00000 0.00000 0.01890 0.11746 0.00000 0.00000 0.01269 0.07887
0.00000 0.00000 0,00003 0.00017 0.00000 0.00000 0.00020 0.00127 0.00000
0.00000 0.06376 0.39634 0.00001 0.00000 0.04281 0.26611 0.00001 0.00000
0.00009 0.00057 0.00000 0.00000 0.00000 0.00000 0.00000 0.00000 0.00002
0.00012 0.00000 0.00000 0.00001 0.00008 0.00000 0.00000 0.00000 0.00000
0.00000
```

Our vector of returns and probabilities correspond one-for-one. Meaning, the first element in our probability vector is the probability of getting the first element of the return vector. We want to reorder the two vectors so that our potential returns are in order from smallest to largest. To accomplish this, we place both vectors into a matrix with the return vector as the first column and the probability vector as the second column. We then row-order the matrix from low to high using the first column as the ordering mechanism. Remember, whenever we move the location of the return elements, we must also move the location of the probability elements! Our row-ordered matrix looks like this:

	Return	Prob		Return	Prob
1	-0.750	0.0000	33	-0.269	0.0000
2	-0.639	0.0000	34	-0.269	0.0000
3	-0.639	0.0000	35	-0.269	0.0000
4	-0.639	0.0000	36	-0.269	0.0000
5	-0.573	0.0000	37	-0.269	0.0000
6	-0.573	0.0000	38	-0.250	0.0189
7	-0.573	0.0000	39	-0.111	0.1175
8	-0.573	0.0000	40	-0.111	0.0000
9	-0.573	0.0000	41	-0.111	0.0127
10	-0.573	0.0000	42	-0.111	0.0000
11	-0.480	0.0000	43	-0.111	0.0638
12	-0.480	0.0001	44	-0.111	0.0000
13	-0.480	0.0000	45	0.054	0.0789
14	-0.383	0.0000	46	0.054	0.0000
15	-0.383	0.0000	47	0.054	0.0002
16	-0.383	0.0000	48	0.054	0.0000
17	-0.383	0.0000	49	0.054	0.3963
18	-0.383	0.0004	50	0.054	0.0000
19	-0.383	0.0000	51	0.054	0.0428
20	-0.383	0.0000	52	0.054	0.0001
21	-0.383	0.0000	53	0.054	0.0001
22	-0.383	0.0002	54	0.054	0.0000
23	-0.383	0.0000	55	0.054	0.0000
24	-0.383	0.0000	56	0.054	0.0000
25	-0.383	0.0000	57	0.250	0.2661
26	-0.269	0.0000	58	0.250	0.0000
27	-0.269	0.0000	59	0.250	0.0006
28	-0.269	0.0000	60	0.250	0.0000
29	-0.269	0.0000	61	0.250	0.0001
30	-0.269	0.0013	62	0.250	0.0000
31	-0.269	0.0000	63	0.250	0.0000
32	-0.269	0.0000	64	0.250	0.0000

[...]

And our final step is to find the return element in our row-ordered matrix, which is equal to or just less than our required return. If our required return is 8%, then the row number would be 56 because the return of that row, 5.4%, is just less than our required return. To assess the probability of failing to achieve that return, we sum all the elements in the probability column from the first row to row 56. In this example, the result is 0.73. And so, the probability of failing to attain our required return, on average, over those three periods, given the investment weights and capital market expectations, is 73%.

Obviously, this level of resolution is far too low to derive meaningful answers. Furthermore, the objective is to *adjust* the portfolio weights in each period to generate the lowest possible failure probability. As should be abundantly clear, this cannot be done "by hand" in practice—this was simply to illustrate the procedure so you may implement the method using the tools of your preference.

Let's increase the resolution and set $N = 60$ with $r_{min} = -0.80$ and $r_{max} = 0.80$. This generates a probability of failing to achieve our 8% average required return of 79%, meaning our choice of portfolio weights was generally poor.

And this is where our optimizer comes in (for interested readers, I have included some R code in the companion resources[5] to illustrate the method). It is the objective of the optimizer to minimize the probability of failure by adjusting the portfolio weights in each period. When we do all of this, we find that our optimal allocation is 100% stocks in year one, 100% bonds in year two, and 100% stocks in year three, which is consistent with our intuition. When we run a single-period optimizer, we find that our optimal allocation is 100% stocks in year one, 100% *alternatives* in year two, and 100% stocks in year three, which is a departure from our intuition. To quantify this point, the multiperiod optimizer yields a probability of failure of 44% while the single-period optimizer yields a probability of failure of 52%! No small difference!

In an effort to be as clear as possible, let us recap the procedure:

1. **Subdivide the total time horizon into subperiods and develop capital market expectations for each subperiod.** There is no need for infinite subperiods, nor to account for the whole time horizon (if it is long). After a while, our capital market expectations should converge to the long-run average and, after that, every subperiod portfolio will be the same.
2. **Subdivide each distribution into sample regions.** More samples yield higher accuracy, but at the cost of higher computation time. Practitioners will need to strike the right balance to accomplish the task at hand.
3. **Estimate a sample return by averaging the value from the left and right side of each region.** Log that return sample in a vector. Start a new vector for each subperiod.
4. **Estimate that sample return's probability by applying the cumulative distribution function to the left and right side of the region and taking the average.** Log that sample's probability in a vector. Start a new vector for each subperiod. Also, and this is very important, the values in this vector must maintain their correspondence to the sample return vectors.

[5]The companion resources can be found at www.franklinparker.com/gbpt-book

5. **Apply a geometric (or arithmetic) return process to each sample return vector such that each return sample passes through each subsequent return sample.** The final vector (which will be longer than the other vectors) is the sample of possible aggregate/average returns.
6. **Apply the chain rule of probabilities to each sample probability vector such that each probability passes through every subsequent probability sample.** The final vector (which will be longer than the other vectors) is the probability of each sample return occurring.
7. **Order the return vector from smallest to largest.** Maintain the correspondence of elements to the probability vector. That is, if you move element 115 in the return vector to position 53, make sure and move element 115 from the probability vector to position 53!
8. **In the final return vector, find the return element that is just under the return required by the goal.** Log the element's position number.
9. **In the final probability vector, sum the probability vector from its first element to the position number ascertained in step 8.** This figure is our estimated probability of failing to achieve our required return.
10. **Change the expected distribution in each period (and also the final, aggregate, distribution) by adjusting the portfolio weights of each period.** An optimizer or Monte Carlo engine can be used to find the intertemporal portfolio combination which offers the lowest chance of failure.

And that is the procedure in a nutshell!

It seems worthwhile to pause here for a word on balancing the computational burden with accuracy. Clearly, the higher level of resolution, the more accurate our assessment of the final probability distribution (in the limit, as $N \to \infty$, we have the actual distribution). However, computational time increases exponentially with increases in resolution—our final vector has a length of N^T elements—so there is a tradeoff to be had here.

Also, we do not necessarily need to define capital market expectations for every possible subperiod to which our investor is exposed. That is, if our time horizon is 10 years, I do not think we should develop capital market expectations for each of those 10 years. At some point, our forecast is no better than average, and in that case, we simply make our capital market expectations equal to our long-run average expectation. We only need to develop capital market expectations for the periods in our near future that depart

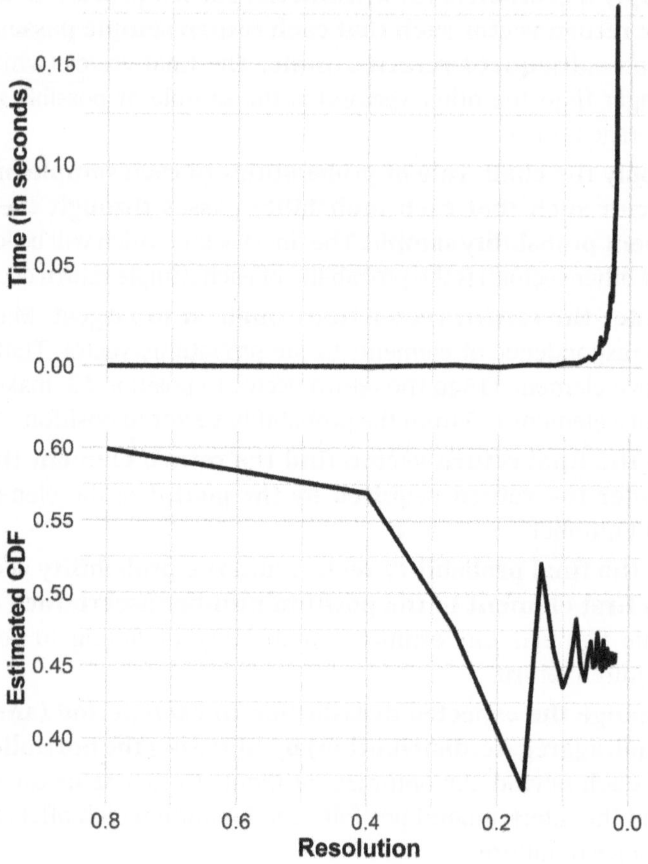

FIGURE 4.2 Trading Computational Time for Accuracy
Example computation times running the optimizer on my average-performance personal computer.

substantially from the long-run average expectation because the difference between the single-period and multiperiod optimizer is only significant for these periods, anyway. When our expectations match the long-run average, the multiperiod solution is the same as the single-period solution.

And let us remember that all of this is just an estimate anyway. While it may be tempting to increase the resolution to very fine levels to get ever more accurate estimates, we start running the risk of "being wrong to several decimal places," as Jean Brunel has cautioned. Is there really a difference in practice between a portfolio with a 43.4532% probability of failure and a 43.4423% probability of failure? I would venture to say that there is likely little practical difference between a portfolio with a 44% probability of failure and one with a 40% probability of failure, so I would need a lot of convincing before I accepted that the extra computational time is worth it (Figure 4.2).

In the end, these are decisions best left to you, the practitioner. You are in the best position to balance these tradeoffs for the application in front of you. In any event, it should be clear that multiperiod optimization is superior to single-period optimization. We would all do well to adopt such a model, even if it does naught but augment existing processes. I would also recommend that practitioners continue to incorporate their own "polishing" procedures to any optimizer. The Black and Litterman model[6] is quite common, but there are also some more recent polishers that appear very promising.[7] Whatever portfolio management procedures are used, the multiperiod approach can serve to help our investors achieve their goals more often.

And that is what we get paid to do.

[6]F. Black and R. Litterman, "Asset Allocation: Combining Investor Views with Market Equilibrium," *Fixed Income Research* (Goldman, Sachs & Company, 1990).

[7]H.P. Pendersen, A. Babu, and A. Levine, "Enhanced Portfolio Optimization," *Financial Analysts Journal* 77, no. 2 (2021): 124–151, DOI: https://doi.org/10.1080/0015198X.2020.1854543.

CHAPTER 5

Real Markets, Real Risk, Real Portfolios

"Foresight is not about predicting the future, it's about minimizing surprise."

—Karl Schroeder

For the latter-half of my childhood, I grew up on a working cattle ranch in central Texas. As you can imagine, there is always something to be done on a working ranch—haul hay, feed cattle, work cattle, fix fence, and so on—and this kind of work in the heat of the Texas sun imparts an appreciation for the tools of the trade. No two tools loom larger on working land than the tractor and the horse.

Tractors are quite handy, of course. You can haul hay, fix fence, and plow fields with tractors. The best thing about a tractor, however, is its reliability. So long as it is well-oiled and full of diesel, you can turn on that tractor and go to work. It does exactly what you tell it to do.

Horses have their own advantages. They are great at reaching those rugged nooks and crannies of land, and almost nothing is better for herding other animals than a good horse. Horses, however, are bigger and stronger than we are, and, unlike tractors, they have a mind of their own. If you wake up to a horse who does not want to work, there really is nothing you can do about it. And, occasionally, a horse gets spooked and decides to buck you off.

In modern finance, replete with our deterministic equations and empirical studies, we have come to view markets as though they were tractors.

In our minds, markets have become a tool that we can reliably use to get our work done—to retire, to send kids to college, to fund our philanthropic gifts. But contrary to our imagination, markets are really much more like horses than they are tractors. Wonderful tools, yes, but markets are bigger and stronger than we are, and very often they would just as soon kick us in the teeth as help us get our work done. Goals-based investing is as much about discarding these incorrect views of markets as it is about adjusting the math of portfolio theory.

As we have explored, there are some silly assumptions pervading the investment literature—unlimited short-selling and leverage are certainly at the top of that list. There is, however, another very damaging assumption for goals-based investors pervading the practical and academic literature: the assumption of Gaussian returns for assets. Of course, many academics and practitioners will be quick to point out that though markets may not be exactly statistically normal, they are "close enough" for our purposes. If returns *are* close enough to Gaussian most of the time, then we could defend the use of such a distribution, I will agree. But is that claim actually true?

Our first clue comes from the S&P 500 index (though any asset would do to illustrate this point). Suppose we were to use the first 1,000 days of returns to calculate an expected volatility, as measured by standard deviation. If returns were drawn from a Gaussian distribution, that would be more than enough to get an accurate expectation. However, what we find is that, no matter how long of a period we use to calculate volatility, any expectation derived from the past is always *very* wrong going forward.

This difference is illustrated in the plot. Here I have repeatedly calculated the standard deviation of returns over the number of days shown on the x-axis, and plotted the result on the y-axis. So, we calculate the standard deviation of daily returns for 100 days, then 101 days, then 102 days, and so on. When drawn from a Gaussian distribution, volatility converges fairly quickly on our expectation, as the dotted line shows. That is, when drawn from a Gaussian distribution, the standard deviation of daily returns is not meaningfully different, whether we use 2,500 days of data or 5,000 days of data, and our standard deviation expectation tends to hold for the *next* 2,500 or 5,000 days of data. This is what we would expect if markets were tractors.

Actual market returns, however, show that volatility seems to never converge toward any given number, as Figure 5.1 demonstrates. In fact, the longer the period of data, the higher volatility seems to get. Note, too, how the data becomes dominated by intermittent "catastrophes." Volatility tends to find a stable point, but then it jumps considerably. Even after 12,000 days of data, calculated volatility has not found an equilibrium and continues to

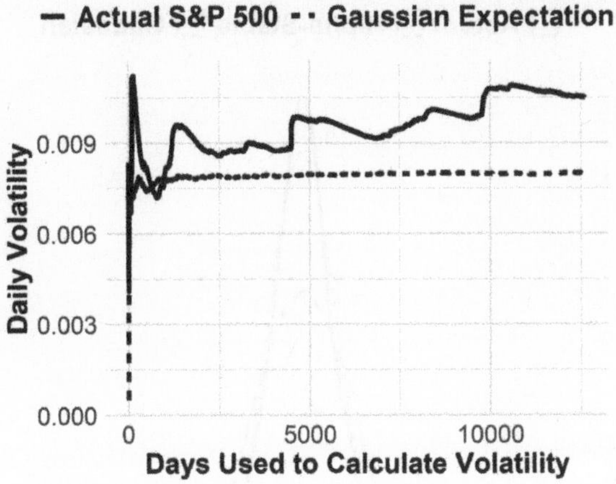

FIGURE 5.1 *N*-Day Volatility of S&P 500, Jan 1970 to Dec 2020

drift higher. Sounds quite a lot like a horse. Most of the time we can get our work done, but every now and then that horse tries to buck us off.

If that is not convincing enough, let's absorb the same data a different, more formal, way. Nassim Taleb calls this *Wittgenstein's Ruler*.[1] Suppose you believe, with 99.9% certainty, that market returns are Gaussian. We can use Bayes' rule to update our beliefs rationally in the face of new evidence. We find that there has been one 10-standard-deviation move in the S&P 500 across the period 1950 to 2012, and two 9-standard-deviation moves.[2] So, presupposing markets are Gaussian with 99.9% certainty (our prior), given these market moves (the new evidence), we must accept that the probability of markets *actually* being Gaussian is 0.0000000000000002%.

In short, there is really no way a rational person can believe market returns are drawn from a Gaussian distribution, or anything close thereto.

Better fitting the evidence of observed returns is a type of distribution known as Levy-alpha-stable, sometimes called just alpha-stable or Levy distributions (Figure 5.2). Among other things, these distributions are characterized by having infinite volatility—there is no point where we can expect calculated standard deviation to settle on a particular value. Our expected volatility, therefore, is *infinite* with these distributions. Of course, this puts

[1]Wittgenstein asked whether you were using the ruler to measure the table or the table to measure the ruler. C.f. N.N. Taleb, *Statistical Consequences of Fat Tails: Real World Preasymptotics, Epistemology, and Applications* (Stem Academic Press, 2020).

[2]J. Voss, "Fact File: Sigma Events," *Enterprising Investor Blog*.

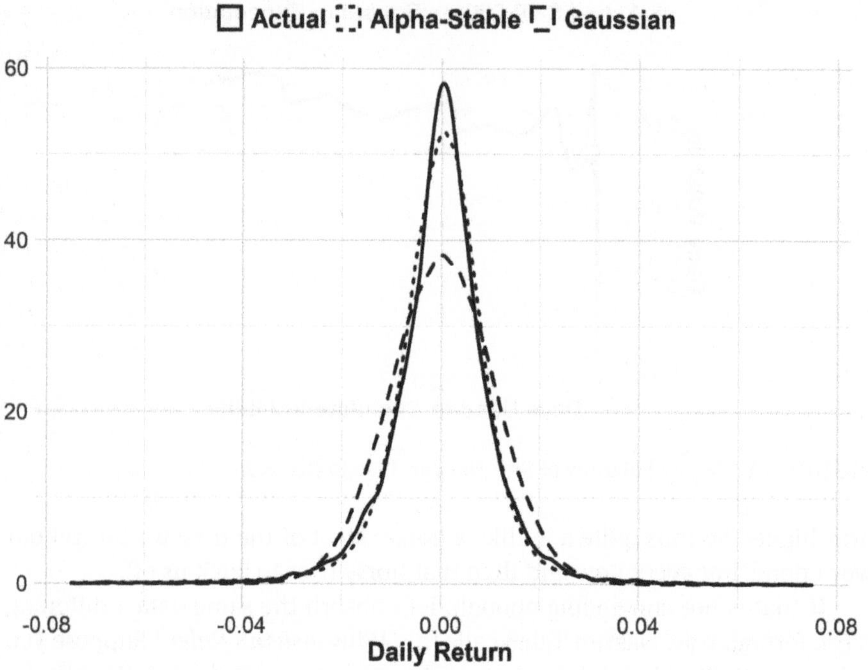

FIGURE 5.2 Daily S&P 500 Returns Compared to Alpha-Stable and Gaussian Distributions

the entirety of mean-variance theory in doubt—if our variance expectation is always infinite, there is no way to find a portfolio with *minimum* variance. Luckily for goals-based investors, alpha-stable distributions have defined cumulative distribution functions! Since that is the central metric with which we are concerned, goals-based portfolio theory allows investors to step away from the Gaussian assumption, at least at the portfolio level.

Another defining characteristic of these distributions is that they have "fat tails." Returns will be very very bad and very very good much more often than the Gaussian distribution would predict. In the illustration of daily S&P 500 returns, note how in the tail of the actual distribution the record of daily returns very closely matches the alpha-stable distribution (Figure 5.3).

For goals-based investors, understanding which return distribution we can expect is extremely important as it yields different outcomes for risk expectations, portfolio allocation and, ultimately, the probability of achieving a goal. For example, suppose you had perfect foreknowledge of the mean and standard deviation of annual returns for a portfolio that was 60% allocated to SPY, 30% to AGG, and 10% to GLD from 2004 through 2020. Even

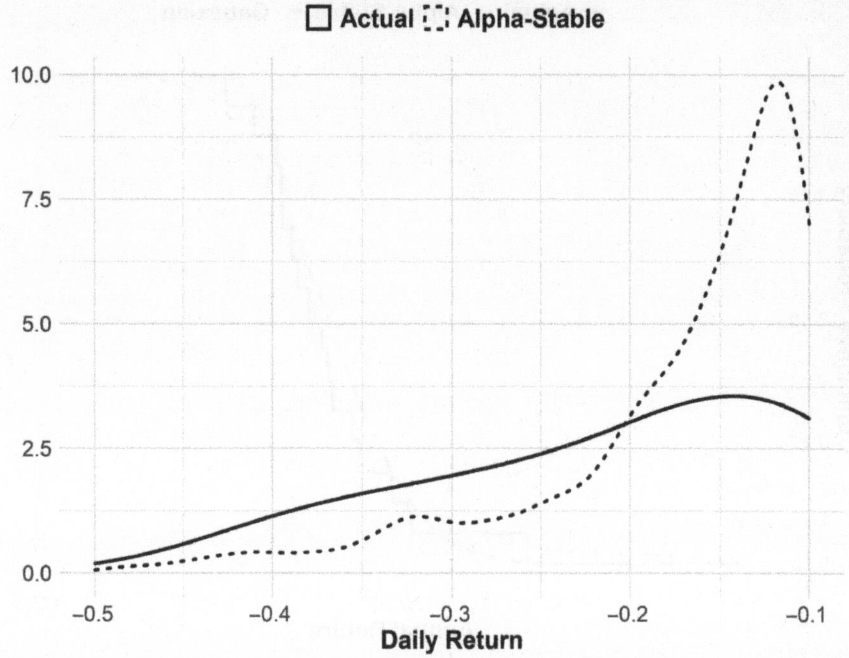

FIGURE 5.3 Daily S&P 500 Returns in the Left Tail Compared to Alpha-Stable and Gaussian Distributions

with perfect knowledge of those parameters, using a Gaussian return assumption would lead you to underestimate the probability of achieving a 7% annual return by 13% points (Gaussian assumptions lead to a 57% probability of achieving 7% or better in any given year). Using the alpha-stable distribution (and assuming perfect foreknowledge of the parameters), we get a probability of 67%—a miss of only 2% points as the actual realized probability is 69%. Gaussian assumptions also underestimate the chances of a severe loss in any given year—an important consideration for investors nearing their goal. As veteran practitioners are well aware, the order of returns matters quite a lot for investments that carry defined time horizons. All of this is illustrated in Figure 5.4.

As a quick aside, my favorite example of the risk in the order of returns is the comparison of two 30-year market periods: 1981–2010 versus 1930–1959. Both market periods returned an average of 12.2% per year, but in the second period our investor experienced staggering losses in the first few years (–25% in 1930, –43% in 1931, and –8% in 1932). Of course, for investors not taking withdrawals, this is not much of a problem. These market drawdowns are, in

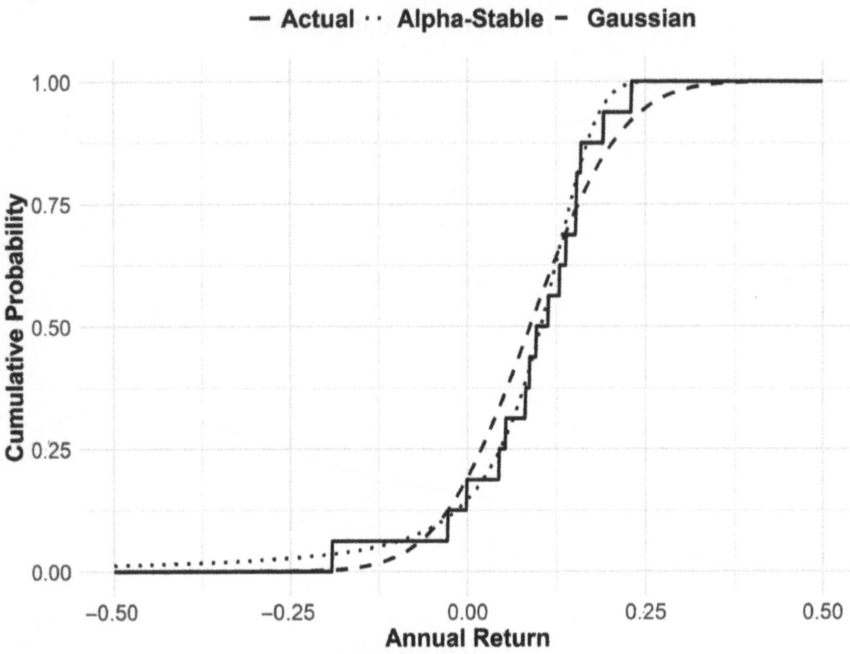

FIGURE 5.4 Cumulative Distribution Function of Actual, Alpha-Stable, and Gaussian Annual Return Distributions
60% SPY, 30% AGG, 10% GLD Portfolio, 2004–2020

fact, beneficial for investors who are actively contributing to an account because they are buying at lower prices early on. However, for investors who are taking withdrawals, those early losses are catastrophic. An investor withdrawing 6% of her initial portfolio value per year from her account would see it depleted within the first decade. A 6% withdrawal rate sounds excessive, yes, until you compare it to the 1981–2010 period. That period saw very good first years (–5% in 1981, 21% in 1982, and 23% in 1983). During that period, our investor not only withdrew 6% of her initial portfolio value every year but also saw her corpus grow by a factor of 10! For goals-based investors, the order of returns and the timing of drawdowns matters!

But even that is not our most serious concern. Of most concern is that the Gaussian return assumption allows us to take a shortcut when organizing goals-based portfolios. When we make the assumption that returns are Gaussian, it is mathematically equivalent to subdivide our total return requirement into annual subperiods, then organize the portfolio to maximize the probability of achieving that return in a single period. In other words, it is the same to optimize the portfolio to achieve a 7% return in the coming year as it

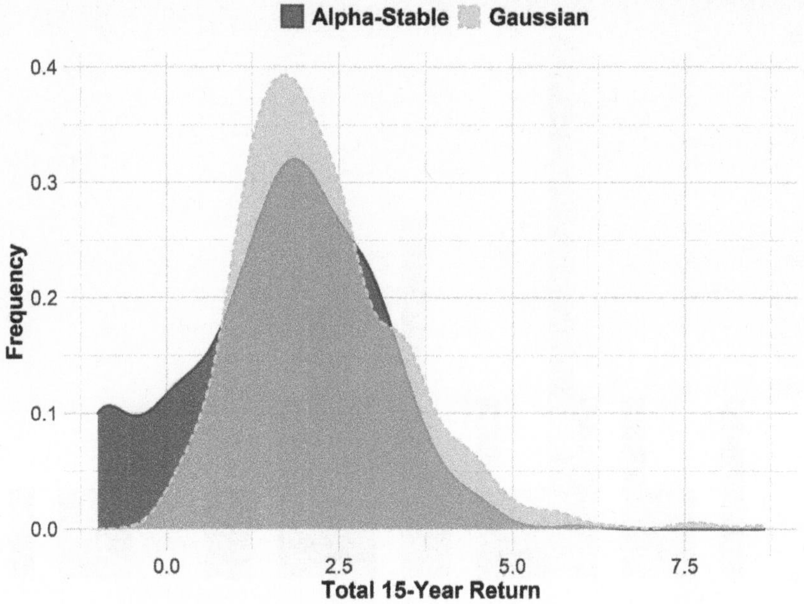

FIGURE 5.5 Simulated Cumulative Returns Drawn from the Annual Returns of Gaussian and Alpha-Stable Distribution
Parameters calculated from the annual return of a 60% SPY, 30% AGG, 10% GLD portfolio, in the period 2004 through 2020

is to achieve a $(1.07)^{15} - 1 = 175\%$ return over a 15-year period. We are allowed to do this because mean and variance scale quite nicely in a Gaussian distribution: a single-year mean can be scaled to a five-year mean by simply multiplying the figure by five. A single-year standard deviation can be scaled to a five-year standard deviation by multiplying the figure by the square-root of five. This shortcut is very handy, but, unfortunately, quite flawed.

If returns are *not* Gaussian this mathematical equivalence across time goes away. As the density plot shows, 15-year aggregate Gaussian returns cluster in a predictably normal fashion, whereas 15-year cumulative alpha-stable distributions cluster entirely differently (bad things happen far more often with alpha-stable distributions, and there are fewer positive outcomes, see Figure 5.5). Of course, this is what we see in the real world, as the histogram of rolling 10-year returns for the S&P 500 demonstrates (Figure 5.6). These aggregate returns do not cluster the way a Gaussian distribution would predict. Rather, they aggregate in a manner much more akin to an alpha-stable distribution.

In truth, that market returns are not Gaussian is a widely known and widely studied fact. Indeed, finding methods and quantitative tools for the

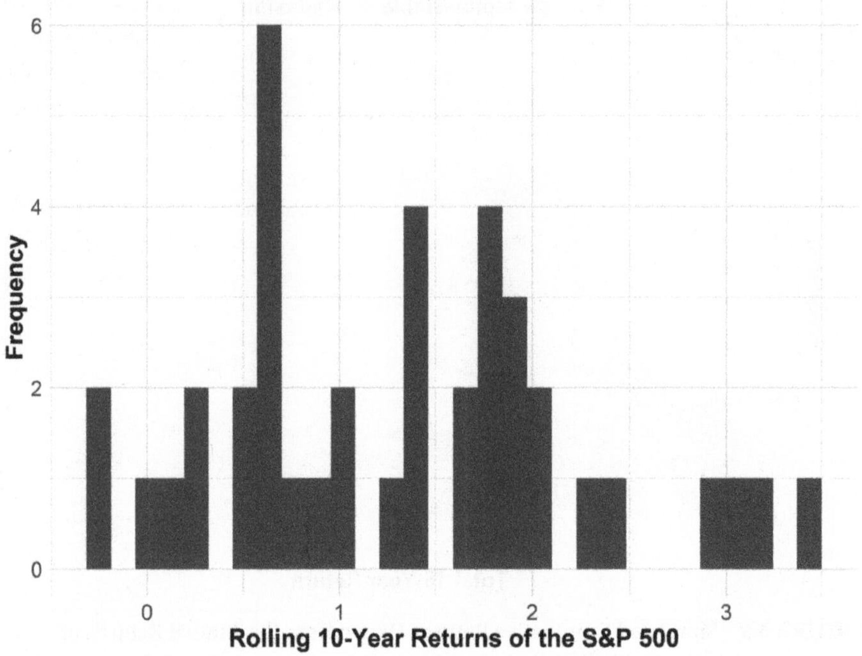

FIGURE 5.6 Rolling 10-Year Returns of the S&P 500 Index
1970 through 2019

combination of non-Gaussian investments into a portfolio was an early project in economics. Nobel-laureates Eugene Fama and Paul Samuelson, as well as famed mathematician Benoit Mandelbrot,[3] along with many others, attempted to find some solutions. They were met with very limited success, unfortunately. Even though the brightest minds in finance attempted to tackle the problem, we really have no practical tools to combine portfolios of alpha-stable distributions. While we may agree that market returns are not Gaussian, abandoning that assumption leaves us with a whole new problem:

[3]E. Fama, "Mandelbrot and the Stable Paretian Hypothesis" *The Journal of Business* 36, no. 4 (1963): 420–429; E. Fama and R. Roll, "Some Properties of Symmetric Stable Distributions," *Journal of the American Statistical Association* 63, no. 323 (1968): 817–836; E. Fama, "Risk, Return, and Equilibrium," *Journal of Political Economy* 79, no. 1 (1971): 30–55; P. Samuelson, "Efficient Portfolio Selection for Pareto-Levy Investments," *Journal of Financial and Quantitative Analysis* 2, no. 2 (1967): 107–122; B. Mandelbrot, "The Variation of Certain Speculative Prices," *The Journal of Business* 36, no. 4 (1963): 394–419; B. Mandelbrot, "New Methods in Statistical Economics," *The Journal of Political Economy* 71, no. 5 (1963): 421–440.

We have no way to understand how weighting investments affects the parameters of the aggregate portfolio's return distribution. Clearly, this is a problem. My genuine hope is that brighter minds than mine will develop a solution in the near future. Absent that, I propose that practitioners use the Gaussian assumption to get close to the right portfolio, then use the alpha-stable distribution parameters of the portfolio to inform risk control and the final probabilities of goal achievement. Obviously, Monte Carlo simulations based on the Gaussian assumption should be abandoned in favor of simulators based on alpha-stable distributions—Gaussian Monte Carlo simulations can be quite dangerous and they are in very common use. Today, most platforms have libraries for both the estimation of the parameters and random-number generation of an alpha-stable distribution—all that is needed for a Monte Carlo simulator—so practitioners can readily upgrade their approach.

Downside risk control takes on added importance in a non-Gaussian paradigm. Those of us working in the industry well know that an average return is only part of our concern, we are also concerned with *when* drawdowns happen, relative to the time horizon for your goal. This was the concern of my first peer-reviewed publication. Coming out of 2008, I had a basic question: How much can you lose in an investment portfolio before you have lost too much? What I learned through difficult experience is that, while markets recover, they may not recover *in time* for investors to accomplish their objectives. Surprisingly, no one had yet taken up this question, so I proposed a simple rule for understanding when portfolio losses are too much to recover from.[4]

The logic runs like this. Suppose we have a bad year in our goals-based portfolio. We now have a new and higher return requirement in the subsequent year, defined as

$$R=\left(\frac{W-\sum_{i=0}^{i=t-1}c_i\left(1+\rho\right)^i}{w*L+w+c+c*L}\right)^{\frac{1}{t-1}}-1,$$

where W is the future funding requirement of the goal, c are the annual contributions to the portfolio, t is the time horizon of the goal, w is the current wealth

[4]F.J. Parker, "Quantifying Downside Risk in Goal-Based Portfolios," *Journal of Wealth Management* 17, no. 3 (2014): 68–77, DOI: https://doi.org/10.3905/jwm.2014.17.3.068; F.J. Parker, "The Erosion of Portfolio Loss Tolerance over Time: Defining, Defending, and Discussing," *Journal of Wealth Management* 19, no. 2 (2016): 23–31, DOI: https://doi.org/10.3905/jwm.2016.19.2.023.

dedicated to the goal, ρ is the annual growth rate of the contributions, and L is the one-year return (loss) we experience in the portfolio. Given our goal variables and a loss we might experience in the portfolio, we now have the new annual return requirement of the portfolio. Going a step further, if we have an estimate for the portfolio's return coming out of a serious loss, and let that stand in for R, then we can take the equation above and solve for the maximum loss our portfolio can weather and still be reasonably expected to recover:

$$L = \frac{W - \sum_{i=0}^{i=t-1} c(1+\rho)^{i}}{(w+c)(R+1)^{t-1}} - \frac{w}{w+c} - \frac{c}{w+c}.$$

What we find using this formulation is that loss tolerance is based on quite a few factors, of which time horizon is probably the most important (though recovery return, R, is also key). As the time until a goal diminishes, we find that a portfolio becomes less able to weather losses, as illustrated in Figure 5.7. Again, this squares with our intuition, but is generally

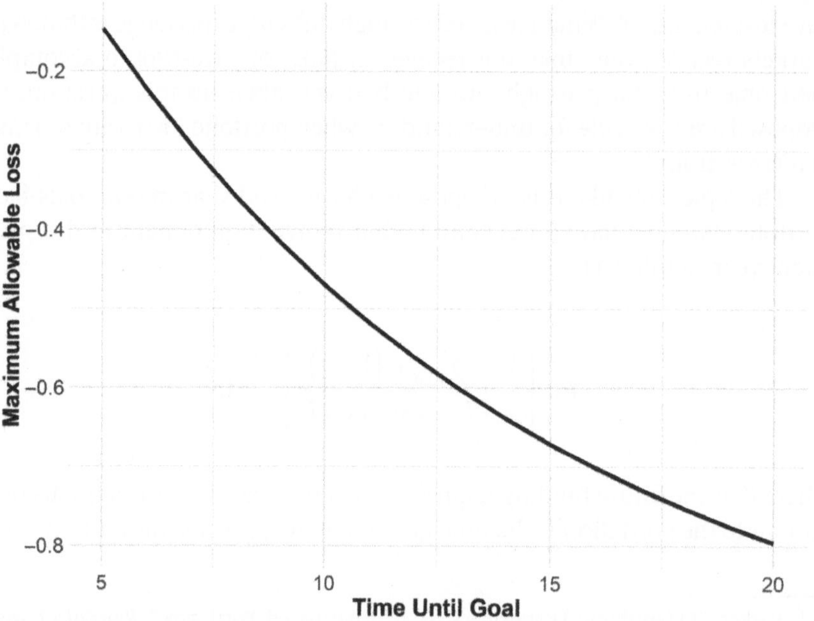

FIGURE 5.7 How Time Horizon Affects Loss Tolerance
Goal is to have $1 with $0.80 in current wealth, no contributions, and a 10% per year portfolio recovery return.

poo-pooed by the academic establishment. Goals-based investors, because of their finite time horizon, must be cognizant of the order of their returns as well as the average of those returns—and this would be true even with a Gaussian return assumption.

The importance of this definition of losses is that it has nothing at all to do with the investor's psychological risk tolerance. This has nothing to do with how comfortable an investor is with risk. Rather, this is an entirely quantitative definition of risk tolerance based on the objective of the portfolio (with an input for a market recovery expectation). In my own experience, I have also found that by understanding losses within the goals-based context, investors become considerably more tolerant of losses. Investors intuitively understand that portfolio losses reduce the probability of achieving their goals, but they rarely know exactly how. That is why all losses tend to feel excessive. However, when placed in this context, investors can know rather than guess how losses affect their ability to achieve a goal, and have a plan to mitigate their risk. Losses, then, are not something to be feared—at least most of the time.

In my original research, I more-or-less hand-waved away the question of how investors go about managing that risk in practice. I proposed that once maximum losses were reached (or almost reached), investors simply exit the portfolio and reinvest again next year. That is a very shallow solution (and the anonymous peer-reviewer told me as much). Stop-losses have their own risks to goals-based investors. Namely, as soon as you exit a position, you have exchanged downside risk for upside risk (notice how goals-based investors are never without some kind of risk!). Downside risk is the risk of loss, of course, but upside risk is considerably less familiar for most investors. Upside risk is the risk that you are in cash when markets start running higher, thereby leaving you without the benefit of that return. It is this upside risk that proponents of buy-and-hold-forever strategies point to when clients call with a strong urge to sell, though they do not exactly call it that.

Upside risk is very real, and for long-term goals it is usually the most acute. However, we should not completely dismiss stop-loss strategies. Of the many risks inherent in them (and there are many), the one I usually hear is, "How do you know when to get back in?" A fair question, and this is a question we will analyze in more detail using the goals-based lens in a moment. But even non-goals-based traders can answer this question satisfactorily: So long as we buy at a lower price than we exited, we come out ahead on the trade. But let's not forget, money is not a single block. We can invest some percentage of our portfolio at lower prices and begin balancing our upside risk with our downside risk.

Let's define our breakeven price as the price at which we must buy back in lest we are forced to buy at a price higher than our exit (and thereby lose money on that trade). For example, if we exited our entire portfolio at \$100/share, then we must buy back in at a price below \$100/share to break even. However, if we account for partial buys, then our breakeven price is defined as:

$$\text{Breakeven Price} = \frac{\text{Stop Price} - \%\text{Invested} \times \text{Price Invested}}{1 - \%\text{Invested}},$$

where %Invested is the percentage of the portfolio (or position) that was reinvested at the Price Invested. If we instead know the new breakeven price we would like to have, we can apply some algebra and learn what percentage we need to invest at a given price to attain our desired breakeven price:

$$\%\text{Invested} = \frac{\text{Stop Price} - \text{Breakeven Price}}{\text{Price Invested} - \text{Breakeven Price}}.$$

Upcoming losses can also be understood in terms of %Invested:

$$\text{Portfolio Loss} = \%\text{Invested} \times \text{Loss to Go},$$

where the Loss to Go is the amount of losses still expected to come in the position (or portfolio).

With this basic framework, a portfolio manager (or trader) with even some insight on markets can then balance downside risk with upside risk. Clearly, there comes a point where upside risk (simply defined as "losing money by buying above our exit point") outweighs downside risk, and vice versa. The point here is not that this basic framework is a panacea for "when should you get back in," but rather, that there is a framework for answering such a question, assuming the practitioner has even a very basic view on capital markets.[5]

My original thoughts on defining maximum allowable losses also led to some interesting discussions around the various quantitative factors

[5]Any active strategy will introduce active risk to a portfolio. Whether that risk—when evaluated in light of portfolio manager skill—is an acceptable one is another matter!

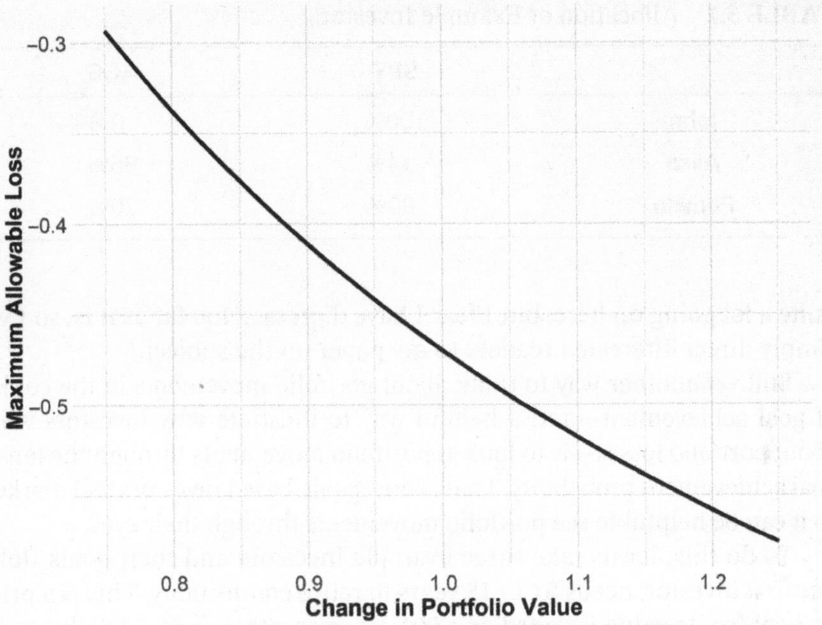

FIGURE 5.8 How Changes in Portfolio Value Affects Loss Tolerance
Goal is to have $1 in in 10 years, with $0.80 in current wealth, no portfolio contributions, and a 10% per year portfolio recovery return.

affecting loss tolerance.[6] Figure 5.7 demonstrates how time horizon affects loss tolerance—showing clearly that losses become less tolerable as the goal approaches (a result we have all known intuitively, though have not been able to quantify). Borrowing the language of options, we could say that this is a form of theta risk, of time decay. However, movements in portfolio value also affect loss tolerance—a form of delta risk. As the portfolio gains in value, loss tolerance increases, and as the portfolio loses in value, loss tolerance decreases, as can been seen in Figure 5.8. There are several other "Greeks" that may well apply to loss tolerance, such as gamma risk, rho, and even a form of duration. Suffice it to say, there is

[6]I am indebted to the anonymous peer-reviewer for this observation, which prompted the subsequent exploration. While I admit there may be little practical application, I do believe that explorations such as this are what build practitioner intuition.

TABLE 5.1 Allocation of Example Investors

	SPY	AGG
John	100%	0%
Alice	14%	86%
Pamela	80%	20%

quite a lot going on here, but I fear I have digressed too far as it is, so I will simply direct interested readers to my paper on the subject.[7]

Still yet another way to think about portfolio movements in the context of goal achievement—and a helpful way to illustrate why investors worry about portfolio losses—is to look at portfolio movements through the lens of goal achievement probability. That is how goals-based investors feel markets, so it can be helpful to see portfolio movements through their eyes.

To do this, let us take three example investors and their goals. John, our first investor, needs $1 in 15 years to retire comfortably. This is a priority goal (so its value is coded as 1.00). He currently has $0.32 dedicated to this goal, and he expects to get 10% returns per year from a portfolio with volatility of 18% over that 15-year period. Alice, our second investor, needs to have $1 in four years to send her child to college, and she currently has $0.95 saved. She expects to get 4% per year from a portfolio with around 9% volatility, and this goal has a value of 0.75. Lastly, we have Pamela. Pamela needs $1 in eight years to fund a bequest for which she has $0.65 today, and she values this goal at 0.22. Pamela expects to generate 7% per year from a portfolio that carries about 16% volatility. Finally, let us suppose that each of our investors is allocated between SPY (the SPDR S&P 500 ETF) and AGG (the SPDR US Aggregate Bond Index ETF), according to Table 5.1.

The plots illustrate how each investor experienced 2020. As practitioners, we are tempted to focus on Panel A of Figure 5.9, which shows the change in portfolio value for each investor from their starting position. John and Pamela, we might be tempted to conclude, were happiest with our work in the end, as they had the largest gain in portfolio value. However, *portfolio value is not how goals-based investors experience markets!* Figure 5.9, Panel B, demonstrates how our investors "felt" their portfolio movements through

---

[7]F.J. Parker, "The Erosion of Portfolio Loss Tolerance over Time: *Defining, Defending, and Discussing*," *Journal of Wealth Management* 19, no. 2 (2016): 23–31, DOI: `https://doi.org/10.3905/jwm.2016.19.2.023`.

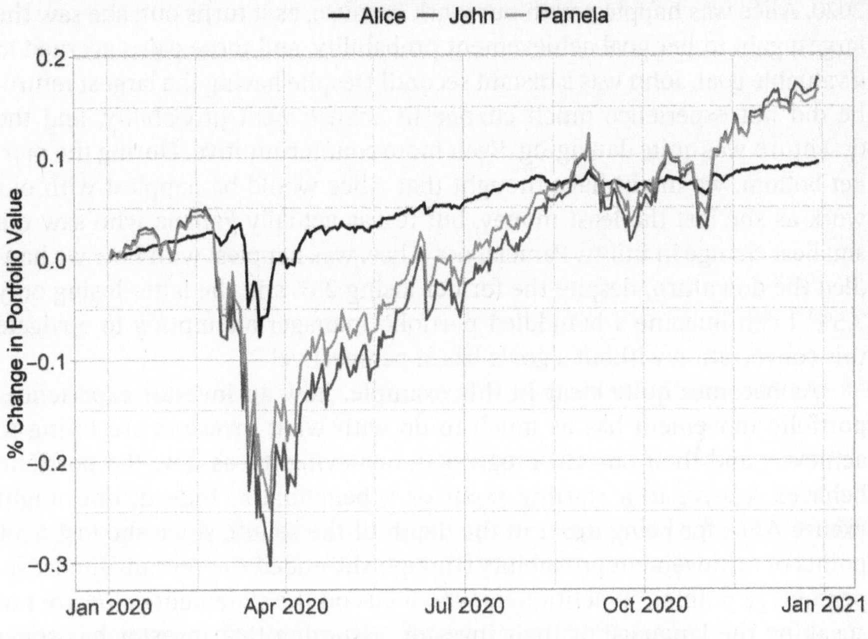

Panel A: Change in Portfolio Value, Relative to the Start of 2020

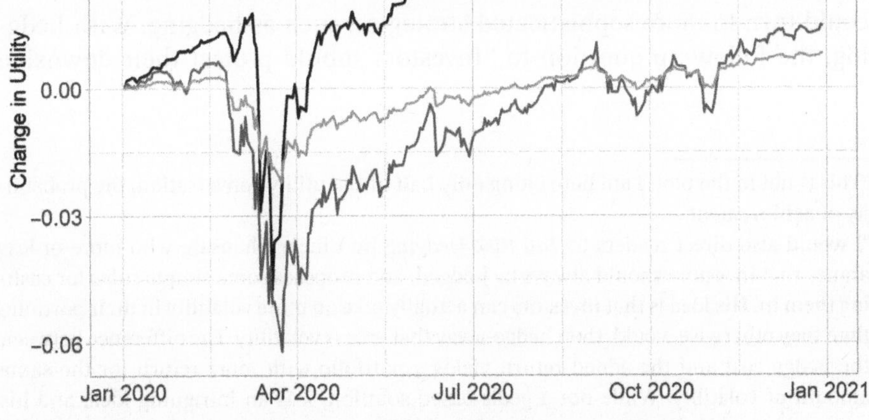

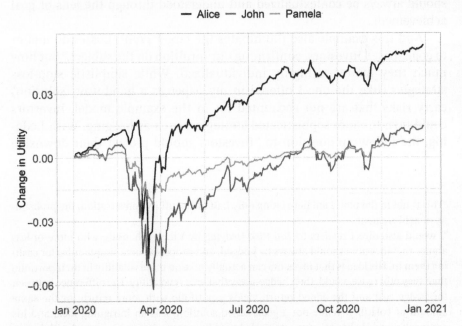

FIGURE 5.9 Example Investors' Experience of 2020
Panel B: Change in Goals-Based Utility, Relative to the Start of 2020
Daily probability of achievement times goal value, relative to the start of 2020.

2020. Alice was happiest with our work because, as it turns out, she saw the largest gain in her goal achievement probability, and those gains accrued to a valuable goal. John was a distant second! Despite having the largest return, he did not experience much change in achievement probability, and the downturn was quite damaging. Even more counterintuitive: During the market bottom, we might have thought that Alice would be happiest with our work as she lost the least money, but it was actually Pamela who saw the smallest change in utility. Pamela, not Alice, was happiest with how we handled the downturn, despite the former losing 25% and the latter losing only 7.5%! I can imagine a befuddled portfolio manager attempting to navigate this conversation without a goals-based perspective!

As becomes quite clear in this example, how an investor experiences portfolio movement has as much to do with what investors are trying to achieve—and their current progress in achieving it—as how the portfolio behaves relative to a starting point or a benchmark. Indeed, one might excuse Alice for being upset in the depth of the selloff, since she lost 5.5% points of achievement probability (though she ended the year up almost six percentage points).[8] Practitioners who focus on the statement value are not speaking the language of their investor, assuming that investor has some goals she is trying to achieve with the funds. Changes in portfolio value should always be contextualized and understood through the lens of goal achievement.

And this example also illuminates the larger point: Losses do matter to goals-based investors, confirming our intuition on the subject,[9] but how much they matter is highly individualized. While simplistic stop-loss strategies (like the one I offered in my paper as a hand-wavy solution) carry risks that are not accounted for in the example model, investors could turn to more sophisticated strategies, such as hedging. With hedging, the follow-up question to "Investors should protect their downside

[8]This is not in the plot. I am here citing only half of the utility conversation, the probability of achievement.

[9]I would also direct readers to *Tail Risk Hedging* by Vineer Bhansali, who more-or-less argues that investors should always be hedged, and proposes some simple rules for cashing them in. His idea is that investors can actually take on more volatility in their portfolio than they otherwise would, then hedge-away that excess volatility. The difference between the hedge cost and the added return yields a portfolio with more return for the same amount of volatility. While not a goals-based solution, it is an intriguing idea, and his approach certainly has relevance to goals-based investors who are concerned with losses.

risk" is, "What are you willing to pay for that protection?" As with everything, we must make tradeoffs. Protecting against excessive losses must be weighed against the cost of doing so. In practice, the most accurate solution to this question would be to include a hedge in a multiperiod optimizer, like the one offered in the previous chapter. Rather than leave it at that, and in an effort to build our intuition on the topic, let's push forward our logic from above to get a sense of what the fair value of a hedge might be to a particular portfolio.

There are four basic outcomes with which we are concerned when hedging. We could pay for a hedge in the portfolio and the market downturn does not happen for the duration of the hedge. In that scenario, we are out the cost of the hedge, and the portfolio must carry a slightly higher return than it otherwise would have to maintain the same goal achievement probability. Let's call that return scenario R_H, and our updated return requirement is $R_H = [W/(1+m)(w-c)]^{1/(t-1)} - 1$, where c is the cost of the hedge and m is the return harvested by the portfolio in a typical year. Of course, we could pay for the hedge and the bad year happens—we bought a hedge and it paid off. Let's call that $R_{H\&L}$. In that scenario, we have incurred the cost of the hedge, but our portfolio loss is offset by the benefit of the hedge. For convenience, let's just say that h is the return of the portfolio when hedged in a bad year, so $R_{H\&L} = [W/(1+h)(w-c)]^{1/(t-1)} - 1$.

We could choose to not hedge the portfolio. We may not get a bad year, so let's call that return outcome R, and $R = [W/(1+m)w]^{1/(t-1)} - 1$. Note that we get the same portfolio return as R_H, except there is no hedge cost. Finally, we could choose not to hedge and the loss happens anyway. Let's dub that return scenario R_L, and $R_L = [W/(1+l)w]^{1/(t-1)} - 1$. And, of course, we have a market view. Let p be the probability of a bad year occurring, leaving $(1-p)$ as the probability of a typical market year. These return scenarios are laid out in Table 5.2.

Now with the details ironed out, we can set up the problem. We are concerned with when the benefits of hedging are equal to the nonhedged scenario.

TABLE 5.2 Return Scenarios

	Hedged Portfolio	Non-Hedged Portfolio
Typical Year, $\mathbf{1-p}$	R_H	R
Bad Year, $\mathbf{p}$	$R_{H\&L}$	R_L

As always with goals-based portfolios, we are using probabilities to measure benefit. We are, then, concerned with the truthiness of

$$p\phi(R_{H\&L}) + (1-p)\phi(R_H) = p\phi(R_L) + (1-p)\phi(R).$$

In these formulations, we will need to input a recovery return and recovery volatility expectation for the portfolio in the ϕ functions for the hedged-and-loss ($R_{H\&L}$) and not-hedged-and-loss (R_L) scenarios, and a more typical return and volatility profile for the hedged-and-no-loss (R_H) and not-hedged-and-no-loss (R) return scenarios. Unfortunately, because the cost variable shows up in two places, there is not an easy algebraic solution, but we can use an optimizer to help us find the hedge cost that makes the above equation true.

Let us consider an illustration. In Figure 5.10, we see how our outlook for the probability of a loss scenario in the coming year affects how much

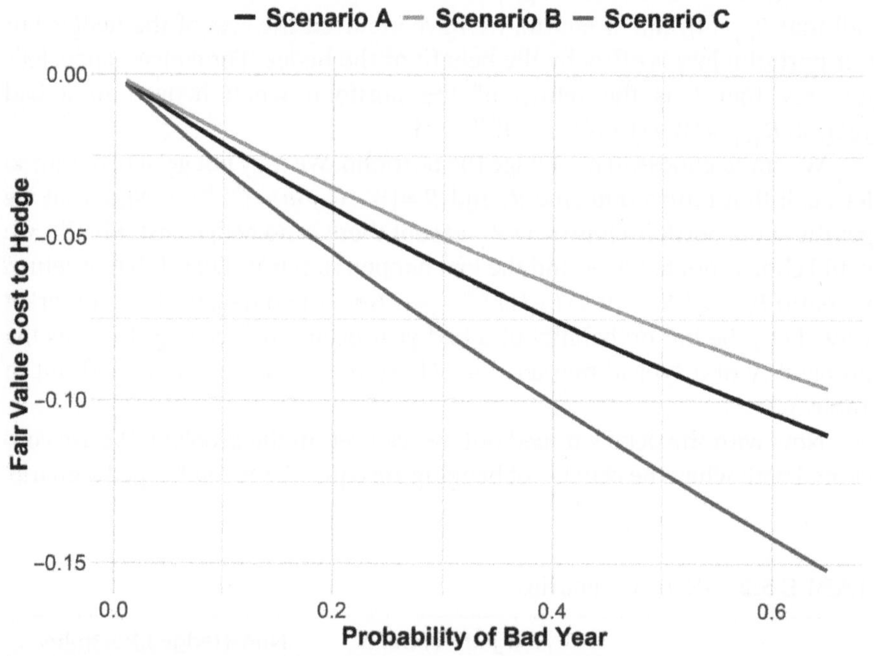

FIGURE 5.10 Effect of Loss Probability on Hedge Fair Value
For all scenarios, the expected portfolio return in a typical year is 8% with a volatility of 11%, and the expected portfolio return after a loss year is 10% with a volatility of 9%. Return distributions are assumed logistic.

we are willing to pay to hedge the portfolio. In all of the illustrated scenarios, the required future value is \$1.00. In Scenario A, our client has \$0.75 dedicated to the goal, a time horizon of 10 years, and we expect a bad year to deliver a loss of 40%. By paying for the hedge in Scenario A, we expect to incur a loss of 25% (plus the cost of the hedge, of course). When we see a 50% probability of a 40% loss, given these figures, we are willing to pay up to \$0.09 to bring that loss down to 25%. Of course, an investor would rather pay less for the hedge, if possible; this is a maximum. A more traditional view might put the fair value of the hedge around its expected value, or the amount of money it saves times the probability of that savings: $(40\% - 25\%) \times 50\% = 7.5\% \times \$0.75 = \$0.06$. However, the more nuanced goals-based perspective shows us that the hedge is in fact worth more to this investor, and the investor then has more pricing power.

Scenario B changes the expected portfolio loss without the hedge to 30% and the hedged loss expectation to 15%. Note here that, in terms of dollar value, the net benefit of the hedge is the same as Scenario A. In both scenarios we are protecting 15% of portfolio value, yet in Scenario B our investor is not willing to pay as much for a hedge. Recall, the probability of goal achievement drops exponentially with losses because they make it ever more difficult to achieve the necessary recovery return. Sensibly, then, the benefits of hedging also grow exponentially. It is not just the net dollar benefit of the hedge with which we are concerned; we are also concerned with where that protection falls on the loss spectrum. Indeed, investors may well be willing to pay a higher price to offset the last 10% points of a 60% loss than they would be to offset the last 10 percentage points of a 15% loss, a puzzling result to traditional theory.

Scenario D shifts the time horizon down to 5 years instead of 10 years, as it was in the previous two scenarios. In addition, Scenario D ups the benefit of the hedge. Without the hedge, we expect a loss of 40%, but with it we can trim that loss down to 15%. Willingness to pay for the hedge grows considerably faster than in the previous scenarios, largely because the time to regain lost ground is much lower.

I want to draw your attention to something very different about this view of hedging costs. This model is heavily driven by goal variables, meaning *every investor will have a different fair value hedging cost.* What's more, every portfolio for every investor is very likely to have a different fair value hedging cost, depending on the goal to which it is dedicated. Fair value is defined as much by *you and your goals* as it is defined by how markets work. I am aware of no other derivative pricing model that individualizes pricing like this. Of course, this has implications for how derivative markets discover price, but I will address some ideas of goals-based market pricing in a later chapter.

As I mentioned above, willingness to hedge should be an asset allocation decision made within the context of a multiperiod framework, as described in the previous chapter. Even so, I wanted to build our intuition around risk management in a goals-based context, as it is different than the more traditional view. I also find it immensely interesting that hedge pricing is dependent not just on our view of markets, as normative theory suggests, but also on our goal variables. Of course, every firm has a unique risk management philosophy, so my purpose here is not to convince you to adopt a different one. Rather, as I have discussed before, we practitioners cannot do our job without first understanding the job that needs doing. Where risk management should be done, it should be done in a goals-based context, just like everything else we do for clients. Goals-based investing really is at the intersection of markets and people. Goals-based risk management is no different.

If anything, the mere understanding that markets are quasi-wild horses rather than reliable tractors should be a benefit to clients. After all, it is them, much more than us, who get kicked in the teeth when things go wrong. In such a model of the world, *the timing and severity of losses matters!* We cannot manage these risks if we do not acknowledge them, and a key outcome of goals-based portfolio theory is to at least acknowledge them. How practitioners go about managing these risks is where real value is added, and I would expect that every firm will have its own approach. Outflowing from this discussion is an understanding that hedge pricing is dependent, not just on our belief about markets (i.e. the selection of the correct return distribution), but as much on the goal our investor is trying to achieve. This gives practitioners an entirely different approach to pricing portfolio hedges and managing risk than more traditional theory would suggest.

Risk management, like everything in goals-based portfolio theory, is individualized.

CHAPTER 6

Insurance Through a Goals-Based Lens

"All good things arrive unto them that wait and who don't die in the meantime."

—Mark Twain

Insurance—and the various insurance products that saturate the marketplace—tend to have either a loyal following or are met with disdain by practitioners. Annuities, as a word, can evoke bristling responses from clients and practitioners alike, while others would sing their praises from the highest mountain if they could. I have myself been pitched countless clever "off label" uses of life insurance, from "it is like owning your own bank" to "it is a rich-man's Roth IRA." And then there is the mundane: life insurance, car insurance, homeowners insurance, even crop insurance.

Insurance is so broad a topic that there is little hope we could do it proper justice in a single chapter. Even so, this is a book about achieving goals, and insurance products very often have a role to play in aiding in their achievement—or at least preventing their failure. Unfortunately, the literature on insurance through a goals-based lens is very limited (this would be a wonderful topic for anyone looking for a research subject), and it is not my intent to fill such a large gap in one sitting. Rather, I would like to view this chapter as a bit of a signpost, both pointing a way for future research as well as offering some direction to practitioners who would like a framework for thinking about the problem (and sifting through some of the nonsense). If all of that is agreeable, we can proceed!

From the prospective of the purchaser, insurance is a simple concept: by paying a fee, certain risks can be moved from me to someone else. The insurance company values the fee (and by pooling risks, it is in a unique position to do so) and the insured values the removal of risk. It is this basic fee-for-risk construct that drives all insurance. Like almost all else in the market, insurance is a transaction that represents an exchange of value. For risks of catastrophic loss—like the loss of a home—the exchange of value may be obvious. However, for other applications—like the purchase of an annuity—the exchange of value may be less obvious. Let's deal with each in turn.

The Maslow-Brunel pyramid helps us intuitively grasp the value of catastrophic insurance. If an event destroys the bottom of the pyramid, none of our higher goals will be achieved—all surviving resources will be dedicated to rebuilding the pyramid from the bottom up.[1] As the goals-based model clearly shows, moving the probability of goal achievement to zero yields considerable loss of utility, especially when done across the whole panoply of goals!

We can model this a bit more technically. Since higher goals are contingent on achieving foundational goals, we can model the achievement probability of the higher goals as contingent on the achievement of the goals lower on the pyramid:

$$u(G) = v(A)\phi(A) + v(B)\phi(A)\phi(B) + v(C)\phi(A)\phi(B)\phi(C) + \cdots.$$

In this structure, the utility of the higher goals can only be achieved if the foundational goal (goal A) is achieved. This is intuitive: If we are unable to buy groceries (bottom of the pyramid) due to the loss of a job, savings that would otherwise have been dedicated to buying a vacation home (higher up the pyramid) is now at risk. We will not be buying a vacation home if we starve to death, so the achievement of that goal is contingent on achieving our goal of eating every day. We will not be donating a significant portion of our estate to a philanthropy if our assets do not survive through retirement. All goals higher on the pyramid are contingent on the achievement of goals that are beneath it.

[1]Of course, at times people are required to purchase insurance (such as a bank requiring homeowners insurance to issue a mortgage), but let us set that aside for now. I want to build our intuition with voluntary insurance purchases, as ostensible as they may sometimes be.

If we look at just the two-goal case (for simplicity), we can model the value of insurance a bit more clearly:

$$u(G) = v(A)\phi(A) + v(B)\phi(A)\phi(B).$$

The utility of our goals-space is the value of goal A times its probability of achievement plus the value of goal B times its probability of achievement *times the probability of achieving goal A*. This last point is what makes insurance sensible. Goal B's achievement is contingent on the achievement of goal A. When we buy insurance, we offset a catastrophic loss by paying a fee. That fee reduces the amount of wealth available to achieve higher goals, but we also gain some increase in achievement probability for our foundational goals, and any goals that rest on them.

This is where the modeling gets a bit tricky. In practice, we should evaluate the cost and benefit of the insurance through the lens of the specific scenario and its achievement probability. I can imagine some levels of wealth at which it would be advantageous to self-insure certain types of risk. However, for the purposes of this much more general analysis, let us assume that the benefit accrues to the foundational goal and the cost is pulled from the higher goal. We are concerned with when the cost is equal to the benefit, from the goals-based perspective. So, let us set u(buying insurance) = u(no insurance):

$$\begin{aligned} &v(A)\left[\phi(A) + \Delta\phi(A)\right] + v(B)\left[\phi(A) + \Delta\phi(A)\right]\left[\phi(B) + \Delta\phi(B)\right] \\ &= v(A)\phi(A) + v(B)\phi(A)\phi(B). \end{aligned}$$

In this equation, we have some gain in achievement probability, represented as $\Delta\phi(A)$ for the foundational goal and $\Delta\phi(B)$ for the higher goal. As we apply some algebra, it is clear that $\Delta\phi(B)$ is negative (hence, a cost), but exactly what level of cost is acceptable depends on a number of factors:

$$\Delta\phi(B) = -\frac{\Delta\phi(A)\left[v(A) + v(B)\phi(B)\right]}{v(B)\left[\phi(A) + \Delta\phi(A)\right]},$$

remembering that $\Delta\phi(B)$ is not expressed here in dollar terms but in percentage points of achievement probability. One would need to convert to actual dollars to get the maximum premium cost our investor would accept.

This relationship is graphed in Figure 6.1, Panel A. Again, it is expressed in terms of probability of goal achievement. To convert to actual dollars,

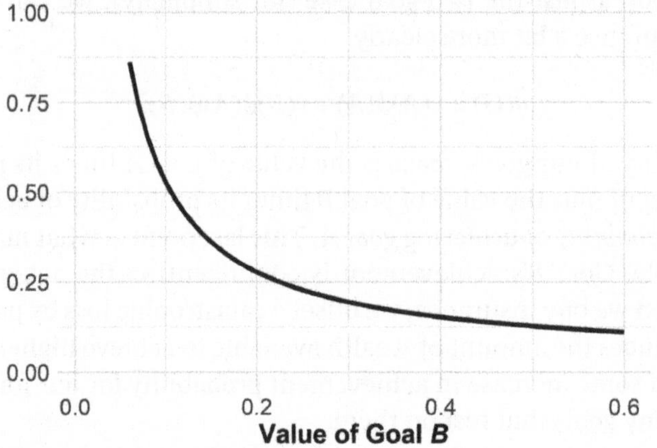

Panel A: As a Function of Goal *B*'s Value

Goal A moves from 95% probability to 100% probability with insurance; goal B carries a 55% baseline probability of achievement.

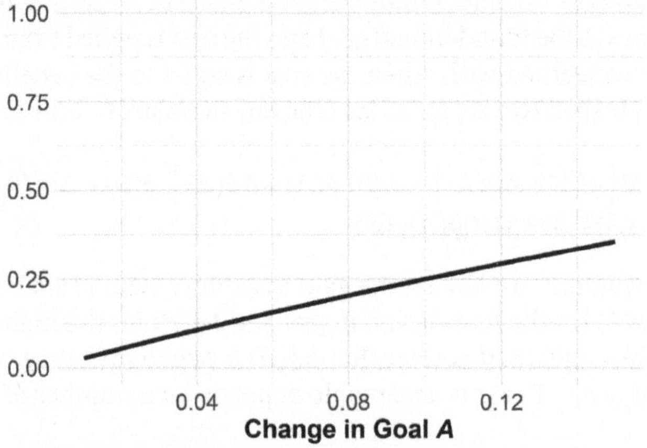

Panel B: As a Function of How Insurance Affects the Achievement of Goal *A*

FIGURE 6.1 Example: Willingness to Pay for Insurance

Goal A has an 85% probability of achievement; goal B has a value of 0.55 and a probability of achievement of 55%.

we would need to apply some algebra (assuming our portfolio is accurately represented by a logistic distribution):

$$w = \frac{W}{\left[1 + m - s\ln\left(\frac{1}{1 - \Delta\phi(B)} - 1\right)\right]^{t}},$$

where m is the portfolio's average return, s is the portfolio's volatility (though in logistic terms), W is the required wealth value to achieve the goal, and t is the time horizon. All of these terms apply to goal B. A simple example: Suppose we have \$62.63 today and we need \$100 in 10 years to achieve goal B, and we can expect to get 8% in a portfolio with 16% volatility. Using the equation above, we would expect our investor to be willing to pay up to \$3.68 in premium to move the probability of achieving goal A from 95% to 100%. That would reduce our probability of achieving goal B by 12.5% points.

Note that this move of five percentage points for goal A is not equal in price across the whole range of achievement probabilities! For example, if we drop our probability of achieving goal A from 95% to 85%, that same five percentage point move (now moving goal A from an 85% chance of achievement to a 90% chance of achievement) is worth a bit more: \$3.94 of goal B's wealth allocation. This is illustrated in Panel B of Figure 6.1.

In this category of specific and catastrophic-type risks, I would also count risks to human capital—a primary rationale for the purchase of life insurance for many investors. The foundational work of Chen, Ibbotson, Milevsky, and Zhu describes the problem this way: "An investor's wealth consists of two parts. Human capital is defined as the present value of an investor's future labor income. . .although human capital is not readily tradeable, it is often the single largest asset an investor has."[2]

Over time, through their labor and receipt of income, people convert their human capital into financial capital, so the risk of loss to human capital tends to decline as we age. The amount of insurance need, in this framework, is simply the present value of future human capital. Hence, the value of life insurance tends to be greater earlier in life than in later (though estate planning concerns often come into the calculus later in life). Given that this idea is widely studied, I will not rehash the techniques here, but interested readers should certainly read the footnoted article as it is an important concept in financial planning.

All of this is a way to think about offsetting very specific and measurable risks to an investor's goals-space, such as homeowners insurance or medical insurance. Of course, not all risks are so measurable and specific.

---

[2]P. Chen, R.G. Ibbotson, M.A. Milevsky, and K.X. Zhu, "Human Capital, Asset Allocation, and Life Insurance," *Financial Analysts Journal* 62, no. 1 (2006): 97–109, DOI: `https://doi.org/10.2469/faj.v62.n1.4061`.

Often, investors wish to offset much fuzzier risks, such as the risk of being wrong about a forecast. To be fair, the problem is not usually framed in that way. Rather, the problem is usually framed as the risk of running out of money. While this is traditionally studied as a form of mortality risk (and it is partly that), I would also argue that this concern is a form of forecasting risk. Let me illustrate my point.

In a very simple model, the amount of money we think is needed to fund a goal is, in no small part, a function of our inflation forecast. If, for example, we expect that $74 of *today's dollars* are needed in 10 years to fund a goal, we must apply some inflation forecast to this figure to generate the final wealth requirement: $\$74 \times (1+i)^{10} = W$, where i is our inflation forecast. If we forecast inflation at 3%, then we need $100 in 10 years, but if we forecast inflation at 5%, then we need $121—quite a difference![3] Of course, actual inflation will be different from our forecast, so how could we offset the risk of being wrong—especially wrong in the wrong direction?

In my view, this is a type of fuzzy risk that investors often want to offset by buying annuities, pensions, or other insurance products with cost-of-living adjustments built into the policy.[4] The premiums charged and payouts of these policies are usually based on mortality risks, at least primarily, but investors often buy them to offset these other, more subtle and visceral, risks. To illustrate the role this risk plays in pricing insurance, let us set up our probability model with this form of meta-uncertainty built in (our required future value is subject to geometric Brownian motion based on our inflation forecast):

---

[3]We will address the fragility of financial planning with respect to inflation forecasts in Chapter 10. As it turns out, this is a very critical assumption in the forecasting of goal requirements!

[4]Though I do not detail the methods here, I would direct interested readers to the foundational work of Moshe Milevsky on annuities, especially:

M.A. Milevsky, "Optimal Asset Allocation Towards the End of the Life Cycle: To Annuitize or Not to Annuitize?" FAS #21-96 (1996). Available at SSRN: `http://dx.doi.org/10.2139/ssrn.1077`.

M.A. Milevsky, *Life Annuities: An Optimal Product for Retirement Income*, CFA Research Foundation Monograph (2013).

M.A. Milevsky, K. Moore, and V.R. Young, "Asset Allocation and Annuity-Purchase Strategies to Minimize the Probability of Financial Ruin," *Mathematical Finance* 16, no. 4 (2006): 647–671, DOI: `https://doi.org/10.1111/j.1467-9965.2006.00288.x`.

$$f(W)=\frac{1}{W\sigma_i\sqrt{2\pi t}}\exp\left(-\frac{\left(\ln W-\ln w-t\left(\mu_i-\frac{1}{2}\sigma_i^2\right)\right)^2}{2\sigma_i^2 t}\right),$$

where W is our forecast for future wealth, μ_i is our expectation for inflation over the time horizon for the goal, dubbed t, σ_i^2 is the variance of our inflation expectation over that time horizon, and w is the amount of wealth dedicated to the goal today. $f(W;\,\mu_i,\,\sigma_i)$, then, is the probability density function of the final wealth requirement.

Clearly, if we misestimate inflation the wrong way and we end up needing more money than we originally estimated ($\widehat{W}$), then our client cannot achieve her goal. So, our actual probability of goal achievement is influenced by the probability that we got our inflation forecast right. We can understand that probability as the cumulative distribution function of $f(W;\,\mu_i,\,\sigma_i)$, or

$$\Pr\left[W\le\widehat{W}\right]=\int_0^{\widehat{W}} f(W;\,\mu_i,\,\sigma_i)\,dW.$$

Our final probability of achievement, then, is:

$$\phi\left(\widehat{W},\,w,\,t,\,m,\,s\right)\int_0^{\widehat{W}} f(W;\,\mu_i,\,\sigma_i)\,dW,$$

where m and s are the return and volatility of the portfolio, $\phi(\cdot)$ is the upper-tail cumulative distribution function for our portfolio, and $\widehat{W}$ is our expected future wealth requirement based on our projection for inflation. With the set up out of the way, we can turn to the meat of the analysis.

We are concerned with how much return our investor is willing to give up to change how uncertain we are about our inflation forecast. Letting α be the minimum probability of achievement our investor is willing to accept, we can let Δm stand in for the amount of return our investor is willing to give up and let $\Delta\sigma_i$ be the change in the uncertainty about our inflation forecast. Plugging these into our equation above, and we have

$$\alpha=\phi\left(\widehat{W},\,w,\,t,\,m+\Delta m,\,s\right)\int_0^{\widehat{W}} f(W;\,\mu_i,\,\sigma_i+\Delta\sigma_i)\,dW.$$

Expanding our $\phi(\cdot)$ function (assumed logistic) and applying some algebra to solve for Δm yields

$$\Delta m = s \ln\left[\frac{1}{1-\frac{\alpha}{\int_0^{\widehat{W}} f(W;\mu_i,\sigma_i+\Delta\sigma_i)dW}}-1\right]+\left(\frac{\widehat{W}}{w}\right)^{\frac{1}{t}}-1-m,$$

which is the maximum amount of return drag our client would be willing to accept, given the inputs.

Unfortunately, this relationship is not particularly intuitive, at least at first glance. Figure 6.2 illustrates the relationship given some example parameters. On the horizontal axis, we have the amount our inflation uncertainty changes ($\Delta\sigma_i$), and on the vertical axis we have the maximum return drag that our investor is willing to accept. As becomes clear, our investor is

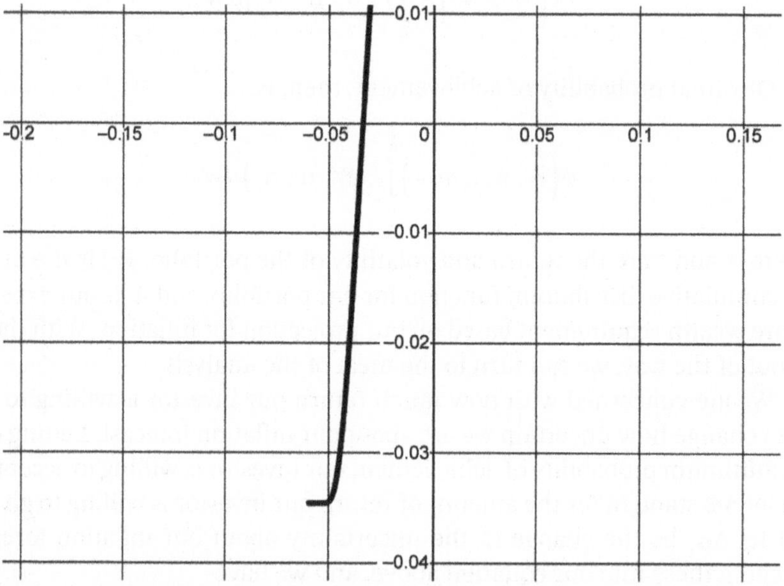

FIGURE 6.2 Willingness to Sacrifice Return to Reduce Inflation Uncertainty
With a goal that is 67% funded, a 10-year time horizon, a portfolio that is expected to deliver a 10% return with 15% volatility, a minimum probability of achievement of 54%, an inflation expectation of 3% with a standard deviation of 6%.

willing to pay to offset a lot of uncertainty, but not necessarily to offset a little uncertainty. In some cases, our investor would not be willing to pay to offset any uncertainty at all, but that would of course depend on all of the various inputs. Interestingly, to completely eliminate inflation uncertainty, our investor is willing to pay quite a lot per year—over 300 basis points in this example! Intriguingly, this is just to offset *uncertainty about inflation*, not even to offset the effect of inflation itself!

We can apply the same logic to the effect of inflation itself. In a similar vein, an individual should be willing to pay up to Δm units of return to offset the effects of inflation itself ($\Delta\mu_i$):

$$\Delta m = s \ln\left[\frac{1}{1-\frac{\alpha}{\int_0^{\widehat{W}} f\left(W;\mu_i+\Delta\mu_i,\sigma_i\right)dW}}-1\right]+\left(\frac{\widehat{W}}{w}\right)^{\frac{1}{t}}-1-m.$$

Again, we can build our intuition on the topic using Figure 6.3. Similar to before, our investor is increasingly willing to sacrifice returns to offset the effects of inflation (the horizontal axis is the change in expected inflation and the vertical axis is the maximum acceptable return drag). Indeed to offset the full 3% inflation, our investor is willing to give up about 300 basis points of annual return.

The point here is simply that investors are, sometimes, willing to pay to offset inflation risks. That rational willingness can justify the use of more expensive financial products, like annuities, within which these types of benefits are usually included. There are other risks, of course, like longevity risk—the risk that I live longer than expected and thereby "outlive my money," A group of researchers has approached this problem with some interesting results.

One group of researchers presented another very interesting look at the role of annuities in consumption goals over time.[5] Their approach was slightly different and very insightful. They analyzed how an investor in the

[5]J. Sun and H. Lan, "Solving the Decumulation Puzzle with Dynamic Asset Allocation and Annuities," *Journal of Wealth Management*, forthcoming (2022).

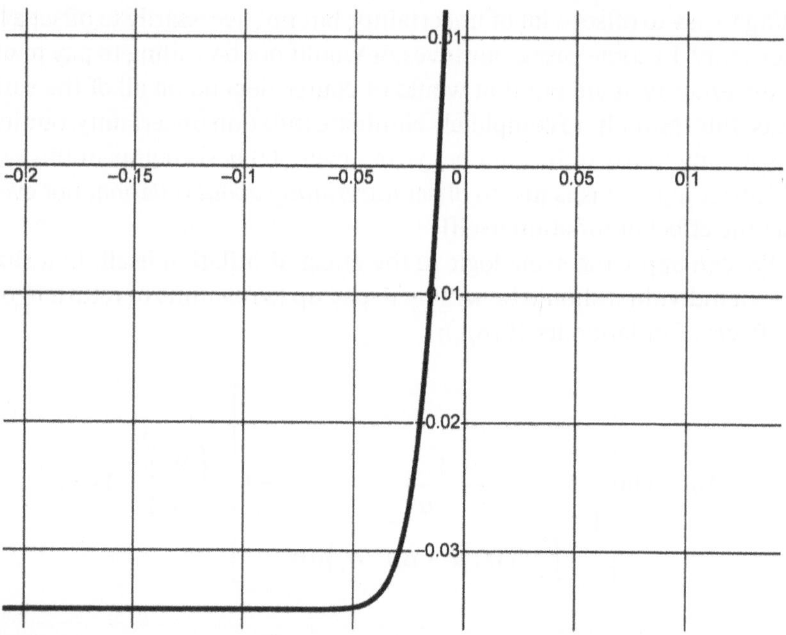

FIGURE 6.3 Willingness to Sacrifice Return to Reduce the Effects of Inflation
With the same parameters as Figure 6.2.

decumulation phase (in retirement, for example) could maximize the utility of their consumption over time. In essence, they sought to answer how much an investor should consume, and how much an investor should allocate to stocks, bonds, cash, and single-premium immediate annuities (SPIAs), using their age and current capital to calculate the risk of outliving their capital. In general, they found that investors should start with smaller withdrawals and increase them every year, and SPIAs will tend to replace a significant chunk of a fixed-income allocation as investors age. SPIAs also appear to be a much more effective way to offset longevity risk than fixed-income allocations in their analysis. And, as the amount of present wealth dedicated to the goal grows, annuities become a more important component in the portfolio.

This last point is consistent with the more formal goals-based framework. As the amount of wealth dedicated to a goal shrinks, an investor becomes more and more reliant on higher-volatility assets (like stocks). An annuity, with its guaranteed payout and smaller uncertainty, is the antithesis of that kind of asset so an investor with low initial wealth will tend to avoid such a solution.

Their analysis is consistent with this one in another way: the pricing of and allocation to insurance products is highly individualized. The premium an investor is willing to pay to offset various types of risk is completely dependent on the goals the investor is trying to achieve and the risks being offset. To the investor, there is a different price to offset inflation risk than the risk that a house burns down. There is a different price to offset the risk of fire in a vacation home than to offset the same risk in a primary residence. No two purchasers of insurance are alike, and no two insurance purchases are alike (even if they are by the same individual!).

There is a lesson here for insurance companies. As technology grows, it may be possible to customize the insurance product as well as the price of that product based on the individual and the need. Differential pricing has long been a practice, but that has largely been based on the types of risks being offset rather than the price an investor is willing to pay. Assuming the insurance company is adding real value by offsetting investor risks, it may well be that investors are willing to shoulder higher costs to lay off those risks. In any event, the cookie-cutter model that has dominated the industry may well be on the way out. Pricing and risk-selection are individualized, just like everything else in goals-based investing.

Admittedly, this is a simplistic way to model and think about insurance, but I hope it communicates the point. Insurance will be viewed through the lens of tradeoffs, and many factors go into understanding and making those tradeoffs. The thrust of this chapter is not to present a hyper-detailed analysis, but rather to demonstrate that goals-based investors are concerned with offsetting both specific and more nontraditional risks. It is clear that people pay money to offset very specific and fundamental risks (i.e. the risk of losing shelter to a storm), and it is also clear that people pay money to offset more subtle risks, like inflation, in real life (so they don't "outlive their money"). This behavior is both predicted and modellable using the goals-based framework.

Research viewing insurance through a goals-based lens is only just coming out. It is still a new perspective. Much work has been done from the perspective of an insurance company, especially in the actuarial sciences, and some very good work from a purchaser's perspective has been done using more traditional models of utility. Analysis from the perspective of the investor, the purchaser of these products, through the lens of achieving actual goals, is a boulevard that needs more light, and researchers are likely to find fruit here. Insurance companies stand to benefit by better understanding and pricing their client. More importantly to me, however, is that individuals stand to achieve their goals more often if they can see insurance within the proper context. Rather than selling insurance through clever marketing ("Be your own bank!"), the goals-based framework can give practitioners confidence that an insurance solution will help our clients achieve their goals more often.

But there is much work to do.

CHAPTER 7

Impact Investing

"The negative idea of Unselfishness carries with it the suggestion
not primarily of securing good things for others, but of going without them ourselves,
as if our abstinence and not their happiness was the important point.
I do not think this is the Christian virtue of Love."

—CS Lewis

A company is asking for an investment from you. Its numbers are incredible—the company projects 65% annualized returns over the next 10 years. What's more, you believe that it can accomplish this. In fact, this is, by your estimate, a conservative projection. One catch: the company employs slave labor in its manufacturing process (overseas, of course).

Clearly, no one would invest in this company (if you find yourself tempted, you should put this book down and read some books on moral philosophy or religion). There is, in fact, *no* financial return that could justify the enslavement of our fellow humans. Given a marketplace of investors who all turn down even such a lucrative offer, we could say that the cost of capital for this business is infinite. And that is part of the point of impact investing—to change the cost of capital for a business so that other businesses take note and change their behavior to reflect the norms and preferences of their investors. Given an infinite cost of capital, businesses will realize that slave labor is not a financially successful practice and abandon it.

We are all, therefore, impact investors, at least on some level.[1] The conversation surrounding impact investing is not really about *whether* it should be done—the illustration above readily demonstrates that we all do it—rather, the conversation is about *what matters to me.* We can all agree that slavery is wrong. But what about fossil fuels? Or gender equality? Or investing in Japanese stocks?

It is here that the industry has taken its usual approach: we build products, then sell them to clients. Impact investing is no different: here is what *we* care about, so you should care about that, too. But goals-based investing starts with the *client's* wishes. It is about the *client's* goals, not ours. I have found that, more than any other topic we may cover, impact, ethical, and environmental, social, and governance (ESG) investing is very personal. What you consider important may not be important to your client. What matters to me in impact/ESG investing is not necessarily what matters to you.

In that way, ethical/impact/ESG investing is a perfect topic for goals-based portfolio theory. As should by now be obvious, investors very often have multiple goals they wish to achieve. As individuals have become more socially aware (and certainly more aware of the potential harms their investment dollars may enable), the goals-space has now expanded to include objectives that are not strictly financial. Impact investing is one example of a nonfinancial, but very real, goal.

Yet these types of goals offer some specific challenges to the practitioner. First, since they are not financial nor futuristic, they are achievable right now. In other words, if your goal is to not invest in oil and gas companies, that goal can be accomplished by simply reallocating away from oil and gas companies. But what is the cost to your long-term financial goals to avoid oil and gas companies in your portfolio? How much has your new probability of achievement changed by adding this restriction to your portfolio? Is that change worth it?

To date, these questions have been given only a superficial treatment. There are those who claim that ESG constraints and impact investing are a long-term good for *any* portfolio—that it is just good investing. There are

[1]Much of this discussion is taken from F. Parker, "Achieving Goals While Making an Impact: Balancing Financial Goals with Impact Investing," *Journal of Impact and ESG Investing* 2, no. 3 (2021), DOI: `https://doi.org/10.3905/jseg.2021.1.014`.

others who insist that investors must be giving up *something* to incorporate any investment constraint, ESG constraints included.

It is not my intent to wade into this debate. In my opinion, an honest review of the literature leaves me as undecided as I ever was. The point for goals-based practitioners is not necessarily to have an answer or strong opinion on this topic. Rather, it is our job, as practitioners, to help investors accomplish their goals. If my client wishes to retire on a rowboat in the middle of Lake Erie, my job is to help her retire on a rowboat in the middle of Lake Erie, not to pass judgment on whether that is a worthy goal. Similarly, if it is our investor's objective to incorporate an ESG constraint or impact mandate, our role is to help her do so, and help her to manage any tradeoffs, not to impose our value judgements onto her decision. With the framework of goals-based investing, we can now advise our clients whether or not they should incorporate an ESG or impact mandate, given their desire to achieve other goals, as well.

We begin, as usual, with an understanding of our client's goals, which includes understanding the time horizon, funding requirement, and total pool of current wealth. From there, we have the client rank her goals from most important to least important, then elicit the value ratios of each goal to the other (this is all covered in Chapter 3). Note that the impact mandate will simply be another goal in the goals-space, listed and understood along with all the rest. The difference is that the impact mandate has no funding requirement, only an allocation requirement, so we have to code it a bit differently in the model.

Pulling the goals-based utility function, let us consider a two-goal case for ease of discussion (so $\{A,B\} \in G$):

$$u(G) = v(A)\phi(A) + v(B)\phi(B),$$

where, as before, $v(A) = 1$ is the value of the client's most important goal, and $v(B)$ is the value of the second-most important goal. In this case, goal B is the impact investing mandate, and goal B is achieved if goal A's portfolio is invested according to the mandate, or not achieved otherwise. Leaning on the logistic distribution to assess probability (for tractability), we can model the two-goal case with the mandate as

$$u(G) = 1 - \frac{1}{1 + \exp\left(-\frac{r - \left(m + \Delta m\right)}{s}\right)} + v(B)\phi(B),$$

where Δm is the return drag of the impact mandate (if there is any), r is the annualized return required to achieve the goal, s is the volatility of the portfolio, and m is the expected return of the portfolio. Again, $\phi(B)=1$ if the mandate (and return drag) are implemented, and $\phi(B)=0$ otherwise.

We can now model the investor's point of indifference—that is, when does the return drag of the impact mandate outweigh its added benefit? This indifference point will give us the maximum return drag our investor is willing to accept to implement the return mandate. Since the utility of the goals-space without the mandate is (recall that $v(A)=1$, so it is not enumerated)

$$u(G')=1-\frac{1}{1+\exp\left(-\frac{r-m}{s}\right)},$$

and the utility of the goals-space with the mandate is (recall that $\phi(B)=1$, so it is not enumerated)

$$u(G)=1-\frac{1}{1+\exp\left(-\frac{r-(m+\Delta m)}{s}\right)}+v(B),$$

then the point of indifference is $u(G')=u(G)$:

$$1-\frac{1}{1+\exp\left(-\frac{r-m}{s}\right)}=1-\frac{1}{1+\exp\left(-\frac{r-(m+\Delta m)}{s}\right)}+v(B).$$

Solving for the maximum acceptable return drag, we have

$$\Delta m=r+s\ln\left[\frac{1}{v(B)+\frac{1}{1+\exp\left(-\frac{r-m}{s}\right)}}-1\right]-m.$$

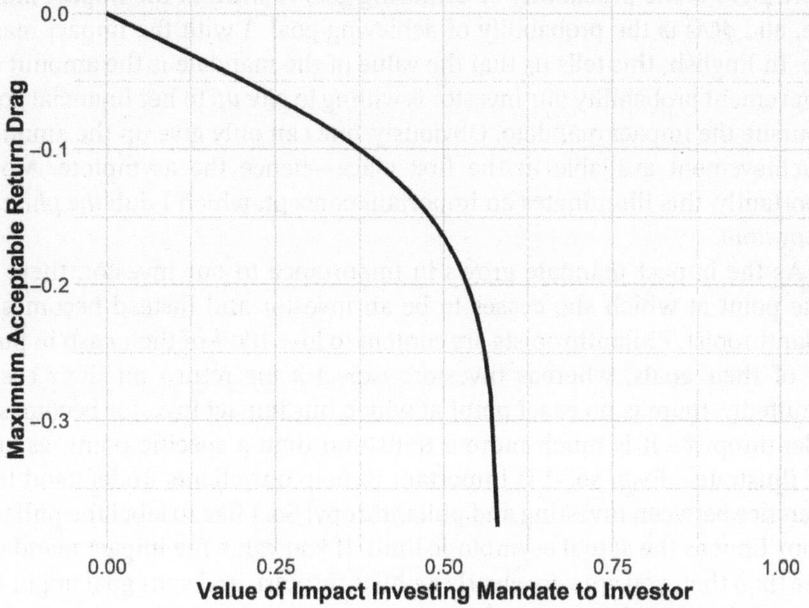

FIGURE 7.1 Maximum Acceptable Return Drag, as a Function of Mandate's Relative Value
Where required return is 6%, expected portfolio return is 8%, and expected portfolio volatility is 6%.

Clearly, the maximum return drag our client is willing to accept is a function of many things: how much return we expect to get from the unconstrained portfolio, how much volatility we can expect, the required return of the goal, and how much the impact mandate is valued relative to the other goal, $v(B)$. In Figure 7.1, everything is held constant except how much the investor values the impact mandate, which illustrates the asymptotic nature of the relationship. As the relative value of the mandate grows, our investor becomes willing to accept absurd levels of return drag.

Mathematically, this asymptote makes sense. Recalling our point of indifference equation from above, we can simplify it in an alternate way:

$$\phi(A') = \phi(A) + v(B)$$

yields

$$v(B) = \phi(A') - \phi(A),$$

where $\phi(A')$ is the probability of achieving goal A without the impact mandate, and $\phi(A)$ is the probability of achieving goal A with the impact mandate. In English, this tells us that the value of the mandate is the amount of achievement probability our investor is willing to *give up* in her financial goal to pursue the impact mandate. Obviously, one can only give up the amount of achievement available in the first place—hence the asymptote. More importantly, this illuminates an important concept, which I dub *the philanthropy limit.*

As the impact mandate grows in importance to our investor, there is some point at which she ceases to be an investor and instead becomes a philanthropist. Philanthropists are content to lose 100% of their cash in pursuit of their goals, whereas investors expect *some* return on their cash. Admittedly, there is no exact point at which our impact investor becomes a philanthropist—it is much more a transition than a specific point, as our plot illustrates. Even so, it is important to help our clients understand the difference between investing and philanthropy! So, I like to label the philanthropy limit as the actual asymptotic limit. If you value the impact mandate more than that, you are very clearly a philanthropist, and your goal might be better achieved in that frame of mind.

The philanthropy limit becomes clearer if we swap the ranking of goals. Rather than modeling the financial goal as the most important, we can label the impact goal as the most important (goal A) with the financial goal as the less important goal (goal B). Similar to before, we can determine the point at which our investor is indifferent to the achievement of the financial goal with the mandate and the achievement of the financial goal without the mandate. Let $\phi(B)$ be the probability of achieving the financial goal without the mandate and let $\phi(B')$ be the probability of achieving the financial goal with the mandate. We can set up the problem as

$$v(B)\phi(B) = v(A)\phi(A) + v(B)\phi(B').$$

When the impact mandate is in place, goal A is achieved, so $\phi(A) = 1$, and we set $v(A) = 1$, per usual. Solving for the investor's value of goal B (which is the financial goal in this setup), we find

$$\frac{1}{\phi(B) - \phi(B')} = v(B),$$

which is a contradiction! $\phi(B) - \phi(B') < 1$, meaning $v(B) > 1$, which directly contradicts our original definition, that the value of goal A is equal to 1 and that the value of goal B is less than the value of goal A: $v(B) < v(A) = 1$.

In other words, *no investment solution exists* if our investor values the impact mandate more highly than the financial goal. In that case, our investor is not an investor at all, but is instead a philanthropist. And this delineation is important because it can spark an important conversation. Namely, is an investment solution the best use of your capital, or would a direct gift to a philanthropic endeavor more readily accomplish your goal?

Of course, direct philanthropy and impact/ESG investing are not the same in practice. The idea behind impact/ESG investing is to decrease the costs of capital via financial markets for businesses with agreeable practices or products, thereby encouraging them to adjust. Direct philanthropy typically sidesteps financial markets altogether, so the net result is different in practice. Financially, however, it is the same to our client to invest in an unconstrained portfolio and then donate the annual return drag we would have been willing to accept to a philanthropic cause. That is, if you stood to gain 8% in the unconstrained portfolio and 5% in the impact portfolio, then receiving 8% return and donating three percentage points of your return every year to a relevant philanthropy is the same financially as investing in the impact portfolio (which returns 5%).

This framework also offers a method for allocating to philanthropic goals. By coding philanthropic concerns as another goal in the goals-space, we can optimize our wealth across goals, and that optimization procedure will yield an amount dedicated to philanthropy—given all other goals and their inputs. Some decision with respect to a probability of achievement function would have to be made, but something simple could stand in for the general case (leaving specifics to the practitioner). A simple proportional funding function may do the trick: If the cause requires $1.00 to fund, and our investor funds $0.80, then the "probability of achievement" is $0.80/$1.00 = 80%.

The goals-based framework also reveals some important dynamics around willingness to pursue an impact mandate. It is not the same in all market environments. If we hold other factors constant and vary our portfolio return expectations, our volatility expectations, and our required return expectations, we find that each affects willingness differently.

Investors tend to be least willing to sacrifice return when portfolio volatility is smaller. As volatility expectations grow, so does an investor's willingness to sacrifice return, illustrated by Figure 7.2(a). This makes some intuitive sense: as volatility expectations grow, the probability of achieving the financial goal shrinks. This makes the utility offered by the secondary goal more important, and so return drag becomes more acceptable. Walking a client through her volatility expectations and asking her to imagine a higher or lower volatility environment may be useful in preparing her for her own

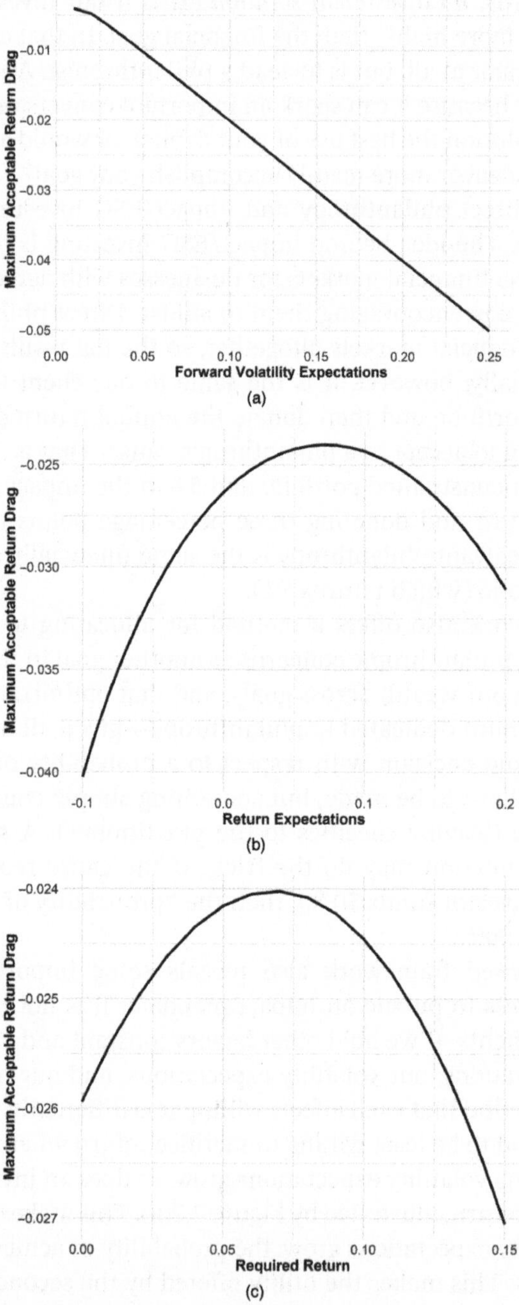

FIGURE 7.2 Other Factors Affecting Willingness to Accept Return Drag. Unless otherwise specified, in all figures required return equals 6%, expected return equals 8%, expected volatility equals 12%, and the value of the impact mandate is 0.05. *(a) Expected volatility; (b) Expected returns; (c) Required return*

shifting sentiment. With regard to accepting return drag, volatility expectations are the second most important factor, after the value of the mandate.

As realized market returns shift the principal value of the portfolio, we can also expect investors to adjust their sentiment toward impact investing, but this shift is not a linear one. This market value adjustment shows up as a new required portfolio return (market gains yield lower future required returns; market losses yield higher future required returns). As Figure 7.2(c) shows, the relationship is an inverted parabola with investors being least willing near where the required return equals the expected portfolio return, and most willing as return requirements move away from this point in either direction. For example, if an investor expects a 6% portfolio return, she will be least willing to sacrifice return around the 6% required return mark, and more willing at the 3% or 9% required return mark. It is a similar case for shifting portfolio return expectations. As portfolio return expectations move away from equality with the required portfolio return, an investor becomes exponentially more willing to accept return drag (again, this is an inverted parabolic relationship, as Figure 7.2(b) shows).

It is not just market shifts that can move sentiment toward return drag. As we have discussed, the relative importance of the goal (impact mandate) is the most important factor. While individual investors may have a relatively constant valuation for this goal, this cannot be assumed for other account types, like trusts. It is not uncommon for a wealth-creating generation to use trusts as a vehicle to pass along wealth to the next generation. For the bequeathing generation, it is likely that their estate goal is nearer the top of the Maslow-Brunel pyramid (i.e. it is not a foundational goal, but more aspirational). The inheriting generation, however, is likely to view their inheritance nearer the bottom of the Maslow-Brunel pyramid—it is likely a much more foundational goal. This means that *each generation will value an impact mandate differently*. In theory, the bequeathing generation should be more willing to accept a return drag to pursue an impact investing mandate, while the subsequent generation should be less willing.

Of course, up to now the drive to pursue impact and ESG mandates has tended to come from the younger generation. However, *we should not assume that to always be true*. For one, the luster of social consciousness can wear away with age or changing social norms. Also relevant: as the second generation learns, through experience, how fragile their corpus of wealth can be, willingness to sacrifice return for an impact mandate may be blunted. An assumption that return-drag tolerance will be always constant is a dangerous one, not just for retaining clients, but also for the liability of trustees.

In any event, people tend to be less tolerant of return drag in their foundational goals than their aspirational ones. Circling back to the generational divide just mentioned, it may well be that younger investors are more willing to give up return for impact mandates, but whether they *should be*, given all of their other objectives, is a separate question. It may well be the practitioner's job to talk through a mismatch between what a client says and what a client should do. People are not always rational, after all.

Furthermore, balancing not just competing psychological interests but also the legal interests[2] (in the case of trusts) of multiple generations is a delicate tightrope to walk. An understanding of the value placed on an impact mandate, not just today but also across various market environments and generations, is absolutely critical—and even then, ongoing adjustments seem likely. Building flexibility in the account and setting flexible expectations with the client are two key components to long-term success in impact investing for goals-based investors.

With impact investing, some of the benefits of goals-based portfolio theory become clearer. Traditional portfolio theory has no guidance for the pursuit of nonfinancial objectives, whereas, as we have just discussed, goals-based portfolio theory offers a rational framework for the management of any potential tradeoffs. It is the broader goals-based approach, however, that lends the most value to clients, and ESG/impact investing is a great foil to see this. Currently, the industry imposes a particular view of ESG/impact investing on the client. That is, an asset manager will build a fund or a portfolio and then sell it to an investor, asking the investor to both buy in to the investment strategy as well as the fund manager's definition of ESG/impact. This is very clearly a top-down philosophy.

But ESG and impact investing are very personal things, and not all investors define it the same way. I have a client, for example, whose father fought in the Pacific theater of World War II. She does not want to own any Japanese stocks. Of course, I have no problem owning Japanese stocks (assuming they are a worthwhile component of the portfolio). But this is *her* ethical constraint, and it is *her* money. My role is not to pass judgment on whether that is a worthy constraint, but rather to help her manage any potential tradeoffs that creates and invest the portfolio according to *her* wishes. In contrast to

---

[2]A proper treatment of trust legalities is well beyond the scope of this book and my expertise. I would, however, highly recommend reading Schanzenbach and Sitkoff's paper, "Reconciling Fiduciary Duty and Social Conscience: The Law and Economics of ESG Investing by a Trustee," *Sanford Law Review* 72 (2020): 381–454.

the current industry approach, this is decidedly a bottom-up, client-centered philosophy.

Every investor is different. Goals-based theory accounts for those differences and offers a framework for managing them. Practitioners would do their clients good to adopt at least some of the methods.

CHAPTER 8

Taxes and Rebalancing

"Experience without theory is blind,
but theory without experience is mere intellectual play."

—Immanuel Kant

I will be the first to admit that a chapter on taxes and rebalancing sounds like a chapter I would skip were I reading this book. I have enough somnolence in my day. Unfortunately, this is where the rubber meets the road and the balancing act of an individual's tax situation, various goals and ethical constraints, the firm's capital market expectations, along with the practical constraints of our chosen investment universe all come together. This is the job, as it were. The other challenge for practitioners and theorists alike is that this is not a simple problem to solve. Putting all of this theory together is a complex task, and each practitioner will likely have her own approach. My objective here is not to lay out *the* right answer, but rather, to sketch a framework for thinking about the problem and present *a* potential solution.

In a perfect world, the solution to the rebalancing problem would be quite simple. However, in addition to the challenges posed by the individualization offered by the goals-based framework, it is very common for potential investments to themselves have varied allocations to subcomponents. A firm building capital market expectations around economic sectors, for example, may have to account for Amazon.com's link to both the technology sector and its link to the consumer staples and consumer discretionary sectors. A given stock will have exposure to multiple factors of concern to factor-oriented firms (i.e., value, size, quality, momentum, etc.), or a blended mutual fund may have allocation to stocks, bonds, and foreign exchange risks. This problem alone makes rebalancing a complicated task. Stacking the added complications brought on by the goals-based framework creates a decidedly nontrivial problem.

The literature on investing in the presence of tax costs has grown quite large. I won't recount all of it here, but suffice it to say that taxes should be considered in an investment strategy. What is most difficult for practitioners, however, is that optimizing for taxes often requires depositing funds into various locked-up account types today, for possible use at some future date. Full tax costs are not generally known at that future date, and thus the full benefits and costs of locking up the funds cannot even be calculated! In addition, many investors find themselves in the distribution phase and must decide how to optimally liquidate these various account types. For the latter problem, there tends to be standard advice in the industry, expected to apply to everyone.[1] As we have learned (and will show through this chapter), "standard advice" should not be applied to goals-based investors. The problem is not standardized, after all![2]

To tackle the problem, let's begin with the basic goals-based utility function with N-number of goals, and $v(i)$ is the value of goal i, W_i is the funding requirement of goal i, and t_i is the number of years within which goal i must be accomplished:

$$u(G) = \sum_{i}^{N} v(i)\phi(\varpi\vartheta_i, W_i, t_i).$$

[1]Interestingly, the order of withdrawals from the various account types does not matter in a constant-tax-rate environment, though there is still an optimal location of assets. See, for example, J. A. DiLellio and D. N. Ostrov, "Constructing Tax Efficient Withdrawal Strategies for Retirees with Traditional 401(k)/IRAs, Roth 401(k)/IRAs, and Taxable Accounts," *Proceedings of the Academy of Financial Services 2018 Annual Conference* (Chicago, IL, USA, October 2–3, 2018).

[2]In addition to the expansive literature on investing in the presence of taxes, there was some good work done recently that analyzes the simultaneous optimization of a withdrawal strategy and investment allocation over the course of an investor's life through a goals-based lens. The authors make some simplifying assumptions, of course, but the result is informative and interesting. See S. R. Das, D. Ostrov, A. Casanova, A. Radhakrishnan, and D. Srivastav, "Combining Investment and Tax Strategies for Optimizing Lifetime Solvency Under Uncertain Returns and Mortality," *Journal of Risk and Financial Management* 14, no. 285 (2021): 1–25.

As in Chapter 4, let us lean on the modified logistic cumulative distribution function with $\varsigma = 0.60$ as our Gaussian-to-logistic scale conversion factor:

$$\phi(\varpi\vartheta, W, t) = 1 - \frac{1}{1 + \exp\left(-\frac{\left(\frac{W}{\varpi\vartheta}\right)^{\frac{1}{t}} - 1 - m}{\varsigma s}\right)}.$$

With any decision, rebalancing included, it is our objective to maximize utility in this form. As markets evolve through time, the weights of each investment in the portfolio also drift and our expected probability of achievement moves from its optimal point. We want to bring the investment weights back to a point where probability is maximized, but doing so typically comes with costs—the largest and most obvious of which is taxes. The costs we incur in the portfolio are a function of how much we change existing portfolio weights, so let's call it $C(\Delta\omega)$, and it generally lowers the amount of total wealth available, though not always! Though we are never able to add actual cash wealth to our pool, if we sell an investment for a loss in a taxable account, we can use the resulting tax credit to offset future taxable gains. That is a very real resource that should be accounted for in our resource pool.

Here is our probability equation, updated with our cost function:

$$\phi(\varpi, W, t) = 1 - \frac{1}{1 + \exp\left(-\frac{\left(\frac{W}{\left[\varpi + C(\Delta\omega)\right]\vartheta}\right)^{\frac{1}{t}} - 1 - m}{\varsigma s}\right)}.$$

Note that when $C(\Delta\omega) < 0$, we have to pay a cost to make the weight adjustments: when $C(\Delta\omega) > 0$, we have a cost (tax) credit. I should note that this approach—adding a cost function that adjusts the current wealth variable—is not the standard one taken in the literature. For most studies of which I am aware, the standard method is to adjust returns (m, in our equation) and adjust volatility (s, in our equation). However, those studies are done using standard mean-variance optimization, and, as we have discussed ad nauseum, mean-variance optimization has no account of the other goal variables, such as current wealth. Furthermore, it is not strictly accurate to adjust the return and volatility variables because those are *expected* return and volatility. They are not realized until the *next* period, and realizing costs happens in *this* period. Hence my preference for linking the cost function to the current wealth variable.

As this equation demonstrates, rebalancing can be simply thought of as re-optimizing the portfolio with tax costs incorporated into the model. As always, the objective of the optimization is to maximize $\phi(\cdot)$, so our rebalancing rule is quite simple. If the rebalance results in a higher probability of goal achievement than its current position, net of all costs, then the portfolio should be rebalanced. If the portfolio yields a higher probability of goal achievement in its current state than it would after rebalancing with costs, then we do not rebalance the portfolio.

Rebalancing using this simple rule calls into question the industry practices of calendar rebalancing and threshold rebalancing. In calendar rebalancing, the portfolio is rebalanced according to a regular period—monthly or quarterly, for example. In threshold rebalancing, the portfolio is rebalanced when the investments are off of their target weight by some predetermined amount—500 or 1,000 basis points, for example. Of course, the traditional mean-variance paradigm has the same "maximize utility" rule for rebalancing, and the calendar and threshold rebalance approach are simple heuristics that allow for the scaling of investment management firms. To date, it has been impractical to account for individual tax situations when rebalancing at scale. As technology and computing power has advanced, the tools now exist (or potentially exist) to individualize rebalancing, but more on that in a later chapter.

With our rebalancing litmus test in place, let us now turn to the more granular problem of rebalancing across sectors, factors, or asset classes when the individual investments have exposure to more than one of the components with which we are concerned. For the sake of discussion, let us say that we are concerned with a factor allocation. Just know that we could replace factors with sectors, asset classes, or any other investment classification system with which the firm is concerned.

At its simplest, we can describe the vector of portfolio factor exposures, $\mathbf{W}_p$, as the internal product of the matrix of investment factor exposures, $\boldsymbol{\Omega}$, and the vector of investment weights in the portfolio, $\boldsymbol{\omega}$:

$$\mathbf{W}_p = \boldsymbol{\Omega} \cdot \boldsymbol{\omega}.$$

From here, if we know the portfolio weights we want and each investment's factor weight, we can solve for the optimal weights to each investment, ω. Unfortunately, Ω is not necessarily a square matrix so we cannot always invert it. We must instead take the left-inverse of Ω (if it exists!):

$$\Omega^{-L}\mathbf{W}_P = \omega.$$

Of course, the original equation could also be solved using a numerical method, filling in possible values of ω that satisfy the equality. Given the uncertainty of a left-inverse always existing (or the difficulty of calculating it outside of a setting involving code), it may be considerably more practical to simply use a numerical method (like a standard optimizer or Monte Carlo simulation).

The optimal values of ω come with a cost, as we have discussed. $\Delta\omega$, then, can be described with an element-wise subtraction of the optimal weights from the existing weights, ω_E:

$$\Delta\omega = \omega - \omega_E.$$

The costs, then, are the sum of tax costs associated with changing each investment position,

$$C(\Delta\omega) = \sum_{i=1}^{N} \Delta\omega_i \vartheta\varpi Q_i,$$

where Q is the short-term tax rate (if the gain/loss is short-term), and the long-term tax rate (if the gain/loss is long-term). Recall that $\vartheta\varpi$ is the dollar-allocation to the goal, so when multiplied by the change of allocation, we have the dollar amount of the change, which then gives the dollar amount of the taxes when multiplied by the tax rate, Q. Note that Q is indexed because each investment's change in weights may trigger different types of tax rates (e.g. long-term vs. short-term capital gains rates).

Drawing from existing heuristics (and common practice), in a rebalance we could simply set the vector of optimal portfolio exposures ($\mathbf{W}_P$) while minimizing tax costs. However, we have no real way to balance the two. If, for instance, we have a tax cost of $100,000, is the rebalance worth it? What if the tax cost is $100? Using only heuristics, we have no way of knowing the point at which the rebalance is worth its cost in taxes.

Alternatively, we could seek to minimize the difference between current portfolio weights and optimal portfolio weights, subject to a declared tax budget. That is, if we know we cannot spend more than $25,000 in taxes on this rebalance, then we minimize our weight differences as closely as possible without breaching this upper tax limit. Or,

$$\min \Delta\omega$$

$$\text{s.t. } C(\Delta\omega) \leq B,$$

where B is the tax budget for the rebalance.

For firms operating with model portfolios, this may be a relevant heuristic. However, it is not really how a goals-based investor should operate. As mentioned, the objective is to maximize the probability of attaining the goal; therefore, both tax considerations and capital market forecasts should be incorporated into the probability equation to determine exactly what the balance between portfolio adjustments and tax costs should be.

Furthermore, almost never does a client come to a firm with only cash to invest. Almost always, her portfolio is already invested and the extent to which that portfolio should be liquidated to accommodate the firm's preferred allocation must be determined. For example, I might be reluctant to sell a highly appreciated tech stock in favor of a tech-sector fund in a taxable account. Though the tech-sector fund provides purer and more diversified exposure, those two considerations alone may not make up for the tax costs incurred by selling the stock (though our equation above would be the final arbiter of such a question). Such practical considerations are rarely of concern to more academic approaches, but goals-based investing is a practitioner-oriented theory. As such, I believe we should consider the problems as they are presented in the real world.

To help illustrate these concepts, let us consider an example. Table 8.1 illustrates a typical tax basis scenario, which will inform our tax cost, or $C(\cdot)$. Note that the differing tax lots are listed because we will very often need to sell down only *some* of a particular security, and it would be best if we could direct the sale of specific tax lots, rather than a first-in/first-out or last-in/first-out strategy. This, of course, requires interfacing with the broker to ensure the correct tax lots are earmarked when sold.

Table 8.2 illustrates a subcomponent allocation matrix, what we have dubbed $\boldsymbol{\Omega}$ in the equations above. In this matrix, we have some securities with pure exposure, but we also have a fund with blended exposure, and one of our stocks also carries blended exposure to the various factors with which we are concerned. Again, this is fairly reflective of what we regularly experience in the real world, and this table illustrates what is quite common: a client

TABLE 8.1 Cost Basis Report

Security Name	Tax Lot	Cost Basis	Market Value	Short-Term Gain(Loss)	Long-Term Gain(Loss)
Stock A	1	$143,584	$237,562	--	$93,978
Stock A	2	$32,564	$84,311	$51,747	--
Stock A	3	$127,167	$97,421	($29,746)	--
Stock B	1	$56,455	$71,922	--	$15,467
Stock B	1	$22,355	$30,951	$8,596	--
Fund A	1	$585,127	$721,311	--	$136,184
Fund A	2	$377,143	$461,021	--	$83,878
Fund A	3	$452,500	$448,301	($4,199)	--
Fund B	1	$352,901	$285,937	($66,964)	--
Fund C	1	$811,000	$1,022,058	--	$211,058

TABLE 8.2 Subcomponent Allocation Matrix

Security Name	Factor 1	Factor 2	Factor 3	Factor 4	Factor 5
Stock A	25%	35%	5%	35%	--
Stock B	100%	--	--	--	--
Fund A	9%	45%	18%	20%	8%
Fund B	100%	--	--	--	--
Fund C	--	100%	--	--	--
Fund D	--	--	100%	--	--
Fund E	--	--	--	100%	--
Fund F	--	--	--	--	100%

has a few positions that the firm does not follow (Stocks A and B, and Fund A) and a target allocation in other funds (Funds B through F). By focusing on factors rather than specific securities, the firm is able to include the unfollowed securities in their capital market expectations.

To properly calculate our preferred allocation, we must also have capital market expectations for each subcomponent (or factor). Those are listed in Table 8.3. At first glance it might seem more effective for a portfolio manager

TABLE 8.3 Capital Market Expectations

			Forecast Correlation				
	Forecast Return	Forecast Volatility	Factor 1	Factor 2	Factor 3	Factor 4	Factor 5
Factor 1	0.08	0.15	1.00	0.85	0.72	0.90	(0.10)
Factor 2	0.10	0.21		1.00	0.75	0.92	(0.15)
Factor 3	0.07	0.14			1.00	0.83	0.05
Factor 4	0.12	0.35				1.00	(0.20)
Factor 5	0.03	0.04					1.00

to build capital market expectations for each security in the original portfolio (i.e. Stock A, Stock B, Fund A, etc.). In my experience, however, this can get quite unruly and is more likely to water down the portfolio manager's expertise than to add helpful granularity. It is far better for the firm to focus expertise on the subcomponents that form the building blocks of most portfolio exposures—there are, after all, only a handful of risk premiums. From there, technology tools can be leveraged to construct more granular forecasts for individual stocks—specifically, the factors present in each security. This gives firms the benefit of maintaining focused expertise while still being able to generate capital market expectations for almost any security with which they may come into contact. Again, this is an important ability for a firm because clients very often transfer in random securities, some of which carry high tax costs to sell, and it may or may not be in the client's best interest to liquidate them. While we may be able to make such decisions "by hand," we cannot effectively scale "by hand" decisions to the level of the firm, and that is part of the promise of goals-based portfolio theory: it gives the firm a method for scaling individualized portfolio decisions.

In our example, our client has transferred in Stock A, Stock B, Fund A, Fund B, and Fund C. As a firm, we have determined the factor allocation of each of these positions, and we are, therefore, able to come up with some forecast of their future return (even though we only have an official opinion on Funds B through F) because we have capital market expectations for the factors which describe those securities.

From here things get a little goofy, mostly because of taxes. First, we need to build our tax cost function, which returns the tax (and other) costs of a proposed security allocation. Next, we build our optimization function,

TABLE 8.4 Portfolio Weights Comparison

	Current	Optimal with Taxes	Optimal without Taxes
Stock A	12%	--	--
Stock B	3%	23%	13%
Fund A	47%	11%	--
Fund B	8%	--	13%
Fund C	30%	63%	74%
Fund D	--	2%	--
Fund E	--	--	--
Fund F	--	--	--

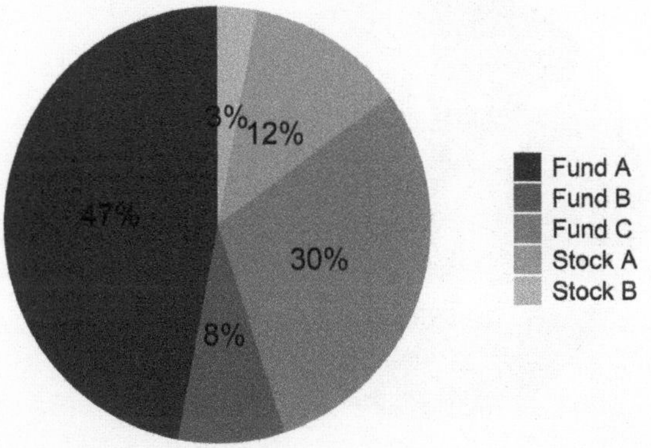

FIGURE 8.1 Current Portfolio Weights

which is the probability function with the cost function added and coupled with our capital market expectations listed at the beginning of the chapter. Finally, we optimize security weights to yield the highest level of achievement probability, the results of which are shown in Table 8.4, Figures 8.1, 8.2, and 8.3. For interested readers, I have included a code example in the companion for the book.

Using this example, we find that it is indeed advantageous to sell down many of the legacy positions, though not all in their entirety. Fund A, for example, moves from a 47% allocation in the portfolio to an 11% allocation, and Stock B moves from a 23% allocation to a 3% allocation (and Stock A gets sold entirely). These changes bump the probability of goal achievement from 39% to 61%, a

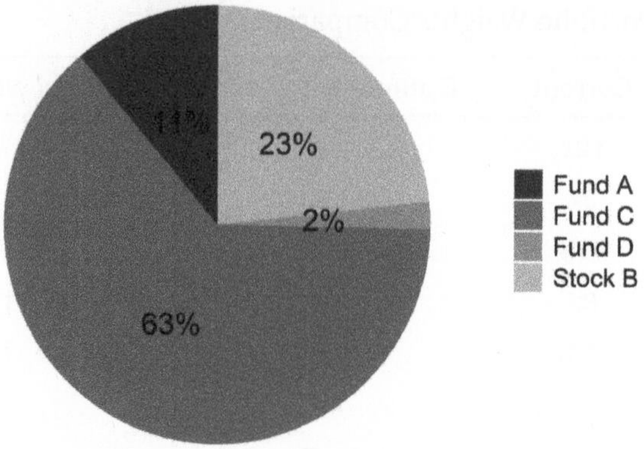

FIGURE 8.2 Optimal Portfolio Weights with Taxes

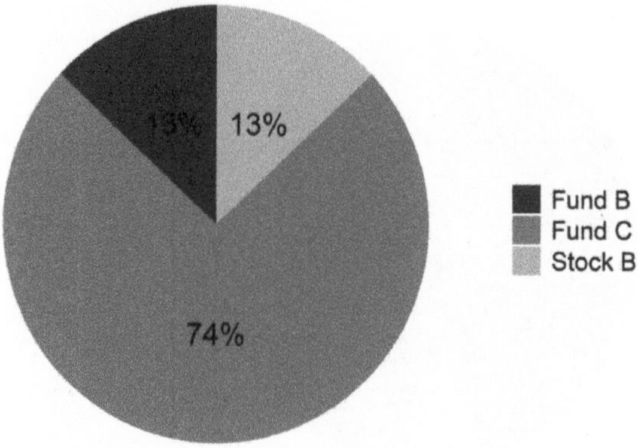

FIGURE 8.3 Optimal Portfolio Weights, No Taxes

considerable increase to be sure. However, if we remove the friction of taxes, the optimal portfolio weights are quite different, as the table demonstrates.[3] Ideally, we would sell all of Fund A along with more of Stock B, and use those extra funds to increase our exposure to Fund C and Fund B. Interestingly, however, there is very little difference in achievement probability. Taxes, while affecting

[3]A result echoed in other studies. See, for example, J. Wilcox, J. Horvitz, and D. DiBartolomeo, *Investment Management for Taxable Private Investors* (Charlottesville, VA: The Research Foundation of CFA Institute, 2006).

our overall portfolio exposure, do not yield much drag on our achievement probability in this case.[4]

A key takeaway here is that rebalancing, just like everything else in goals-based investing, is unique to the individual. There is no hard-and-fast rule about when it is advantageous to rebalance, or when it is advantageous to sell legacy positions. We cannot say that quarterly rebalancing is better than monthly rebalancing. We cannot say that threshold rebalancing is better than scheduled rebalancing. Rather, the portfolio manager must determine when the benefits outweigh the tax and transaction costs in each individual account. When that is the case, that account should be rebalanced, but not otherwise.

Of course, other transaction costs should be considered, too. While free-to-trade stocks and ETFs are quite common in the industry now, this does not mean that trades are free in actual practice. First, free-to-trade programs are generally funded with a payment-for-order-flow program. Such programs tend to result in *slightly* higher execution prices than would otherwise be incurred. That does not mean that such programs are always a net detriment to the client, the opposite is likely true: clients may get cheaper net trade prices than they would get through a commission-based program. For larger portfolio sizes and trades, however, that is unlikely to be the case. Obviously, ample due-diligence is warranted here to determine which approach minimizes overall trade costs.

Commissions and execution price aside, the bid–ask spread is another friction that can add up. Every round-trip trade has the client pay the difference between the bid price and the ask price, and this alone can (and should) limit the number of trades executed in a portfolio. For many liquid and widely traded securities, this is usually of little concern (the bid–ask can be less than a penny in most blue-chip US stocks, for example). However, for less liquid securities, or in times of extreme market stress, the bid–ask spread can really add up, and for some classes of securities (like bonds), the bid–ask can be quite large. In any event, that cost to trade is real and should be included in the model. I prefer to include it in the cost function, using an average bid–ask spread percentage as an estimate for trade costs.

---

[4]This is consistent with the results of S. R. Das, D. Ostrov, A. Casanova, A. Radhakrishnan, and D. Srivastav, "Combining Investment and Tax Strategies for Optimizing Lifetime Solvency Under Uncertain Returns and Mortality," *Journal of Risk and Financial Management* 14, no. 285 (2021): 1–25. They find that the tax optimization component adds only a few percentage points of goal-achievement probability. Of course, for very highly appreciated stock, these result would likely shift considerably.

In any event, trade cost due diligence—beyond the standard tax awareness—is one place where advisors can add considerable value—it requires specialized knowledge and experience, and most laymen are barely aware of the nuance imbedded in it. Firms with a method for segmenting portfolios and/or directing trades through the appropriate program can add real value to their clients. And, while this may be a very "inside baseball" conversation to have with a client, delivering a legitimately better service into the marketplace is not usually about doing one big thing, it is typically a culmination of many little things aggregating into something people recognize as truly better than the competition.

Accounting for costs—tax and transaction costs, most notably—is clearly of high importance for goals-based investors. It is also a very individual consideration, especially when the portfolio manager also considers existing tax credits and liabilities (which I have not discussed here), and the individual nature of tax brackets. In the US, for example, short-term capital gains are taxed as income (long-term gain rates are constant). The estimation of a client's effective tax rate for the *coming year* clearly requires some time spent with the client, and likely her accountant, too. It is, honestly, too important a consideration to ignore (per the academic tradition), or to approximate via a model portfolio (per the practitioner tradition). In the end, taxes and rebalancing requires a very individualized approach.

There are some tax heuristics we can draw from some excellent studies done by other researchers. It is worth noting that, counterintuitively, there is a *benefit* to taxation. Investors have a partner to help them bear some of the pain of investment loss, and that partner is the taxman. Suppose you are taxed at a rate of t and the standard deviation of pretax returns is σ, then the standard deviation of after-tax returns is $\sigma(1-t)$—less than our pretax volatility![5] This means that, all else equal, portfolios held in taxable accounts can hold higher equity exposures than nontaxable accounts to realize the same level of after-tax volatility. Higher equity exposure also helps to offset the effects of tax drag over time by delivering higher returns than we would otherwise be willing to bear.

And this highlights the importance of the asset location decision. Given the myriad types of accounts, each with its own tax treatment, where should various types of investments be located? The general wisdom, if you think of

[5] S. M. Horan, and A. Al Zaman, "Tax-Adjusted Portfolio Optimization and Asset Location: Extensions and Synthesis," *The Journal of Wealth Management* 11, no. 3 (Winter 2008): 56–73.

all accounts and assets as one pool of wealth, is to hold assets such as bonds, REITs, and some types of hedge funds in tax-advantaged accounts. Passive stocks or even restricted shares should be held in a taxable account, generally speaking.[6] Of course, tax-advantaged accounts are almost always preferred to taxable accounts for goals with an appropriately long-term time horizon.

Yet even the bifurcation into tax-advantaged and taxable is overly simplistic, especially in light of more sophisticated planning structures, such as charitable-remainder trusts, generation-skipping trusts, variable life insurance policies, captive insurance companies, foundations, grantor-retained annuity trusts, and so on. The possibilities and combinations are nigh endless. Again, asset location is an area where well-informed practitioners can add considerable value—a value that would not exist if taxes were not an issue.

Asset location, while an important consideration to any financial planning effort, and carrying the benefit of tax efficiency, has the downside of being yet another real-world friction to ongoing rebalancing and plan adjustments. We must also consider investment liquidity. Since the goals-based model assumes that investors rebalance both across investments and also across goals, we need to deal with each of these frictions.

For many investors—especially higher-net-worth investors—private investments will comprise a significant portion of their investment portfolio. I recently reviewed a few proposals from big-name private wealth managers, and 20% to 30% in illiquid alternatives was not unusual (nor was such a suggestion inappropriate). These investments have the potential to deliver both noncorrelated and higher returns when compared to many public securities. However, they come with the disadvantage of illiquidity—once the cash is in, we cannot get it out until the specified time period has passed.

From a goals-based perspective, liquidity risk is basically the same as the risk of not having a fully funded goal within the right time horizon. If I need $1 to accomplish my goal, and I have $0.75 in liquid securities and $0.25 tied up in illiquid investments that do not mature for another three years, then I cannot fund my goal, even though I have the proper amount of wealth on a monthly statement. Not having liquidity when I need it is functionally the same as not having the money at all. Portfolio managers need to manage liquidity risk just as they would manage shortfall risk. That requires forethought and planning, as well as a clear understanding of when goals must be funded.

---

[6]W. R. Reichenstein, "Calculating a Family's Asset Mix," *Financial Services Review* 7, no. 3 (1998): 195–206.

As mentioned, asset location is another way that goals-based investors may be curtailed in their ability to rebalance. For example, in most tax jurisdictions, it is not uncommon to have funds both inside and outside a retirement account, or inside and outside a trust. Our goals-based model assumes that investors can rebalance across goals (and across accounts), but that is often not so simple in practice. We cannot rebalance funds out of an IRA to finance college tuition objectives without significant tax consequences, for example.

Whereas portfolio managers can manage liquidity risk, asset location is a risk that is considerably harder to manage. Tax benefits often warrant the use of such investment vehicles, and it is very difficult to foresee all changes in market regimes and goal priorities (or the addition of new goals). However, we do have some tools at our disposal, and with expert knowledge and creativity, advisors can add considerable value to their clients by deftly managing this ongoing risk.

Our current pool of wealth can also be broken down into its constituent components. First, there is current financial wealth. These are what we usually think of when we think of current wealth: account values, marketable assets, illiquid assets, and cash. An ability to borrow could also be included here, though I would be inclined to only include low-interest-rate borrowing power, certainly not consumer credit. Current financial wealth also includes the present value of all future savings—what we would think of as human capital. It is these last two, borrowing power and human capital, that can be tapped to help facilitate rebalances that would otherwise be impractical due to asset location and/or asset liquidity. To illustrate, let's bring back our example from Chapter 3.

If you recall, our client has four goals: maintaining lifestyle, funding her children's estate, purchasing a vacation home, and naming a building for her alma mater. Let's say this client took our advice and did what we suggested. She now has a vacation home and is on her way to achieving her other goals with a reasonable level of confidence. Two years have now passed. About a month ago, there was a critical loss in the client's business that requires $352,000 to fix, and it must be dealt with within the next six months. Assuming all accounts grew in line with our original capital market expectations (a nice wish!), our client now has the following assets:

- $4,392,954 in her living expenses account
- $187,063 dedicated to the children's estate
- $700,000 in a vacation home (approximate value, all of which is equity in the home)
- $93,080 in the naming rights account

Because our client's current living expenses depend on the business's cash flow, fixing the business is a top priority. Both future living expenses and fixing the business have a value of 1—the most important value in our goals-space.[7] Adjusting the goals-space and value ratios to account for the updated situation and then re-optimizing yields an optimal goal-level allocation of wealth of

- $352,000 to fix the business
- $3,985,069 to fund future living expenses
- $323,113 to the children's estate
- $592,375 to the vacation home
- $107,701 to the naming rights goal

And here we have an example of how we can add value as advisors. The vacation home has a value of $700,000, and our optimizer suggests we pull $108,000 of cash from of the value. With marketable securities, we could simply sell down a partial amount of the account. With an illiquid investment like a vacation home, however, we cannot sell a portion of the "account." We can accomplish this, however, by recommending a modest cash-out refinance, rather than an outright sale of the home.

Our advice, then, is to reallocate $407,000 from the living expenses account and to take $108,000 of equity from the vacation home. The $515,000 in cash is then used to fund the business fix and increase the children's estate funding, and about $10,000 is redirected toward the naming-rights goal. And, by the way, even after pulling $407,000 from her living expenses goal, our client still has a 71% probability of achieving it.

This is one, admittedly simple, example of how advisors can add ongoing value to their clients. By keeping an open and creative mind, making a habit of solving hard problems, and gaining confidence in your ability to solve them, the ongoing occurrences in the lives of our clients need not be catastrophic or even out of the ordinary.

As with everything else in goals-based investing, taxes, rebalancing, asset location, and the changing goals-space are as individual as the clients themselves. Only with a clear understanding of our clients, expert-level

[7]More technically, we should code all goals to be contingent on the business fix, as the business must be maintained to continue their funding. I have chosen not to do that here because the result is similar, and the math is much more complicated. We can, in my opinion, forgo some small benefit to maintain simpler models.

knowledge of the myriad considerations of importance, and models that better represent the real world can we genuinely help our clients achieve their financial goals.

I have always thought that creativity requires two components. First, creativity requires creative thinking—a tough skill to teach. I have met many a brilliant person who can solve equations in a heartbeat, but were I to ask them to solve a problem where the math must be applied differently, or a problem without a mechanical answer, they become frazzled. Creativity is either had or not, for the most part. Second, creativity requires a medium of expression, and that requires us to be intimately familiar with the tools of whatever trade we find ourselves in. Generating clever solutions to client problems requires a deep knowledge of the tools that could be used to solve them. The most creative-thinking person in the world cannot compose a piece of music if she does not understand the ins-and-outs of instruments and harmony. Similarly, we cannot solve client problems without a deep well of knowledge to draw from. That, coupled with creative minds, can generate substantial value on behalf of clients. Indeed, there are fewer moments in the client–advisor relationship where the advisor can add as much value as specialized knowledge and creativity surrounding asset location and structuring decisions.

Taxes and rebalancing may be boring, but it is the heart and soul of good wealth management.

CHAPTER 9

Goals-Based Reporting

"I don't understand you, you don't understand me.
What else do we have in common?"

—Ashleigh Brilliant

I remember, early in my career, I was excited to show a client what a good job we had done in the recovery post-2008. Through some effective stock picks, we had generated substantial alpha relative to the market as a whole. During the meeting, I pointed out the alpha figure and, much to my disappointment, my client responded, "What does that mean?" Unfortunately, rather than take the hint, I dove headlong into an explanation, equations and all, of how important alpha was as a risk-adjusted measure of returns. It did not help. My client did not care about his risk-adjusted performance relative to a benchmark. My client cared about achieving his goals! Alpha, to him, was a meaningless statistic.

So much of our current client reporting paradigm is consistent with the quip at the top of the chapter. We, as an industry, spend inordinate time and ink presenting metrics and data that *we* care about, and quite little on what it is the client cares about. Financial plans are a staple, of course, and that is good. But when it comes to monthly or quarterly performance reporting, the financial plan is drawered, and the meaningless metrics come back in force.

I want to explore how we might update our reporting to be consistent with a goals-based framework, to move away from the myriad meaningless metrics toward the metrics real people actually care about. I do not claim that this is the only way reporting should be done; by contrast, I am a bit of a neophyte when it comes to the challenges of client reporting. Like most practitioners, I rely on my technology services to generate and deliver reports without much second thought. This discussion is my attempt at a second thought on the matter, and it is my sincere hope that this discussion prompts others to add their wisdom and experience to the conversation. Hopefully, then, the industry can coalesce around a new and more meaningful norm for client reporting.

Rather than walk through the deficiencies of existing reports and how we might fix them, let's begin this discussion with a blank slate. Given the goals-based framework, what information is relevant and meaningful to the investor? As we have discussed, goals-based investing sits at the intersection of the "big world" and the investor's world. It stands to reason, then, that we need some reporting on both. First and foremost, an investor cares about her world—the world of her dreams, wants, wishes, and needs. Is the portfolio manager helping her achieve those objectives or not? But those objectives can only be achieved with the help from the big world of capital markets because the big world represents the opportunity set from which our investor can draw. If, for instance, the opportunity set only offered below-average returns, it is important our investor understands that the firm's sub-par performance relative to her need is not necessarily due to insufficient skill on the part of the portfolio manager, but rather due to a poor opportunity set (and the inverse is also true, so this cuts both ways!). Good goals-based reporting should strike the right balance between the two (Figure 9.1).

In my mind, proper goals-based reporting opens with a quick summary of the client's goals, and the client's current financial picture with respect to

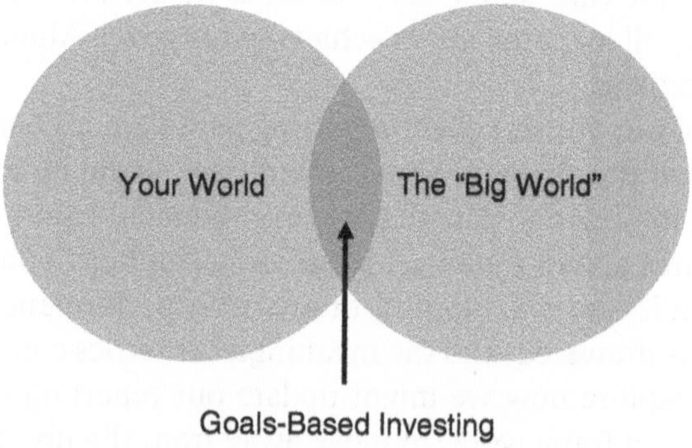

FIGURE 9.1 Goals-Based Investing

them, as shown in Table 9.1. Front and center is the only metric that *really* matters: our client's forecasted probability of goal achievement. I imagine this figure generated from the firm's capital market expectations and the client's goal variables; however, I also recognize that firms could jury-rig their CMEs to produce figures here that are higher than they really should be. Rather than the objective measure that it should be, this could easily be a subjective measure—but more on that in a second. For now, let's admit the tension inherent in how the figure is generated but remain committed to its presentation. It is *the* point of all this, after all.

Next, I've laid out the goal variables our client has specified: the required future balance to fund the goal, the time horizon within which the goal must

Example Goals-Based Reporting Summary

Progress Toward Your Goals - Summary

	Retirement	**Vacation Home**	**Philanthropic Endowment**	**Wealth Building**
Expected Probability of Achievement *end of last period*	68.5%	58.4%	48.4%	*N/A*
Expected Probability of Achievement *end most recent period*	68.8%	62.7%	45.8%	*N/A*
Current Balance *as of 30 Sept 2021*	$3,781,989	$354,232	$113,948	$243,000
Required Balance	$6,000,000	$550,000	$1,000,000	*N/A*
Time Horizon	12.25 years	6.75 years	22.5 years	*N/A*
Required Return *most recent period, annualized*	3.84%	7.62%	10.38%	*N/A*
Actual Return *most recent period, annualized*	7.12%	8.43%	4.32%	6.33%
Bechmark Return *most recent period, annualized*	5.93%	9.21%	3.77%	6.18%

be accomplished, and the current account balance dedicated to the goal. From there it is a simple matter to calculate the required annualized return. I think it important to consistently reflect the client's objectives, as stated by them. It gives both the investor and the advisor a chance to review these figures and have a conversation, restating them if necessary. Furthermore, it contextualizes the figures to follow, namely the portfolio's actual return over the previous period, which is compared to, primarily, the return required by the client's goal, but also the benchmark return (the opportunity set from which the client can draw). By flanking the actual portfolio performance with both what is needed and what was offered, our investor can immediately see both how they are doing and whether that is from good or bad portfolio management.

In our Vacation Home sample goal, for instance, our client attained a return much better than needed. This gained ground for her in achievement probability, moving from a 58.4% chance last period to a 62.7% chance this period. While this portfolio underperformed its benchmark by 78 basis points, that is less concerning since we simultaneously outperformed the return required by a greater margin, 81 basis points. Of course, consistent and significant underperformance relative to a benchmark might be a signal that a portfolio manager should be replaced, which is why the information needs to be presented, but that should not be the primary focus of reporting, in my view.

Relative performance is also contextualized by the gain/loss in goal achievement probability at the top of the page. By outperforming our required return, our client should see gains in her achievement probability over time. Underperformance does the opposite. Again, rather than a focus on how many basis points of under/overperformance the portfolio realized to a benchmark, presenting portfolio performance along with how many basis points of achievement probability have been gained/lost contextualizes the portfolio manager's work more appropriately. Portfolio losses can also be contextualized more meaningfully with these metrics. Investors do not fear losses in the abstract, they fear not achieving their goals. Investors intuitively understand that portfolio losses mean a lower probability of goal achievement, but without the actual figure they are left guessing (and usually guessing for the worse). By doing that quantitative work and showing investors plainly how much portfolio moves affect their achievement probability, practitioners will likely find the nature of their conversations changing. Long-dated goals, for example, are considerably less affected by portfolio losses than most investors think. The underperformance of our example philanthropy portfolio did little to move the needle of achievement probability, and that should reassure our investor somewhat.

One important goal metric that is not included in the summary report is the goal's relative value. As I discussed in previous chapters, this is an elusive figure, and I am not sure that presenting it is particularly clarifying for an investor. That is not to say it should not be reviewed—it absolutely should be oft reviewed. Rather, because it does not carry intuitive meaning to our client, it is a metric that only we as practitioners care about in the end, and so I am inclined to exclude it.

That said, we cannot assume that goal values are constant through time. I have an intuition that an individual's value for a goal, relative to the others in the goals-space, is inversely proportional to how likely it is to be achieved. In other words, as the achievement of a foundational goal becomes more and more likely, I would expect individuals to want to shift resources away from that goal toward other goals with less relative value and less probability of achievement. This is an exogenous factor for the goals-based model, though we can adjust for it through time by revising the value-of-goals metric on an ongoing basis and reoptimizing wealth across the goals-space. Some research here may be warranted, as, for the time being, this is just an hypothesis.

Graphics can further highlight important goals-based metrics and help to contextualize not just the current reporting period but also the progress of our investor across the lifetime of our relationship. I do find that the more traditional asset allocation and portfolio growth graphics are useful, but I believe they should be presented on a secondary basis to goals-based ones. Again, asset allocation is an important variable to communicate, but it is not particularly meaningful to most investors. It should be viewed in the context of goals-based achievement metrics.

In the next figures, we have three examples of how visuals can augment the central points. Figure 9.2 (Panel a) is how our example retirement goal has progressed over the 3¾ years that our client has been with us. In this plot, we see our client's account value plotted, not against a benchmark (though one could be added), but primarily against the required growth curve that was set when we started. This plot clearly shows that the portfolio has grown more than the goal requires, and certainly helps to conceptualize the recent portfolio loss—we are still well above where we need to be.

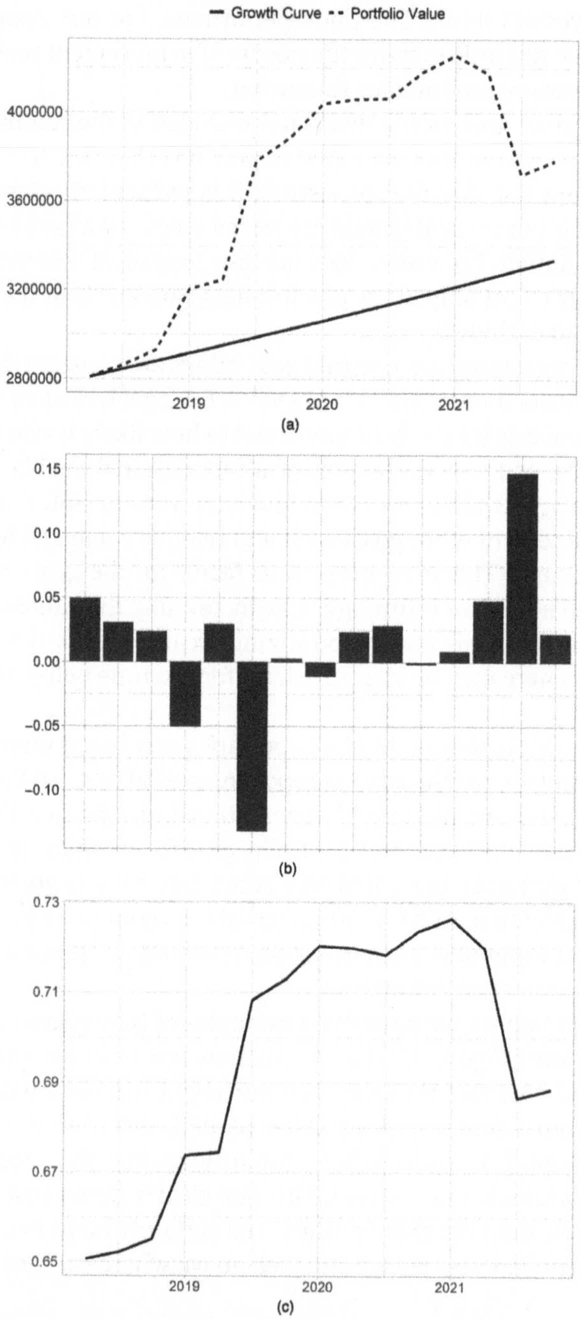

FIGURE 9.2 Sample Retirement Goal, Goals-Based Graphics: (a) Account Value Relative to the Required Growth Curve; (b) Quarter-Over-Quarter Over/Underperformance Relative to Required Return; (c) Probability of Goal Achievement over Time. All values are simulated.

Figure 9.2 (b) presents similar information, but with an adaptation. Instead of the original required line, we update the required return at the end of every quarter. This is to reflect the idea that we are rebalancing and reoptimizing on an ongoing basis, so our required return is always in flux. Is the portfolio manager able to maintain her performance relative to that *ongoing* shift in requirement, rather than the static one presented in Figure 9.2 (a)? A line delineating the average over time might be appropriate here, as well.

Finally, Figure 9.2 (c) presents the central figure with which clients (and we) are concerned: how our client's probability of goal achievement has evolved over time. Ideally, this figure increases every year until the account has grown enough to fully fund the goal. In a way similar to Figure 9.2 (a), presenting the probability of goal achievement through time also conceptualizes the recent portfolio drawdown. While it has damaged the probability, we are still further along than we were when we started.

Deguest, Martellini, and Milhau[1] also suggest including the maximum expected shortfall of a goal. To calculate this figure, we look at the outcomes that fall short of the goal requirement and take their average (this is the conditional shortfall); then we divide by the probability of the shortfall:

$$\text{Expected shortfall} = \frac{E\left(1 - \frac{\widehat{w}_T}{W} \middle| \widehat{w}_T < W\right)}{1-\phi},$$

where $\widehat{w}_T$ is the simulated portfolio value at the end of the goal horizon, T, W is the wealth required to achieve the goal, and ϕ is the probability of achieving the goal. $E(1 - \widehat{w}_T / W | \widehat{w}_T < W)$, then, is the average shortfall of the portfolio for all worlds in which the portfolio fails to achieve the goal. Generating this figure requires simulating possible portfolio paths and so it is subject to errors in model choice and errors in forecasts (or outright hacking). It is also not intuitive. Even so, it can be a useful figure once trained a bit.

With all of these figures, we are trying to place portfolio movements within the context of a client goal. Over time, Figures 9.2 (a) and (c) will also capture another important result of the goals-based framework. Recall how the probability mass in a portfolio's distribution of returns is pushed well above the required return. This means that, over time and on average, goals-based portfolios should outperform their required returns by some

[1] R. Deguest, L. Martellini, and V. Milhau, *Goal-Based Investing: Theory and Practice* (World Scientific Publishing, 2021).

significant margin. This is, of course, how our probability increases every year, and how the difference between the portfolio's required return and actual return in the first graph will come to diverge so significantly. This is, in part, the purpose of the middle plot—to show how a portfolio manager is adapting to the very fluid nature of our required return target, to "normalize" the reporting on an ongoing basis.

An investor focus on different metrics will also pace a different focus on portfolio managers. If clients do not judge a firm by risk-adjusted returns, but rather by how well they help them to achieve goals, then we should reward or punish portfolio managers by different metrics, too. How do we know if a portfolio manager is good at her job if alpha is not our objective? To what should we hold the manager to account if benchmark returns are not our primary concern?

One thing goals-based practitioners should value quite highly is accuracy of forecasts. Our client's goals depend on being fairly right about markets most of the time. If we are consistently wrong in our capital market expectations, we are not adding value, we are destroying it. Happily, the goals-based framework gives us a very convenient metric by which to judge the accuracy of forecasts. Despite the apparent complexity of the problem, we make a very simple forecast every single period. We forecast that our client's required return will be hit some specified percentage of the time. We can judge the accuracy of our forecasts, then, using a Brier score. A Brier score is the average of squared deviations of our forecasts from what actually happened, or

$$\text{Brier score} = \frac{\sum_{t=1}^{t=N}(p_t - O_t)^2}{N},$$

where p_t is the forecasted probability of achieving the required return in a given period and $O = 1$ if our return was actually attained and $O = 0$ if our return was not attained, t is the evaluation period (a month, quarter, or year, for example), and N is the number of periods over which we are measuring.

A Brier score, then, is much like golf: lower scores are better and higher scores are worse. Random predictions, coupled with random outcomes, will generate a Brier score of 0.33, and this is our threshold. A portfolio manager with a Brier score greater than 0.33 is doing *worse* than chance. A portfolio manager with a Brier score of less than 0.33 is doing better than chance. One study found that a Brier score was closely related to portfolio outperformance, and a score of less than 0.20 was necessary to consistently produce alpha.[2] While alpha is not necessarily relevant to goals-based investors, the accuracy of our capital market expectations *is absolutely critical*. Hence, some method for judging this accuracy is needed.

Now, whether this information is displayed on a client report is another question altogether. It is certainly part of how a client should judge a portfolio manager, along with the other metrics with which we are all familiar. A secondary space on the statement could be dedicated to this question: "How good is your portfolio manager?" Although it is unlikely most clients will understand how to read all of those metrics, a Brier score could potentially be included here. For internal use, however, among the firms, this score could be quite valuable as a way to evaluate portfolio managers that is consistent with the goals-based framework (whereas more traditional metrics may not be).

There are downsides to a Brier score, of course. They can be hacked, and they do not take into account the extremity nor cost of wrongness. For example, suppose the probability of a portfolio going to $0 is 10%. If I were evaluated by a Brier score alone, the optimal strategy is to predict the probability of this event as 0% in every period. Though my Brier score would be quite good, 0.10, my real-life results would not be. After 10-ish periods, all of the portfolios I managed would now be worth nothing and our investors would likely be filing lawsuits. It is doubtful that "I had a good Brier score" will suffice as a defense. Obviously, some real-world wisdom, good faith, *and oversight* is required to ensure portfolio managers are not gaming their metrics.

Another potential goals-based portfolio manager evaluation tool, one that could help offset the deficiencies of a Brier score, is a metric that accounts for a goal's value and also the gain/loss in probability of achievement over multiple periods. Keep in mind that this is a first pass, but something like a value-weighted average of our client's gain/loss in achievement probability. It could look like this

$$\text{PM value added} = \frac{\sum_{t=1}^{T} \sum_{i=1}^{N} v_t(i) \cdot \Delta\phi_t(i)}{T},$$

---

[2]J. A. Cerniglia and P.E. Tetlock, "Accelerating Learning in Active Management: *The Alpha-Brier Process*," *The Journal of Portfolio Management* 45, no. 5 (2019): 125–135. DOI: `https://doi.org/10.3905/jpm.2019.45.5.125`.

where T is the number of time periods over which we are measuring, N is the number of goals in our client's goals-space, $v_t(i)$, is the value of goal i at time t, and $\Delta\phi_t(i)$ is the change in probability for goal i in time t. A metric such as this would reward portfolio managers who delivered portfolio results that directly increased investor utility, which is, at the end of the day, how a firm is judged by its clients whether consciously or unconsciously. As well as offsetting some of the Brier score deficiencies, this metric also discriminates between what is more important and what is less important to our client. As we have discussed, aspirational goals have low probabilities of achievement, but since they also carry lower value to the investor, this metric weights progress toward that goal appropriately low. Portfolio managers, then, can be rewarded for delivering value where it is most needed.

There are deficiencies to goals-based reporting, many of which I am sure will not be clear until they are implemented. Iteration will be key; I do not hold any of these ideas as gospel truth. I can imagine that a reporting rubric with achievement probability as the centerpiece will push investors to focus on this figure, perhaps obsessively. I could see investors unhealthily caught up in the volatility of the achievement probability metric. Were it adopted as industry standard, the industry would, no doubt, find ways to artificially suppress the volatility of this figure so as to ease the minds of their fee-paying clients. No doubt lower volatility of this figure would be financially rewarded over higher volatility (I even sense a peer-reviewed paper or two on the subject).

Even so, putting a focus on probability of achievement, and contextualizing portfolio results within that framework at least puts the focus on the right metrics. To the extent that this yields an unhealthy obsession is more a commentary on how metrics drive behavior, whether rightly or wrongly, than whether the metric is measuring something meaningful. Clearly, this is *the* meaningful metric; all else is secondary. Can it, as a metric, be abused? Of course. But let's not throw out the baby with the bathwater. The metric is valuable, but no metrics should be obsessed over. Just as with all else in life, wisdom and context matter quite a lot.

There are other complications, of course. For example, I am unsure how to account for the human capital problem in these metrics. They are included in the model so the data is there, but should that be included on an official client report? Client reports are (and should continue to be) sacrosanct. Something like the discounted value of all future savings, with its considerable nuance and uncertainty, may not be appropriate to include in so important a document. Excluding it also leaves out critical assumptions that did drive the portfolio allocation decision of the portfolio manager. I admit to being at an impasse. There is a strong argument for and a strong argument against. This tension would extend to any and all of the financial planning assumptions we might tap to produce these metrics (inheritance, projected dates of death, and so on). No doubt regulators will have the final word on questions such as these.

This also brings up reporting on impact and ESG objectives, if there are any. As we have discussed, impact and ESG objectives are very often important and personal goals to investors. It would be appropriate to include the progress toward their achievement. That said, impact reporting is an entire book unto itself, currently with varied opinions and debates of its own. I doubt my ability to properly tackle such a discussion. However, it would be appropriate, on some level, to adopt best practices for such reporting, and include them on a client statement. Especially when returns are being sacrificed for the accomplishment of an impact objective, ignoring it altogether seems inappropriate—even if it is just a line item on a goals-based statement for the time being.

Lastly, clients often have a pool of wealth with no specific objective. I have labeled this as "Wealth Building" in our sample statement. While I have not enumerated it, I would propose that such a portfolio be reported as we have traditionally reported investments. What's more, I do not want to give the impression that the rest of a performance/activity statement should be thrown away. Quite the contrary! Let's keep what is working and what is familiar. I am proposing firms *add* goals-based reporting metrics and bring them to the fore of investor reporting.

I would be surprised by the current lack of goals-based reporting except for the technology investment that I know it will take. Keeping up with multiple goals for every client in the firm's book is no small task. It is a multiplicative problem: for every 100 clients, each with five goals, the firm must actively track progress on 500 individual objectives. No small feat, to be sure. Most investment managers will find this unruly, so we will have to rely on our technology partners to help us make this possible. The competitive edge for the investment advisor is obvious. For the technology firm that gets this right, the competitive edge is even more apparent, but more on that in a later chapter.

For now, let us conclude with some agreement that goals-based reporting is an obvious addition to the current reporting structure for individual investors. Firms stand to better communicate their value in a way that clients understand (unlike my failed attempt to sell alpha to one of my early clients). And clients stand to gain the metrics and figures that are most relevant to them, not tangled up in the financialese that "sophisticated" reporting has become.

CHAPTER 10

Fragility Analysis of Goals-Based Inputs

"You are only entitled to the action, never to its fruits."

—Bhagavad Gita

"We usually just put in 3% for an inflation estimation. It doesn't really matter too much, anyway," a trainer responded to my question about the new financial planning software the firm had brought on. It carried numerous assumptions: the returns and volatilities of various assets, the future inflation rate, medical cost increases, even future tax estimations. As a young financial advisor, I understood few of the other inputs, but I could grasp inflation, so that is what I asked about. Despite my trainer's answer, I later played with the inflation assumptions in the tool and found that, contrary to his response, the inflation assumption *does* matter. It matters quite a lot, in fact. In a few of the simulations I ran, the difference between a 3% inflation rate and a 5% inflation rate over 25 years was the difference between retiring with near certainty and not retiring with near certainty. Counter to my intuition, adjusting the market return assumptions by the same 200 basis points had a much smaller effect. This left me with a question: Which assumptions matter most to goals-based investors? We know that all our myriad forecasts are wrong to some extent. With limited time and resources, what should we, as practitioners, focus on getting as right as possible, and what can we leave for broader approximations?

I really had no way of effectively answering this question, so I sat on it for years—until I came upon Nassim Taleb's theory of fragility. Most practitioners are familiar with Taleb's iconoclastic style and more laymen-oriented work, such as *The Black Swan*. His book *Antifragility* is a must-read, but it was his technical work on the topic of system fragility that triggered a possible path to answer this latent question of mine. In 2012, with some coauthors, Taleb published a paper for the International Monetary Fund offering a simple heuristic for detecting fragility in any modellable system.[1] These ideas were later expanded into more technical definitions,[2] but the heuristic is sufficient for our needs.

In a nutshell, Taleb argues that linear increases in event significance often result in exponential increases in harm to the system. As an example: running a stop sign at 15 miles per hour is a fender-bender—likely a few thousand dollars in damage. Running a stop sign at 45 miles per hour is a hospital visit—likely tens of thousands of dollars in bodily damage, not to mention the possible loss of life. A 3x increase in event size (speed) resulted in a 10x to 20x increase in harm (financial cost and bodily risk). In derivatives trading, this is known as gamma risk, or convexity.

Taleb uses this starting point to suggest a simple rule. Take a model of the system. Perturb the inputs, one at a time, equally to the upside and downside. Take the average of the output and subtract it from the baseline. If the result is negative, then negative convexity is present and the system is fragile with respect to that input. If the result is positive, then positive convexity is present and the system is antifragile (that is, it gains from extreme movements). If the result is 0, then the system is robust (immune to movements). What is more exciting is that the accuracy of the system model is of secondary importance. As Taleb and Douady put it, "A wrong ruler will not measure the height of a child, but it will certainly tell us if he is growing." It is not the absolute result with which we are concerned—that is, we are not concerned whether 8 comes out if 4.5 goes in. Rather, we are concerned with the drama associated with the changes—if 8 comes out when 4.5 goes in and 25 comes out when 5 goes in, we have some ground to say that getting this input right is very important.

---

[1] N. N. Taleb, E. Canetti, T. Kinda, E. Loukoianova, and C. Schmieder, "A New Heuristic Measure of Fragility and Tail Risks: Application to Stress Testing," *IMF Working Paper 12/216*, 2012.

[2] N. N Taleb and R. Douady "Mathematical Definition, Mapping, and Detection of (Anti) Fragility," *Quantitative Finance* 13, no. 11 (2013): 1677–1689. DOI: `https://doi.org/10.1080/14697688.2013.800219`.

More formally: Let $f(\cdot)$ be your model of a system and let α be an input to your model (since we are perturbing the model one variable at a time, α represents any input to the model). From here, we perturb $f(\cdot)$ by $\pm\Delta$, or some constant amount, and subtract the baseline from the average result:

$$\Xi = \frac{f(\alpha - \Delta) + f(\alpha + \Delta)}{2} - f(\alpha).$$

As mentioned above, when $\Xi > 0$ the system is antifragile with respect to α, when $\Xi < 0$ the system is fragile with respect to α, and when $\Xi = 0$ the system is robust with respect to α. Of course, each input will affect the system differently, so it may be antifragile with respect to one input and fragile with respect to another.

In the context of financial planning and goals-based investing, once we understand which variables create the most fragility in our system, we can know where we need to most direct our focus and expertise. The goals-based utility model carries five basic inputs, and we will test each one: (1) current wealth, (2) future required wealth, (3) time until the funding is needed, (4) expected portfolio return, and (5) portfolio volatility. There are, in fact, some hidden variables in each of these, as well. How much wealth is required to fund a goal is itself a function of our inflation projection, and our current wealth dedicated to a goal is a function of the goal's value relative to the other goals in the investor's goals-space as well as the number of dollars in an account. If we include the present value of future human capital, current wealth becomes even more nuanced as that calculation carries even more assumptions! Ultimately, the goals-based model is intricate. Teasing apart each variable is admittedly difficult and quite possibly fraught. Even so, I believe that some light on the question is better than no light.

First, we must build a model that approximates the real world. As mentioned above, this fragility test has quite a lot of tolerance for model inaccuracy (in fact, it assumes the model is inaccurate), which is an immense relief! This allows us to simplify the problem considerably, and can even justify the use of a Gaussian return assumption, which we know is an entirely inaccurate way to model real-world returns.

Leaning on a Monte Carlo approach, let's model our baseline future value as

$$\widehat{W}_j = w\left[1 + \sum_{i=1}^{i=t} \Phi^{-1}(\varepsilon_i, \mu, \sigma)\right],$$

where $\widehat{W}_j$ is the future wealth value in the jth simulation, w is the current wealth value dedicated to the goal, t is the time horizon within which the goal must be achieved, $\Phi^{-1}(\cdot)$ is the inverse cumulative distribution function, ε is a uniform random variable that takes values between 0 and 1, μ is the location parameter of the distribution (mean), and σ is the scale parameter (volatility). In essence, this equation simulates the life of a portfolio, starting at the present value and ending at some number of years in the future. Each time subperiod is generated by pulling a randomly selected percentile from the distribution, then applying the aggregate growth factor to the present value of the portfolio.

Using this stochastic simulation approach, we can set J equal to some high number of simulations and thereby assess the probability of meeting our future goal by counting the number of trials that meet or exceed our minimum required future wealth value, then dividing that number by the total number of trials simulated, J. More formally:

$$\frac{V_{j=1}^{j=J}\left(\widehat{W}_j \geq W_{req}\right)}{J},$$

where $V(\cdot)$ is a counting function, returning the number of occurrences where the parenthetical statement is true, or the number of times we hit our goal (simulated wealth is greater than or equal to the minimum required wealth). This equation simply returns the probability of success, which is *the* litmus test for goals-based investors. Harm, to goals-based investors, is failing to achieve their goals.

Once we have the baseline probabilities, we can begin adjusting each input in turn and measure the change in goal achievement probability. This should give us a sense for which variables are most important. To get a true apples-to-apples comparison, we will adjust each variable by varying percentages rather than some arbitrary number. This will keep some consistency across the various variable types.

The results of our fragility test are displayed in the plot. The vertical axis in Figure 10.1 is the fragility measure (Ξ)—recall that negative values indicate the model is fragile with respect to that input. This can also be thought of as a measure of average harm of being wrong. Alternatively, Ξ can be thought of as a measure of convexity for a particular variable. The more negative the figure, the more being wrong can hurt you. Alternatively, the more positive the figure, the more being wrong can help you. The horizontal axis

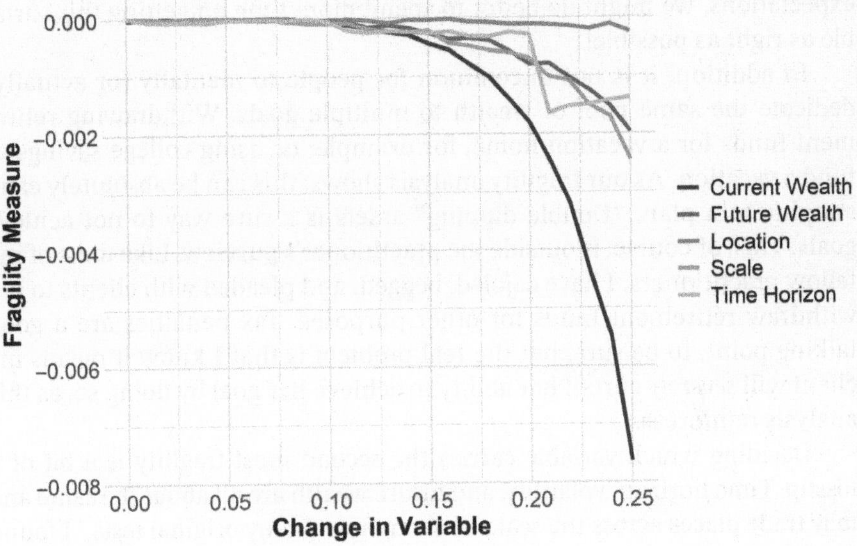

FIGURE 10.1 Fragility Test Results

is the percentage by which we perturbed the variables, which can be alternatively thought of as our level of wrongness.

What becomes immediately clear is how fragile goals-based investors are with respect to their levels of current wealth. More than any other variable, being wrong about the amount of current wealth available to achieve a goal is, by far, the most damaging. This is unfortunate since current wealth itself involves so many variables. Total account value wealth is often what we think of when we discuss this variable, but it also includes the present value of all future savings. That present value of future savings contains numerous assumptions, such as a growth rate for savings, a discount rate, and we typically do not even consider those events that could cause a serious drop in savings rates (like poor health, divorce, or unexpected children).

The amount of current wealth dedicated to a goal also includes the allocation from the total pool of wealth derived from the optimization engine. This, of course, relies on an accurate gauge of the relative value of one goal to another. Goal valuation, then, is also an input to current wealth. All of these calculations are within the practitioner's purview, and, though practitioners tend to spend most of our time on developing capital market expectations, we might do better to spend more time on getting this variable as right as possible!

In addition, it is not uncommon for people to mentally (or actually) dedicate the same pool of wealth to multiple goals. Withdrawing retirement funds for a vacation home, for example, or using college savings to fund a vacation. As our fragility analysis shows, this can be absolutely catastrophic to a plan. "Double dipping" assets is a sure way to not achieve goals. This, of course, is outside the practitioner's purview. Like most of my fellow practitioners, I have cajoled, begged, and pleaded with clients to not withdraw retirement funds for other purposes. Tax penalties are a good talking point, to be sure, but the real problem is that I know it means my client will *severely* curtail her ability to achieve her goal by doing so, as this analysis reinforces.

Deciding which variable carries the second most fragility is a bit of a tossup. Time horizon, volatility, and future wealth are all about the same and may trade places across the scale of wrongness. In my original tests,[3] I found future values to be the second most fragile, whereas in this one I found volatility to be second most fragile. The other goal variables all matter, of course, and some of the (minor) differences are likely from where one chooses to place the variables in relation to each other in the various tests. In the end, all of these variables are about equally important, but I will take them in the order that this test ranked them.

Second most fragile is our estimation of the scale parameter (volatility). Getting that wrong is not nearly as bad as getting current wealth wrong, but goal achievement is certainly fragile with respect to it. We discussed in a previous chapter how market returns were decidedly non-normal, and what that means to goals-based investors. Viewed in that light, that volatility—or the spread of possible outcomes—carries the fragility it does should both come as no surprise and also as a warning to practitioners. If the volatility of possible outcomes is not definite, but rather infinite, as is the case with alpha-stable distributions, this fragility analysis shows that employing the correct distribution model—or at least employing risk controls informed by the correct distribution model—is extremely important. Indeed, that volatility carries the

[3]Much of this discussion is drawn from my original paper on the topic: F. J. Parker, "Knowing What to Worry About: A Goals-Based Application of Fragility Detection Theory," *Journal of Wealth Management* 20, no. 1 (2017): 10–16. DOI: `https://doi.org/10.3905/jwm.2017.20.1.010`.

fragility it does is why investors fear mistimed extreme drawdowns in their portfolio. Investors instinctively know that markets can rob them of their ability to achieve goals just as much as they can grant them the selfsame ability. This is intuitive. What is not necessarily intuitive is how to organize a portfolio of investments or trading rules around such facts—hence the discussion in our earlier chapter.

Of course, portfolio volatility is itself a function of numerous inputs. The volatility of individual investments, their correlations to one another, and how that volatility scales through time, all interact to produce what we see as portfolio volatility. Time on these variables is well spent by practitioners, and, likely, volatility is the least predictable of them all! We can take some comfort in how the exponential nature of the harm only really begins to take hold for higher levels of wrongness (above the 15% level). We don't need to be right to five decimal places. There is a 30%-point range within which to reasonably forecast: that is, if realized portfolio volatility is 16%, any forecast within the 11% to 21% range will probably do just fine. If, however, we forecast 15% and realized volatility is 30%, our client has a problem. The point is, getting it about right is acceptable. Getting it blatantly wrong is not.

Future wealth is the next most fragile variable. It seems somewhat obvious on the face of it: If we estimate that you need $1 in 20 years, but in fact you need $1.10, we are more likely to have a shortfall. The trouble here is that estimating an exact future value requires triangulating several variables. For longer-lived and longer-term goals, like funding a lifestyle, we do not dedicate a lump sum to "buy" that goal one day,[4] unlike a piece of real estate or philanthropic gift. Therefore, calculating how much we need to properly fund an ongoing goal is really a function of our capital market expectations over the future period within which the withdrawals are active, and, more importantly, how strongly inflation erodes the purchasing power of our wealth.

Inflation really cannot be understated. Over a period of 20 years, the difference between a 3% inflation rate and a 5% inflation rate is the difference between needing $1.00 and $1.46 when it comes time to fund the goal—a 46% higher wealth requirement. What is worse and more realistic: for goals requiring ongoing distributions where the money is *already* saved, inflation does even more damage. Assuming markets deliver about the same returns,

[4] Brunel calls these "fuzzy goals."

an investor needs *double* the amount of money to maintain the same ongoing distributions in a 5% inflation rate scenario versus a 3% inflation rate scenario.[5] To maintain buying power in a 3% inflation scenario, we need $25 for every $1 in distributions, and in a 5% inflation scenario we need $50 for every $1 in distributions (assuming a 7% portfolio return for both scenarios).

Clearly, understanding how much wealth we need to support an ongoing spending goal is heavily dependent on inflation. Hence, this is a variable that is worth spending time on. Unlike my original training with the financial planning software, inflation estimates really do matter quite a lot.

Time until a goal is about as fragile as our required future wealth estimates. Fortunately, of all the variables, this is probably the least troublesome. For the most part, this is outside the purview of the practitioner. Clients typically have an idea of how long they can wait until they need the funds. Life happens, of course, but that is difficult to plan for ahead of time. Some goals do maintain their distance from now, like estate goals, for instance. Rarely do people know the year of their death, so an estate goal may always be 7–10 years from now. That is okay, in my view, and, unlike the other variables in the calculation, the practitioner can let this variable be what it is.

Both future wealth and time horizon operate within about the same "wrongness window." That is, for both variables, being 15% wrong is only slightly more asymmetric to the downside. Once our wrongness moves beyond that level, convexity takes over and downside wrongness begins to dominate.

Finally, and surprisingly, estimates of portfolio return carry the least fragility in the calculation. This is surprising to me since, if the uncountable number of annual capital market expectations that are produced every year

---

[5]If we expect that our investor leaves the inflation rate in the portfolio to compensate for the lost buying power, then our withdrawal rate is governed by our market returns minus the inflation rate:

$$\frac{\text{Withdrawal}}{\text{Corpus}} = \text{Market return} - \text{Inflation rate}.$$

Solving for our required corpus gives:

$$\text{Corpus} = \frac{\text{Withdrawal}}{\text{Market return} - \text{Inflation rate}}.$$

Of course, this does not capture the very important role of volatility in shaping sustainable withdrawals!

is any guide, firms spend an inordinate amount of time pinning down a return estimate for capital markets. Obviously, having some idea of returns is important. We do need an input into the probability function, after all. But, counter to our intuition and our focused efforts, this is a variable where being wrong is not all that harmful. As this analysis shows, firms would do considerably better to spend their time and energy pinning down more accurate inflation forecasts, and still better to spend time understanding their clients and the nature of their client's current wealth. Of course, inflation forecasts do not have the same sizzle as a take on market returns, and, to be fair, clients expect a story around market returns in the coming period. When asked, responding "returns aren't an important variable" is probably a sure way to be fired by a client. When asked whether portfolio return estimates are important, can you imagine if my trainer had responded, "It doesn't really matter too much, anyway"?! Yet that response would have been more accurate with respect to market returns than it was for inflation forecasts!

Time is a valuable resource, especially in the money management business. Dedicating the proper time to the proper questions is what we as practitioners are paid to do. While we do need forecasts for all of these variables, it is better to understand which forecasts require our detailed attention and which can be more roughly estimated. Forecasts are, of course, wrong by some degree no matter how hard we try, but each forecast carries a "wrongness range" within which we need to operate. If we are consistently falling outside of that range, then we are doing our clients a disservice. For most variables, as this analysis reveals, falling within 15% of the realized result is probably sufficient, though getting current wealth more right would be better.

A few grains of salt the reader should take along with this chapter. First, we should remember that fragility analysis is really a measure of convexity; a comparison of how much more damaging being wrong in one direction is relative to the other direction. Obviously, for all of these variables it is better to be wrong in one direction than the other. It would be generally better, for example, to overestimate coming inflation by 15% than to underestimate it by 15%. This builds a cushion into portfolios and, more importantly, aligns with the tried-and-true advice "under promise and over deliver."

I cannot claim, however, that purposefully overestimating variables like inflation in the name of prudence is always a net benefit. Recall that we are required to allocate wealth across goals as well as to investments within them. Purposefully overestimating important variables will send more wealth to priority goals and less wealth to aspirational goals. This means that less important goals will be considerably less likely to be achieved. In short, purposefully misestimating variables yields a misallocation of wealth both across goals and across investments. Of course, investors could theoretically rebalance wealth from one goal to another as inflation actualizes over the years, but that is curtailed by real-world frictions like varying account types. We cannot realistically pull wealth from an overallocated retirement goal that is executed using a 401(k), or an overallocated college savings goal that has been tied up in a 529 account. Such withdrawals carry prohibitive tax consequences and penalties. In the end, the practitioner must employ experience and wisdom along with quantitative techniques to find the right balance of caution and accuracy in the estimation of critical variables.

Lastly, it is worth noting that my original fragility analysis found a slightly different order for the variables. That analysis was conducted with different baseline assumptions, implying that the fragility of a portfolio may be itself somewhat dependent on our baseline scenario. This is consistent with fragility theory, so it is not particularly noteworthy. Interestingly, in that original analysis, it was misestimation of present value that created the most harm—consistent with the analysis herein. This should again encourage practitioners that a clear understanding of a client situation is absolutely time well spent. After current wealth, my original analysis found that wrongness of future value was second-most fragile, then time horizon as the third-most fragile. In that analysis, I did not extend wrongness as far as I did in this one. At lower levels of wrongness, this order still holds in the current analysis. Finally, location then scale round out the model's fragility in the original analysis, which differs from the current results. This is a hint that, again, the baseline assumptions will influence the relative importance of the variables.

I am of the mind that understanding where our models are fragile is a critical piece of our own self-review and self-due-diligence. However, we should remember that it is part of a larger picture, part of an overall understanding of our mental maps that can help guide decision-making only when viewed in the proper context, and when properly internalized. The internalization is important because that is what feeds practitioner intuition. Intuition based on nothing is a detriment, as behavioral finance has shown us. But intuition founded in well-thought-out quantitative techniques is of immense value. That is when it becomes the lens through which an effective practitioner sees everything else. Building our intuition around fragility carries an immense value. More than anything, it provides the practitioner with a "spidy-sense" when working with and building the myriad models that occupy our daily lives.

CHAPTER 11

Human Risks

"Man is an enigma to himself."

—Carl Jung

Goals-based investing was born in the private wealth management space, driven by practitioners looking for solutions to the problems they encountered every day—problems of which academics seemed unaware. Nowhere does this ring more true than in those decidedly more human risks—the risks faced by individuals and wealthy families that have nothing at all to do with organizing an investment portfolio. With the technical bits of the theory out of the way, I would be remiss if I did not cover a few of the more human aspects of goals-based investing. There are enough to cover a library of books, and I do not intend to recount all of the wonderful resources already in existence. Rather, having spent time in the family office space, serving families and listening to family members from around the globe, I have found that there are a handful of very human risks that can legitimately threaten the long-term growth and preservation of wealth. I do not claim to be an expert here, only to offer my small perspective on a very big topic.

While goals-based portfolio theory does allow for aspirational goals for which high-variance outcomes are preferable, I suspect that many entrepreneurs would read most of this book as a "stay-wealthy" approach (as opposed to a "get-wealthy" approach). And that is true. This is not a book about how to play option markets more profitably, or how to build a better startup. This is a book dedicated to the people who are tasked with the preservation and growth of wealth . . . implying that wealth exists already. It is a truism to say that maintaining wealth is a prerequisite to achieve future goals for which more wealth is a requirement, rather than less.

For almost any family, it is the training of the next generation that becomes most critical for the maintenance and prudent growth of family wealth. Each family has a different perspective on this topic, as well they should, but in all cases it should be well noted that staying wealthy requires a different skill set than getting wealthy. While that may seem obvious, I have noted that some wealthy families struggle with this. As counter to the prevailing wisdom as this sounds, the numbers favor getting wealthy: you can fail 99 times, win once, and you are wealthy. However, those stats work against you once you have won. Now you have to win 100 times out of 100 lest you lose it all. It is usually the wealth-creators who have the greatest trouble shifting mindsets once they have built their business or after a significant liquidity event. And that is my point: maintaining that wealth requires a different skill set from building it. Families that fail to build that skill set tend to fail to maintain their wealth long-term.

In my view, it is the maintenance skill set that must be imparted to the second generation. Entrepreneurship is valuable, do not hear what I am not saying! Entrepreneurship is one of the most powerful forces in the world—a force we can thank for giving us the modern world. For the children of wealth-creators, however, pushing hard to teach entrepreneurship can put the focus on the wrong point. First, entrepreneurs are a unique breed with a unique set of attitudes and skills, and those do not always transfer to the next generation. Second, a focus on entrepreneurship can lead to excessive risk-taking with what is now the family's—as opposed to "my"—wealth. Without the commiserate skill set and disposition, such a focus can lead to the erosion of wealth rather than its creation. Growing an existent operating business is often critical to the long-term success of a family, and many of those skills can be taught, but a focus on starting and growing something completely new should be incorporated only after diligent thought and self-assessment.

But most importantly, an incessant focus on a "get wealthy" approach leaves the second generation without the skills needed to be effective shareholders and/or operators. It is not uncommon for a wealthy family to be both the primary shareholders and executives of a sizable business. Without the necessary skills to be effective operators and shareholders, the business can suffer, and the family's wealth will suffer along with it.

Before I address effective shareholding, we must first address the primary risk to a family's wealth that owning and operating a business presents. Yes, it is a concentrated asset, but that is a distant number-two risk with known techniques for managing and mitigating. The first concern, by a mile, is who will operate the business after the founder has retired or passed away. It is very common for the family to choose someone from within their ranks. However, studies show that this is, generally, a poor choice. Firms that choose a family member to replace an outgoing CEO tend to book higher expenses and lower revenue growth—to name but two variables—than their peers who experience a similar transition. Though, there are some things that mitigate these effects, like a family-member CEO who attended a prestigious university.[1]

Since it is the long-term well-being of the family at stake, the first question families should ask themselves is whether they *want* to operate a business. Moreover, as hard as it may be to question, the family must honestly ask whether the next generation has both the desire and skill to do so. The data shows that this is a long-term headwind to family wealth, so it is, at a minimum, a question that should be very carefully considered, even if answered in the affirmative.

There are advantages to both owning and operating a business, to be fair. Family-owned-and-operated businesses gain an executive who is loyal, at least ostensibly. Frictions between shareholders and the day-to-day of the business operations can theoretically be reduced, making long-term planning and the execution of a vision seamless. For families who wish to impart their business with ethical objectives, a family member operator is much less likely to push back or scuttle such efforts. In some cases, the family business is so scattered that only a family member or long-term executive (who is practically a family member) can get their hands around it. And, the family legacy can be preserved.

If we are honest, it is really this last point that is most pressing for families. There is, very often, a feeling of duty, both to previous generations and to future generations to pass along, not only the ownership, but also the maintenance of the family business. That is a very noble sentiment, to be sure. Duty is a powerful motivator, and the idea that someone without the family's last name would run *our* business can seem anathema to many families. Such sentiments, as well intentioned though they may be, carry inherent

[1]F. Perez-Gonzalez, "Inherited Control and Firm Performance," *The American Economic Review* 96, no. 5 (December 2006): 1559–1588. We should note that it may not be the prestigiousness of the university that creates the effect. Rather, it may be that children interested enough in the operation of a business are motivated to build the requisite skill set to do it.

risks of which families should be well aware. None of this to say that families cannot take such a risk, but rather, if they are to be taken, families should be conscious of them and actively take steps to mitigate them.

The central risk to a family-run business is the dual role of shareholder and operator. Ideally, those roles would be separate because, said simply, the executive of a business is the employee of the shareholders. When a shareholder with extensive family influence is also the operator of the business, the emerging social dynamic makes effective shareholding very difficult, even if not impossible. It is easy for other shareholders to become "lazy shareholders." Lazy shareholders may show up to meetings, but they are generally checked out and unconcerned with the business at hand. They assume their executive is doing everything right and will tell them where and what to sign.

Lazy shareholders are unengaged. They are unconcerned with the goings-on of the business and they are loath to do the homework required of a shareholder. If they have learned to read financial statements, they are unlikely to do so with a critical eye, and if they have not, they are unlikely to be motivated to learn. Lazy shareholders tend to carry a "send me a check" attitude (which can be interpreted by others in the family as entitled), and they are certainly not asking their executive about the mismatch between the story being told in the boardroom and the story being told by the financial statements. Lazy shareholders are a very real danger to a family business.

Effective shareholders, by contrast, are engaged. They come to the meeting prepared, having read and understood the financial statements they received (or are making efforts to do so—I have also found that those with the least skill in reading financial statements often have the most skill in reading the person, arguably the more important skill). They come to ask questions of their executive, attempting to suss out the real challenges in the business, the things keeping the executive up at night. Effective shareholders hold their executive to account, all while recognizing the extreme challenge that it is to run a business well. Effective shareholders are concerned with the morale of their employees. They are concerned with the growth plan and vision of the business. They are concerned with how their business is perceived in the marketplace. They are concerned with an unusual uptick in accounts receivable or an increase in current liabilities. In short, for anything that has to do with the future viability of the business, effective shareholders will press in to ask for a clarification and an outlook.

Asking difficult pointed questions and holding an executive to account is not so easy when that executive is your brother, your father, your sister, your cousin, or your mother. *That* dynamic becomes considerably more difficult—almost impossible, I would argue. To do so effectively requires a mutual respect and understanding, both inside and outside the boardroom. Family members who are operating the business must be humble about their position as employees of the shareholders. In the boardroom, those shareholders are their boss, though they also happen to be family members. Shareholders must also carry humility and respect, but without restraint from doing their job. In the end, the shareholders must be free to fire any family member running the business. If that is not on the table, then the shareholders really are a rubber-stamp organization—a fact they will perceive even if it is never explicitly stated.

It is important, too, that shareholders remember that they are not operators (except in some circumstances). Operating a business is an exacting job. Operators are constantly putting out fires, both big and small, all while trying to execute their vision for the business. Shareholders who want to be operators are but another thorn in the side of an effective executive, and effective executives will not stay on long if they are micromanaged by their shareholders—family or otherwise. Thus, it bears repeating: shareholders are not operators.

Effective shareholding in a family business is about (1) setting a long-term vision with milestones, (2) keeping the business executive accountable to the vision and to those milestones, and (3) governance. It is not unreasonable, of course, for shareholders to adopt the executive's vision, and to set milestones with the executive's input (this would all be preferable). But once those are set, it is the role of the shareholders to make sure progress is being made. If progress is not being made, the shareholders should be provided reasons why and a plan for how to get back on track. And it is always better for the executive to point out when progress has not been made. If shareholders have to point out that progress toward the business's vision has stalled, it is a red flag: either the executive does not know progress has stalled (bad) or does not care (worse).

Good governance is about setting the limits within which the executive is free to operate. Shareholders should never be concerned with how many paper clips are at the receptionist's desk or the type of envelopes used to send out invoices. It bears repeating because this is oft forgotten: *Shareholders are not operators*. Setting governance is, if you'll excuse the nerdiness of this metaphor, like the Prime Directive in *Star Trek*. In *Star Trek*, ship captains had to abide by a set of rules, imposed by the admiralty, called the Prime Directive. A ship's captain is free to accomplish the mission in any way—as long as her actions do not violate the Prime Directive. A captain who accomplishes missions and does not violate these rules is considered a good captain. *So it is with an executive.* If an executive is hitting set milestones and acting within the rules the shareholders have established, then she is a good executive, by definition.

Of course, occasionally Captain Kirk would do something that violated the Prime Directive. When that happened, he was required to call the admiralty as soon as possible and explain the circumstance, why he violated the rules, and what he expects the potential fallout to be. The admiralty would then help manage the fallout, determine whether any punishments were appropriate, up to and including termination, and then move on with life. We should not expect executives to never break the rules, but we should also not expect them to break them excessively. There is a distinct difference between being a bold leader in a tough position and having a wanton disregard for the rules. Ultimately, effective shareholders must be wise enough to judge the difference.

Doing the job of a shareholder is not, nor should it be, easy. The shareholder is the last line of defense against a failing business. When shareholders abandon their posts, they put not only their personal wealth at risk, *but also the livelihood of every employee in the business.* I cannot stress this enough. Every employee in your business likely has spouses and children. Some have ailing parents at home. Your failed business will cost them months, if not years, of lost income and benefits, not to mention the stress and heartache of finding a new job while attempting to feed their families. *It is your job as a shareholder to ensure your business is run well.* If it is not run well, that is your fault. You will pay the cost in lost wealth, and your employees and their families will pay the cost in added stress and lost wages.

Capital is like water, it flows "downhill," toward value. A poorly run business is on a hill of sorts, and the higher the hill, the harder it is to collect capital. In a poorly run business, money will always feel as though it is flowing away, like water down a hill. There will always be a reason, of course: this happened, that happened, it was a bad quarter, et cetera. But you, as a business, are interacting with capital markets, and capital markets are famously unforgiving. Once water begins to run downhill, it is terribly difficult to push it back to your favor. Better to address problems early and head-on.

Of course, we cannot discount the importance of education, as well! Sometimes shareholders simply lack the training required to understand how cash moves through a business. Without some training, within the setting of a board meeting, with an often-foreign vocabulary, and an executive who is likely to know considerably more than most about the operations of the business, shareholders can feel understandably overwhelmed and frustrated—or simply give up and sit back. Building an ongoing program of education for shareholders, to give them the requisite skill set to do their jobs, is critical to the long-term growth of the family wealth. Clearly, any education program must meet shareholders where they are, and seek to move them to the needed level of sophistication given the task at hand. It does no good for a shareholder to learn about the specifics of a distribution business if the family operates an oil and gas business. Again, this is a place advisors can add considerable value.

To be fair, many family shareholders are not engaged because they know nothing they say or do will actually matter. A family member CEO who is also a majority shareholder is not fire-able and everyone knows it. Why bother learning to read the financial statements? Why bother asking the tough questions? Why even bother going to the meeting? Unengaged shareholders tend to be a signal that the relationship between shareholder and executive is not as it should be. While it is true that family shareholders may be unengaged because they simply do not care or because they are entitled, more often than not an understanding of *why* that is the case reveals a deeper dynamic. When things are going well, being a shareholder is boring. Yet as soon as everyone has to forgo checks or, worse yet, has to start putting money *in* the business to fix problems, even the most disinterested family members will become interested in what is going on. Everyone will be an effective shareholder then, hopefully before it is too late. But if those habits and skill sets are not built before a crisis, those shareholder meetings can easily descend into bickering sessions, and the real work is unlikely to get done.

Family governance, as a field, has tried to fill this gap with mixed results. Families can spend significant time and money writing a family constitution only to have it collect dust somewhere, unread. That is not to say that family constitutions have no value. I think they do, but family constitutions are much like the US constitution. The document itself has grown and changed, informed by case law over centuries. The rules laid out in the document itself are only a small part of the picture. It is the ethos surrounding the constitution that binds Americans together. It is what the constitution stands for that matters more than the words on the page—it is the narrative of the country's founding, the lore surrounding her founders, and the feelings all of this evokes that carries water for an American. The constitution is America, in that sense.

So it is with families. Families need more than a document that says what they cannot do and how to resolve disputes, especially if that document is unchanging and sterile. A document such as this is less a glue and more of a bludgeon used to win arguments. That is a negative narrative, and is unlikely to produce healthy dynamics. Families need a *positive* narrative that binds them together, a sense of *who they are* as a family. Families should begin there. The family constitution, then, can be distilled from that ethos, that narrative, and *then* it is alive and meaningful. It becomes more than a document of rules and regulations, it becomes the founding document that evokes a family narrative.[2] With an effective narrative, the family is bound together by something other than wealth. With such a narrative, and an underpinning document that supports it, difficult circumstances can be navigated much more readily. Rather than pull families apart, crises can *deepen* the family lore, *add* to the narrative, and thus *strengthen* the bond that holds everyone together.

Indeed, that is part of the point of family governance, and good governance is very important. Governance is, after all, what helps to hold humans together across long periods of time. Consider Alexander the Great. After his conquests, all power and authority for his newly formed empire was vested in him. When he died suddenly and without a clear heir, his empire was divided among his generals, who then fought amongst themselves for a generation after his death—leading ultimately to the breakup of one of the largest empires the world had yet seen. Rome, by contrast, had built a system of laws, administration, courts, and institutions that came to both signify and wield the power of the senate (during the republican period) or the emperor (during the imperial period). When an emperor died, the organization that was Rome was not under threat because Rome was not contained in one person. Rome had governance; Alexander the Great did not.

Getting all of this right is hard. Quite frankly, doing all of this well is considerably more difficult than building an effective investment portfolio. But families should not expect to do it all alone. This is another place trusted advisors can add real value. For one, advisors can help educate family shareholders. This entails teaching the language of business, like how to read income statements and balance sheets, how to ask effective questions of your executives, and how to square the story being told with the story the numbers tell.

---

[2]I am indebted to Dominik v. Eynern for the concept and importance of a family narrative. See, for example, D. Eynern, "Narrative Embedded Family Governance," *Family Hippocampus Whitepaper* (2021), https://family-hippocampus.com/narrative-embedded-family-governance/.

Advisors can also help dig up and instill the family narrative, creating environments where these stories are told and taken to heart.

Once the narrative is built, families should spend plenty of time determining their own long-term vision. In my mind, everything is on the table in this discussion. Who is it you want to be as a family in 30 years? Do we want to continue being operators? Do we want to transition to shareholders? Do we want to sell the business altogether? Do we want to be philanthropists? Do we want to be art collectors? What is important to us? And so on. This vision should be consistent with the family narrative and values, so this is a second step. For families without a clear vision, or who have trouble developing a clear vision, outside advisors can help facilitate the conversation.

I want to stress that this is the *family's* vision. This should not be the vision of one family member, even if that family member is the wealth-creator. Yes, that person has a say, but if the wealth-creator wants to see that wealth maintained through generations, other family members must have an equal voice in the go-forward plan.

With the vision set, the next step is to develop an implementation plan. That plan may involve everything from transitioning roles of family members and/or executives, to selling a business, to beginning an art collection, or starting a foundation.[3] Families operating in unfamiliar territory would do well to seek out and bring on specialist advisors to help set and manage the implementation plan.

Quite a lot goes into building an implementation plan. There are likely tax consequences to adjustments in wealth allocation or in the structures that hold the family wealth. Where the family should domicile to best accomplish their objectives is a heavy consideration, and there is much that goes into that decision (not the least of which is where people want to live day-to-day). Again, when building the implementation plan, ample input and honesty is required from family members, but everything is on the table. Just because the family has always lived in California, for instance, may not mean that they should continue to do so.

From there, families should hold themselves (and their advisors) accountable to the plan. Ensure milestones are being hit. If they are not being

[3]Starting a self-sustaining foundation is not as straightforward as advertised, and typically involves ongoing work and continuous funding. A foundation that has a 5% payout requirement is unlikely to survive long-term without ongoing infusions of capital (see Bernstein Wealth Management Research's 2005 report, "Looking Beyond Perpetuity: Customizing a Private Foundation"). Families embarking on such an endeavor should do so thoughtfully and with an understanding of the long-term commitment.

hit, a clear understanding of why and what needs to change is a must. This requires intellectual humility and respectful honesty from members of the family and from their advisors.

The implementation stage can also provide roles for family members who have otherwise felt their contributions are not meaningful. For example, a family member who has little business acumen, but considerable artistic talent may do well to lead the art collection efforts alongside the family's art advisor. I would stop short of suggesting that family members themselves operate in an unfamiliar field on behalf of the family without the aid of a specialist (they can represent themselves if they wish). Unless this family member were specifically trained in art collection, or had held such a post before, it would be better to partner with an outside advisor. The family member will then learn the ropes from an expert, effectively represent the family to the advisor and in the field, and be willfully engaged in the business of the family. More importantly, the family member has the opportunity to gain the most valuable wealth of all: daily purpose. The family, in turn, has a representative in the field who solely represents their interests, has confidence that the process is run by an expert, and gains an engaged member of the family council.

And it is in this process that family governance kicks in. Keeping with our example of art collecting, though it could apply to most any objective, the role of the family as a whole is to set the governance structures within which the art advisor and family member can operate. So long as milestones are being hit and the family's representatives are operating within those constrains, *then they are doing a good job, by definition*. The family can change the definition, or the milestones at any time, but they should not be deciding how the job is done, day-to-day. Trust your fellow family member, and trust the family's advisor. If you do not trust your advisor, get a new advisor. If you do not trust the family member, make clear that the advisor works for the family, not any one family member. Decisions will ultimately be within the purview of the advisor, anyway, so your mistrust of your fellow family member can be mitigated, though not eliminated, as a concern.

Trust is an absolute must, but there are different layers of trust. There is, "Is this person trying to screw me?" kind of trust. I think of that as the first layer. Anyone who does not pass that first layer should not be anywhere near your family resources, whether they be a family member or no. The second layer of trust is, "Can this person do what they say they can do?" You can have the first layer of trust and not the second, or the second without the first. In any event, without *both* layers of trust, the relationship does not work, and that applies to family advisors and family members. While most families have the first layer with one another, they may not have the second. An advisor can help to ameliorate that situation. However, if families do not have the first layer of trust, it is better to not delegate tasks to one another at all and instead rely entirely on outside advisors.

A family's advisors often gain considerable loyalty from the family they serve, as well they should. That loyalty and level of trust is very important. But we must recognize that loyalty can also be a liability. Occasionally, advisors have such a deep relationship with the family and are such good and genuine people that the family becomes blind to the advisor's inability to accomplish the task at hand. Because the advisor has the first layer of trust in spades, the family may assume that the second layer of trust is automatically present. Or, the family may be well aware that the advisor has grown ineffective but feels too guilty changing course out of loyalty.

And it is here that we would do well to remember that wealthy families are humans, too. A family cannot, indeed should not, sacrifice their future for loyalty to an ineffective advisor. Our world works because we all add value to each other's lives, and, in my view, it is immoral to expect someone else to live their life for your benefit. Therefore, any advisor who expects a family to exist for her own benefit is immoral, at least in my view. If value is no longer going both ways, then it is time to part ways.

There is a respectful and humane process for doing this, of course! For long-time advisors, ensuring expectations are clear, milestones are clear, and consequences are clear can be key. This gives the advisor a chance to renew her value and become reengaged. In that case the family has won a trusted and loyal advisor! Keep her! If, however, the advisor founders and continues to miss her objectives, an exit plan can be constructed that is fair to both the advisor and the family. Obviously, all of this can apply just as readily to the family's operational executives, as well.

So, a family that develops their long-term objectives, develops a plan to accomplish their objectives, and maintains oversight and monitoring of their objectives is running a goals-based process. Just as the process can be applied to financial wealth, it can be just as effectively applied to more human goals, as we have just seen. Again, however, I will stress that it is considerably harder to do for nonfinancial objectives. Unlike for financial wealth, there is no equation that yields the right answer. The additional complication is amalgamating the myriad goals of various family members, each with its own place on the Maslow-Brunel pyramid. At the moment, techniques for blending the goals and priorities of many people into cohesive communal goals is much more art than science.[4]

Though I have now written a book on the topic, I must admit that it is almost never poor investment decisions that lead to the loss of wealth for families. By far the biggest risk to families are the human risks. Those risks are what tend to decimate family wealth through time, and it is a very real problem. Dynastic wealth is, despite the common social perception, quite rare. One study looked at how many of the families from the original 1982 Forbes 400 wealthiest people list were still on the list in 2014. Only 28% of the people on the list in 2014 were either on the original list or were family members of someone on the 1982 list. Even more damning, families who were on the Forbes top 400 list in 1982 held only 39% of their original wealth by 2014.

Even famous families are not exempt from intergenerational wealth erosion. The Rockefeller family, who held nearly 2,000,000 times the per capita GDP of the United States in 1920, today owns less than 50 times per capita GDP. The Hunt family owned almost 400,000 times the per capita GDP of the United States in 1982, and today they own about half of that. In fact, the top 10 wealthiest families (names most people would recognize) owned an average of just over 200,000 times per capita GDP in 1920. By 1955, the average wealth of those top 10 had dropped to less than 50 times per capita GDP—an aggregate loss of 75% in 35 years![5]

Dynastic wealth, with only a few exceptions, is a myth.

As counter to popular culture as this is to say, wealthy families have the deck stacked against them. Staying wealthy is a different skill set from getting wealthy, and the basic numbers work against their efforts. Passing a family-owned business to a family member is, statistically speaking, a bad decision, but also quite common. Creating a family of effective shareholders

[4]Simple voting is not a clear answer, unfortunately. Kenneth Arrow showed in 1950 that for ranked-choice voting of three or more alternatives, there is no voting system that can convert the preferences of individuals into a communal ranking. See K. Arrow, "A Difficulty in the Concept of Social Welfare," *Journal of Political Economy* 58, no. 4 (1950): 328–346.

[5]All of these figures are from R. Arnott, W. Bernstein, and L. Wu, "The Myth of Dynastic Wealth: The Rich Get Poorer," *Cato Journal* 35, no. 3 (Fall 2015): 447–485. Per capita wealth compensates for the effects of purchasing power, so is a better apples-to-apples comparison than nominal dollar figures. Though, family office professionals do not need the data as they have the experience. The saying "shirtsleeves to shirtsleeves in three generations" is cliché for a reason.

is difficult. Maintaining family cohesion is even more difficult. Structuring and maintaining effective family governance in the midst of these challenges is also very difficult. Not to mention, taxes, specialty advisors, attorneys, and investment fees alone create a significant headwind.[6]

But it can be done. I have personally seen families do it well. Wealth can be preserved through future generations. It takes a vision, a direction, *a goal*. Steps must be taken to accomplish that goal, and an effective implementation plan is needed. That plan must be monitored and adjusted as time moves forward. Effective and purposeful reporting is important at this stage, as is good help. And this whole approach is, fundamentally, the same approach used to accomplish financial goals. The same framework applies, even if not exactly the same tools.

[6]The authors of the study mentioned earlier also found that the average wealth growth of the original Forbes 400 wealthiest people list was about a quarter that of a passive, low-fee 60/40 portfolio. In other words, the wealthiest families in the world made about 5% points per year *less* than a typical market portfolio. Some of that is, of course, lifestyle spending, philanthropic efforts, and poor investment decisions. But some of that may be attributable to a "wealth tax" extracted by investment firms, law firms, advisors, etc., which can doom wealthy families to sub-par returns.

CHAPTER 12

Prudent Investing with High-Variance Assets: An Experimental Chapter

"Yeah man, they call gambling a disease, but it's the only disease where you can win a bunch of money."

—Norm Macdonald

One of the most disconcerting results of goals-based portfolio theory is that gambling is, at times, rational. I admit my own struggle with this result, and I have yet to implement a "gambling" portfolio with clients. Yet I cannot deny the mathematical and practical logic of the result—brutal intellectual honesty requires nothing less. Therefore, some treatment of the method for prudent investing using lottery-like investments seems reasonable, even if its actual implementation is not yet feasible. I have included this chapter, then, as a sort of working document—a record of early thoughts on a topic that I see gaining credibility and consideration in the coming years. I would urge my fellow practitioners to read this chapter reluctantly and with extreme suspicion. And, as usual, do not take any of this as investment advice! This is all very experimental.

Let's quickly review the relevant points. Modern portfolio theory, and its goals-based adaptations, generally assume no endpoint to the efficient frontier.

This can only be true if (1) an investor can invest borrowed money without limit or cost, and (2) can sell securities short without limit or cost. Besides the fact that this is entirely unrealistic, this also creates a contradiction. If a goals-based investor can borrow without limit or cost, why not simply borrow enough money to accomplish the goal? Clearly, these are absurd assumptions.

When short sales and leverage are bounded (or eliminated, as is most common in practice), an endpoint to the efficient frontier must exist. Under that real-world constraint, it is possible that the portfolio's required return (r) is greater than the expected return of the last portfolio on the efficient frontier (μ), and probabilities of achievement then are had by increasing variance rather than decreasing it—hence the break with modern portfolio theory. I refer to these portfolios as $r > \mu$ portfolios. Of course, mean-variance theory would simply declare these portfolios "infeasible" (no solution exists), or would keep you exposed to the last portfolio on the frontier rather than let you depart from it.

It is for those $r > \mu$ portfolios that this chapter is concerned. In the realm of high-variance, low-return assets—assets traditionally considered the very definition of imprudent and irresponsible—what is prudent and responsible investing?

"Prudent and responsible" is relative. Again—and I cannot stress this enough—we are talking about goals that are not highly valued. These are goals at or near the top of the Maslow-Brunel pyramid. We typically call these goals aspirational. Goals-based theory certainly does not recommend high-variance solutions for more foundational goals.

And investors *regularly* have aspirational goals. I would even venture to say that aspirational goals are as common as foundational ones, and sometimes it is the aspirational goals that are more often discussed. There are several important reasons why a theory should incorporate them. First, they exist. To deny their existence or label someone irrational for having such goals just does not serve the needs of real people. Are practitioners really supposed to simply disregard some of the most exciting objectives a client may have? Of course not! And, indeed, most practitioners do not disregard them, and so are left fumbling around in the dark, or are reliant on heuristics to guide them.

I am not being hyperbolic here; traditional portfolio theory assumes that investors are always and everywhere variance averse; it assumes that variance-seeking behavior is irrational, by definition. In *Modern Portfolio Theory and Investment Analysis*,[1] the authors frankly state that the required

[1]E. J. Elton, M. J. Gruber, S. J. Brown, and W. N. Goetzmann, *Modern Portfolio Theory and Investment Analysis* (Hoboken, NJ: John Wiley & Sons, 2009).

return of the portfolio must be less than the maximal return offered by the efficient frontier, thereby eliminating solutions for aspirational goals via a simple optimization constraint (namely, that $r \leq \mu$). I am not picking on these authors; they are presenting the theory as it is. But while these are not unreasonable assumptions most of the time, they are unreasonable assumptions all of the time.

The second and most important reason aspirational goals should be included in a theory is to offer a budget with respect to them. Understanding exactly how much wealth should be allocated to them, at the expense of other goals, is no small matter. While it may sometimes be rational to gamble, it certainly is not rational to gamble *everything*. But where is the line? At what point can we say, "It is rational to gamble this much but not a dollar more"? Without firm theory, we simply do not know.

Now, while maximizing variance is a rational objective in $r > \mu$ portfolios, return matters, too. Even when the required return of the goal is 10%, a portfolio that delivers a 9% return is still preferable to one that delivers an 8% return when the variance of the two portfolios is the same. In other words, the optimization objective is to maximize *both* return *and* variance, though variance will get priority. We can analyze this tradeoff using some basic rearranging of our probability function and a little insight from adapted modern portfolio theory. Using the logistic cumulative distribution function,

$$\phi = 1 - \frac{1}{1 + \exp\left(-\frac{r - m}{s}\right)},$$

where r is the goal's required return, m is the expected return of the portfolio, and s is the expected volatility of the portfolio. We can solve for m:

$$m = r + s \ln\left(\frac{1}{1 - \phi} - 1\right).$$

Adapted MPT suggest that goals-based investors could simply declare the minimum probability of goal achievement they are willing to accept, in which case ϕ in the equation above becomes α.[2] If, for example, I decided

[2]This point is discussed in Chapter 2.

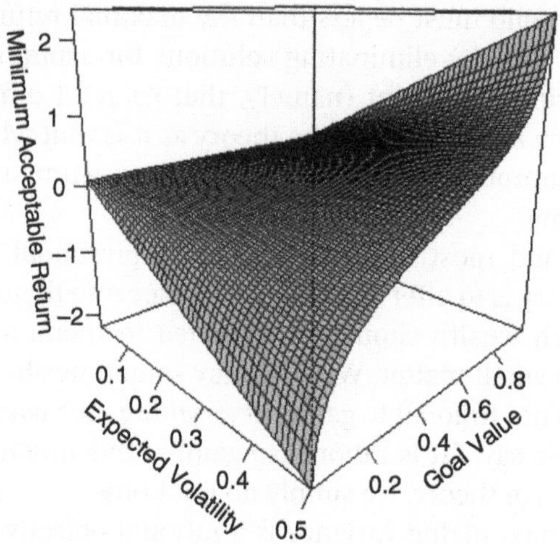

FIGURE 12.1 Volatility–Return Tradeoff
When $r = 0.10$, and assumed logistic distribution.

that a 60% probability of achievement is the absolute minimum I am willing to accept for this goal,[3] then $\alpha = 0.60$. I would enter the market attempting to get $r + s\ln(1/(1-\alpha)-1)$, but I would accept more return if it were offered (since α is the *minimum* probability of achievement I am willing to accept, and per our axiom of attainment I would prefer a higher probability of achievement to a lower). This adapted form in Figure 12.1, then, represents the volatility–return tradeoff for $r > \mu$ portfolios, and it shows that (1) when possible, investors would prefer a higher return if offered, and (2) that investors are willing to give up return to gain *higher* volatility. Of course, this is entirely counter to traditional portfolio theory, which posits that investors are always and everywhere variance-averse.

This simple realization immediately explains quite a few "anomalies," we see in financial markets. Investors who buy call options on very volatile stocks, for example—so-called YOLO trades (which stands for "You Only Live Once"). Or maybe even why lottery tickets are so popular. I spend some time analyzing how goals-based portfolio theory may offer a bridge between

[3]This is really the closest that goals-based portfolio theory gets to a risk-aversion parameter. It is a clever solution, as we have discussed, but it also has some problems. Namely, relying on this parameter means that sometimes no valid portfolio solution will exist.

normative and behavioral economics in the next chapter. What is important for this discussion is that investors may rationally pursue higher-variance outcomes, and they may trade expected return to help them gain it. As the plot shows, for goal values less than 0.50 (that is, where $r > \mu$), increasing volatility decreases minimum acceptable returns, which is the inverse of what happens for goal values greater than 0.50 (where $r < \mu$). Of course, goal values of 0.50 yield indifference to volatility.

This is an overly simplistic view, to be sure. Typically, lottery-like investments do not have bell-curve payoffs. Our expectations should follow a much "bumpier" distribution, like a Pareto or binary distribution. Most outcomes will fail to return what we need, but the few that succeed will pay off big. Angel investments are the first investment to come to mind that fits this outline, so let us attempt to build our intuition on the topic using this familiar asset class. To be clear, it is not my intent to write a treatise on angel investments, my intent is only to build our intuition on the topic using angel investments as a foil.

One study found that 52% of angel investments failed to return even 1x the investor's capital, and a mere 7% returned 10x or more.[4] It is, of course, the big wins that pay for all of the losers. Indeed, if we calibrate a Pareto distribution based on these figures, we find that the expected value (the mean) of the distribution is infinite! Don't get too excited because the *most common* outcome (the median) of this distribution is a loss of 87% of our wealth. The outcomes are quite dispersed!

For goals-based investors, then, the question is how many of these types of investments should be in an aspirational portfolio. It is tempting to say "as many as possible," but here is the problem: If we allocate limited wealth to more investments, we need each investment to pay off even bigger than it would have to if we only allocated to one. Requiring larger payoffs means accepting lower probabilities of achievement. Yet, betting all of our wealth on one seems imprudent, as well. Said more concretely: suppose we have $100,000 and we need $500,000 to achieve our aspirational goal. We need a 5x return from our angel portfolio. Betting all $100,000 on one startup feels unwise, but if we spread our wealth to 10 different startups, then that means we need a 50x return from one of them. Of course, a 50x return is considerably less likely than a 5x return. Hence the tradeoff.

---

[4] R. Wiltbank and W. Boeker, "Returns to Angel Investors in Groups," SSRN (November 14, 2007), `https://ssrn.com/abstract=1028592`.

Let us approach the problem with some simplifying assumptions. Let's assume that the probability of a given return for any angel venture is subject to a Pareto distribution:

$$\Pr\left[R > r_{req}\right] = \left(\frac{m}{r_{req}}\right)^{\alpha},$$

the probability of realizing a return R that is larger than our required return, r_{req}. Our required return is influenced by the number of investments in the aspirational portfolio, n, so $r_{req} = Wn/w$. Clearly, the higher n, the higher multiple needed to attain our goal. We further have our location parameter m (which can also be thought of as the minimum possible return, but must be greater than 0), and the tail persistence parameter, α. Using a Pareto distribution to model angel investment total returns is not unreasonable. Nothing I have said so far is absurd.

My next assumptions are going to draw some ire. If we further assume that the wins and losses in the portfolio of angel ventures are not correlated (which is not true in real life), and we assume that each portfolio can only have one win (which is also not true in real life), then we can use the binomial distribution as an overlay to help us determine how many "at bats" we need to maximize our probability of achievement. Again, none of this is true in real life, but the math is hard enough with these simplifying assumptions, and, as I have said, my purpose here is not to write a treatise on managing a portfolio of angel investments. We are simply trying to build our intuition around the inherent tradeoffs of aspirational portfolios.

The binomial distribution is

$$\frac{n!}{k!(n-k)!}p^k(1-p)^{n-k},$$

where n is the number of investments in our portfolio (our "at bats"), k is the number of wins we need in the portfolio (and $k = 1$ in our case), and p is the probability of achieving that win for any given "at bat." Since the Pareto distribution returns the probability of attaining our required return (a win), we can use the Pareto distribution to generate the p for our binomial distribution.

Putting it all together, we have the probability of achieving our aspirational goal as a function of the number of investments made, our starting wealth, ending wealth, and the Pareto parameters:

$$\phi(n, W, w, m, \alpha) = \frac{n!}{(n-1)!}\left(\frac{mw}{Wn}\right)^{\alpha}\left[1-\left(\frac{mw}{Wn}\right)^{\alpha}\right]^{n-1}.$$

We cannot vary w, W, m, or α, as those are set by the market and our investor. All we can vary is the number of investments made, or n. Thus, we are attempting to find the n that returns the maximum probability of achievement.

What we find, illustrated in Figure 12.2, is quite interesting. For $\alpha = 0.17$, which calibrates the distribution to model the market data mentioned above, we find that just four investments maximize our probability of goal achievement (not far off from the generally suggested six to ten). However, as alpha grows, we find that the optimal number of investments shifts higher and higher. For $\alpha = 0.25$, the optimal number grows to 12, and when $\alpha = 0.45$, we find that the optimal number is as many as possible (probability continues to grow as we further subdivide our wealth to investments). Our maximum probability, however, also shrinks as α grows.

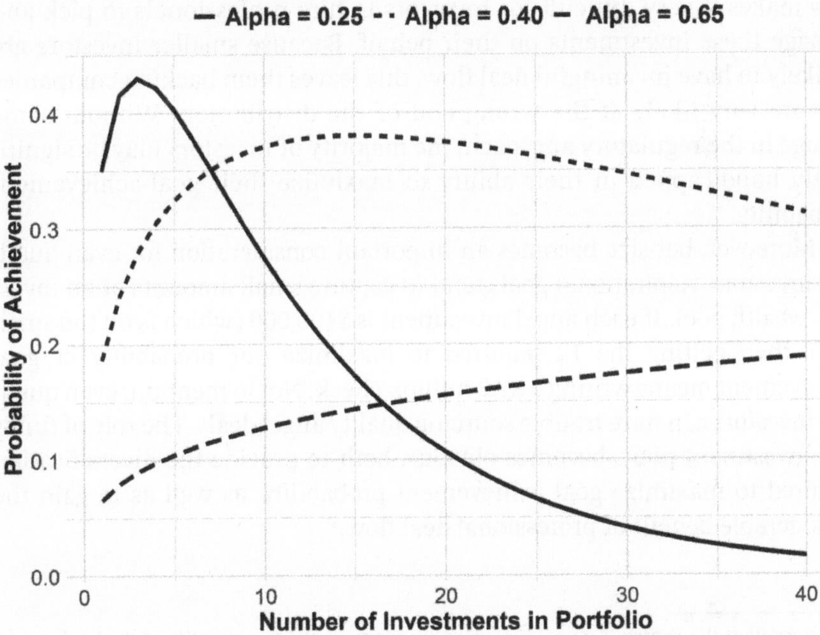

FIGURE 12.2 Number of Investments to Maximize Achievement Probability for Various Values of Alpha
where $W = 1, w = 0.20, m = 0.01$.

In any event, this demonstrates that "high variance" is not *really* the objective in aspirational portfolios since these types of investments tend not to follow Gaussian distributions (or any form of bell-curve shape, generally speaking). Indeed, higher moments (like variance) do not even exist in the distributions with which we are concerned. Rather, when dealing with extreme events and low probabilities, so many other factors come into play, not the least of which is the firm's view of the broader marketplace (read as: the firm's choice of distribution to model the scenario and the believed parameters of that distribution). In the case where power-laws dominate (like angel and venture investing), maintaining persistence in the tail of the distribution becomes important (lower α generates more persistent tails, higher α means the tails decay more quickly). Prudent angel investing, then, is about finding the right balance between tail persistence and portfolio diversification (with the probability of meeting some minimum return as the litmus test, of course).

Goals-based investors potentially face several challenges to angel investing. First, regulations in the United States prohibit nonqualified investors from investing in some types of private companies and funds. This makes it very difficult for investors to hire professionals to pick and manage these investments on their behalf. Because smaller investors are unlikely to have meaningful deal flow, this leaves them backing companies that are very likely at the wrong end of the distribution. Without some change in the regulatory approach, the majority of investors may be significantly handicapped in their ability to maximize their goal-achievement probability.

Moreover, bet size becomes an important consideration for even qualified investors. Aspirational goals tend to capture small amounts of an investor's wealth pool. If each angel investment is $100,000 (which is on the small end), then getting the 12 required to maximize our probability of goal achievement means writing a $1.2 million check. Not to mention, even qualified investors can have trouble sourcing quality angel deals. The role of funds and investment pools becomes obvious, both to provide the diversification required to maximize goal achievement probability, as well as to gain the considerable benefit of professional deal flow.[5]

---

[5]Because all of the return in angel investing comes from the top quartile of deals, the marketplace of funds will also tend to fall into quartiles, with the top quartile of funds attracting the best deals. It becomes important to seek out and back the best funds/deals, and avoid the bottom quartile (where all the losses are). Easier said than done, of course.

Our analysis of angel investments hints at another financial asset that is subject to a heavy-tailed distribution, one in which the persistence of the tails appears to matter quite a lot. An asset that has grown as an aspirational investor favorite: bitcoin.

Bitcoin is a bit of a conundrum from a traditional finance perspective. It has grown immensely popular. On July 1, 2014, there were just over 20,000 tweets about bitcoin, and on October 6, 2021, there were just under 200,000 (and that was not even the peak of 363,000 in one day). And individuals are not just talking about it, they are putting their money on the line. On January 1, 2012, there were just over 5,200 bitcoin transactions. On October 11, 2021, there were 280,000 transactions (with bitcoin over $57,000 per coin, that represents almost $16 billion in one-day trading volume).[6]

Traditional economic theory would struggle to explain why investors would hold an asset with neither cashflow nor expected return, only extreme volatility. Of course, we understand that goals-based investors are willing to accept significant volatility for its own sake in some cases, so this is not a conundrum to us. Bitcoin, however, is a classic example of a very non-Gaussian distribution, and it can be much better described by an alpha-stable distribution. For alpha-stable distributions in which our required return is less than the investment's return, increasing the scale parameter does have a significant effect on increasing the probability of achievement, but those benefits tend to wane after the initial bump (see Figure 12.3). Increasing tail persistence—the alpha parameter in the distribution—carries a very linear effect (see Figure 12.4). The higher alpha becomes, the higher chance we have of achieving the goal.

For aspirational portfolios, the objective is to increase scale (which is the non-Gaussian version of volatility), and also to increase tail persistence. Counterintuitively, then, we should expect investors to seek out tail-*heavy* distributions, rather than avoid them. In foundational portfolios (where $r < \mu$), tail persistence can be quite damaging, as the left tail will loom much larger than the right tail (very bad events can do more damage than very good events can give help). For aspirational portfolios, the opposite is true: The left tail does less damage than the right tail helps (good events help more than bad events hurt). Which explains, quite readily, the interest in bitcoin for aspirational-oriented portfolios.

Portfolio questions such as this bring up unique problems—problems that are unfamiliar to most portfolio managers. Harder still: modeling the

[6]Data from `www.bitinfocharts.com`, accessed on 11 October 2021.

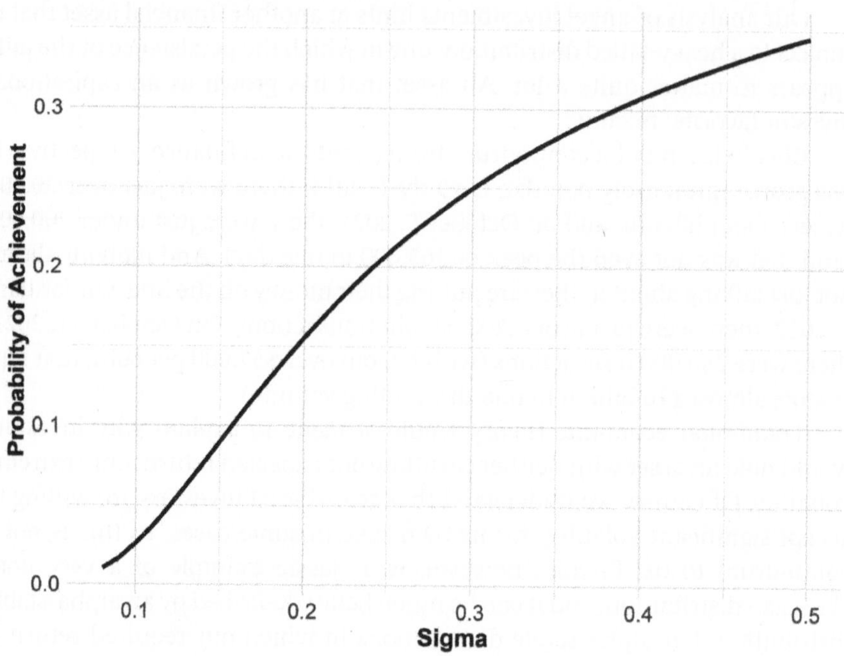

FIGURE 12.3 Effect of Scale in Alpha-Stable Distributions

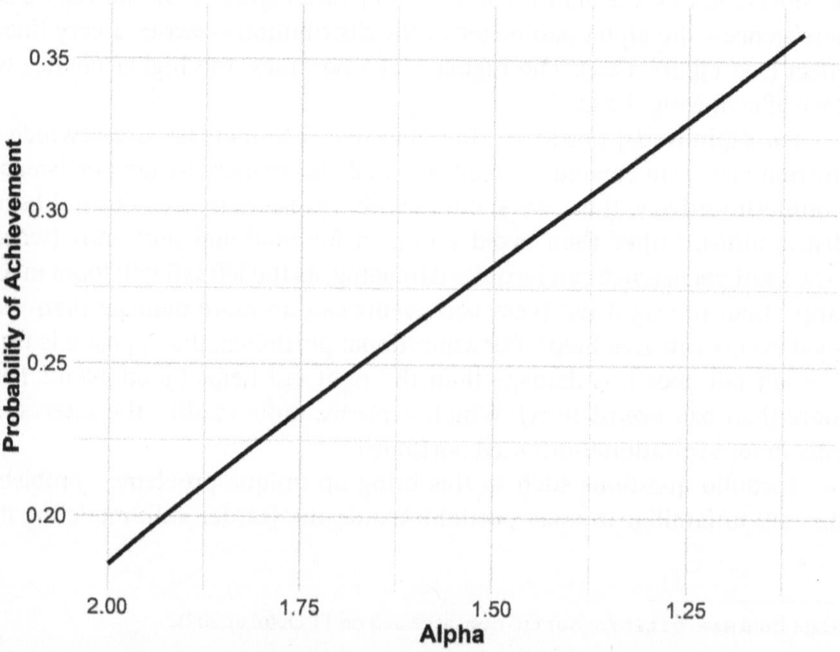

FIGURE 12.4 Effect of Tail Persistence in Alpha-Stable Distributions

potential returns of lottery-like investments requires the use of a much wider range of return distributions, and that puts us in a realm with few practical tools. As we discussed in Chapter 5, there are precious few tools for organizing portfolios of non-Gaussian distributions. Even worse, each category of investment (angel investments, cryptocurrencies, option contracts) is likely to require a separate type of distributions, compounding the modeling problem! At the moment, however, this question may well have little practical use as existing regulations are a significant headwind facing investors and their advisors who seek to advise on these portfolios.

On a more basic level, I must admit that I struggle to apply “prudence” to the pursuit of lottery-like investments. There is clearly much work to be done to help develop tools and theories for the prudent management of assets with the explicit purpose of increasing the dispersion of outcomes. Almost a whole century of research has been dedicated to *decreasing* the dispersion of outcomes, even in portfolios of high-volatility assets like angel investments. For minds steeped in the traditional approach, such as mine, breaking the mold is going to be an ongoing process of research and trial-and-error. It is clear, however, that portfolios managed in this way are an important component of the goals-based portfolio management tapestry. To date, the financial industry has been unwilling to offer solutions for aspirational goals, and some (most?) of that reluctance is the regulatory headwind such an approach is sure to generate. Regulators, even more than practitioners, are slow to change the accepted view. Advisors, then, should sail cautiously through these waters—there may well be dragons!

CHAPTER 13

As a Bridge Between Normative and Behavioral Finance

"We build too many walls and not enough bridges."

—*Isaac Newton*

Of all the tools goals-based portfolio theory adds to the practitioner's toolbox, I find myself most excited about what it may do for economic theory more broadly. Today, economic theory is split into two camps. There are the normative economists who focus on how we *should* behave. Then there are the behavioral economists who focus on how we *actually* behave. To date, each has a legitimate critique of the other. The normative economists acknowledge that people often violate rational rules of behavior, but they continue to insist that the rational course is the one prescribed by traditional theory. The behaviorists acknowledge that normative theory may well be rational, but it certainly isn't practical, nor is it often reasonable. Behavioral insights not only reveal how we actually behave, but they are a better predictor of the actions of people in the aggregate.

Goals-based portfolio theory offers another lens through which we can view the apparent dichotomy of behavior and rationality. Indeed, I am convinced that people are not as irrational as we have so far believed. Rather, if we simply better understand their motivations, if we better understand what goals people are attempting to accomplish in the real world, then many of the normative-behavioral paradoxes melt away. In this way, goals-based portfolio theory offers a bridge between traditional normative theories of economics and more descriptive behavioral theories. Certainly, I should not be so bold as to assert that humans are always and everywhere rational. There are many real-world situations where complete rationality is not only impractical, but entirely impossible.[1] Even so, it is my objective in this chapter to illuminate just a few examples that may sketch an outline of this theoretical bridge. I should say: This chapter is directed toward theoreticians much more than practitioners. So, any readers who are uninterested can skip this chapter with no loss of narrative.

To illustrate how the goals-based utility framework might help build this bridge, I have applied it to three classic normative-behavioral utility paradoxes: the Friedman-Savage puzzle, Samuleson's paradox, and the St. Petersburg paradox. I also include a discussion of the experiments that apparently show that individuals do not weight probabilities objectively—a central component of several behavioral theories. Finally, I show how a market composed of goals-based investors might influence price discovery. Indeed, many pricing anomalies may not be anomalies at all—they may be the aggregate result of goals-based investors behaving rationally.

GAMBLING, INSURANCE, AND THE FRIEDMAN-SAVAGE PUZZLE

As a child, I remember my grandparents occasionally buying lottery tickets. They never spent significant money on them, of course, but buying a few tickets every week was a regular ritual for them. Since they owned two cars and a home, I feel it is safe to assume that they also purchased insurance. And, so, we have an example of our first paradox: real people who bought insurance and lottery tickets at the same time!

[1]Satisficing models fall into this category, for example. Since people cannot know everything, decisions will necessarily be based on limited information. Individuals, then, get "enough" information to make a reasonably informed decision, even if it may not be the exactly optimal one if all information were known. See, for instance, D. Navarro-Martinez, G. Loomes, A. Isoni, D. Butler, and L. Alaoui, "Bounded Rational Expected Utility Theory," *Journal of Risk and Uncertainty* 57, no. 3 (2018): 199–223. DOI: https://doi.org/10.1007/s 11166-018-9293-3.

For most laymen, this does not seem a paradox at all. *Of course* people both gamble and take steps to protect their assets; this is common experience. Yet, normative economics does not allow for this. In normative theory, people are assumed to be everywhere averse to risk. Consider the following choice sets:

1A. $50 with certainty, or
1B. A coin flip: heads pays you $200, tails makes you pay $100.

Both of these offers carry the same expected value of $50, but the second one carries risk. It does seem silly to accept choice 1B when you could grab the $50 for sure—especially if you are playing this game over and over again, as investors do. Risk aversion simply means that you require more payoff than the certain outcome to prefer the risky to the certain choice. Something like:

2A. $50 with certainty, or
2B. A coin flip: heads pays you $300, tails makes you pay $100.

In this second choice, 2B offers $50 more than choice 2A in expected value. This is a risk premium. When playing the game repeatedly, and putting the law of large numbers on our side,[2] we can harvest that extra return and come out further ahead than if we repeatedly chose 2A.

People are assumed to be risk averse in normative economics because it can be shown that people with risk-loving attitudes will accept a *negative* risk premium for the risky choice. That is, they would accept less of a payoff than the certain outcome simply *because* it is the riskier choice. Something like:

3A. $50 with certainty, or
3B. A coin flip: heads pays you $150, tails makes you pay $100.

[2]The law of large numbers is a very controversial topic in both goals-based utility theory and traditional economics. Understanding when it does and does not apply is of prime importance. This is a point Vineer Bhansali makes in his book *Tail Risk Hedging: Creating Robust Portfolios for Volatile Markets*: "We really get one chance to save for retirement. . . The reality is that markets take one path, so the law of large numbers is no insurance against market crisis." More broadly, this has become known as the ergodicity problem. For an insightful treatment, see O. Peters, "The Ergodicity Problem in Economics," *Nature Physics* 15 (Dec 2019): 1216–1221. DOI: `https://doi.org/10.1038/s41567-019-0732-0`.

Here, 3B offers an expected payoff of $25 whereas 3A offers an expected payoff of $50. By choosing 3B, we are giving up an expected $25 per flip to choose the riskier outcome—that is a negative risk premium.

Normative theory does allow for an individual who prefers risk for its own sake. That is, there may well be people who would gamble because they enjoy gambling and are therefore willing to pay to do it. However, in normative theory, individuals are not expected to be *both* risk-averse *and* risk-loving at the same time. Why, then, did my grandparents buy both insurance and lottery tickets simultaneously? How could they be both risk-averse and risk-loving at the same time?

This is known as the Friedman-Savage paradox, after the authors who were first to describe the problem.[3] They also proposed a solution, suggesting that an individual's utility curve bends from concave (risk-averse) to convex (risk-seeking) along various points of wealth, and that there are points along that curve where people are willing to take risks with small amounts of wealth (such as a lottery ticket) and avoid risks with large amounts of wealth (such as a house).

Richard Thaler proposed another solution, one that is foundational to the goals-based methodology. He suggested that people divide their wealth into mental "buckets" and that each bucket has a different risk tolerance. In some buckets, people are considerably more risk-averse and in other buckets people may be risk-seeking. Using our theoretical language, those buckets are simply goals, and some goals are valued highly enough to warrant less risk-taking while others (higher on the Maslow-Brunel pyramid) warrant more risk-taking. This is no longer considered controversial and has almost become part of traditional theory.

Gambling, however, is still controversial. Nowhere in normative economics is gambling considered rational. People may do it, as described by behavioral models, but that is because people are irrational. Yet, goals-based portfolio theory not only acknowledges gambling behavior but considers it rational in some circumstances, as we have already explored. I admit, this is tough for me to accept, but it is a plain fact of the math. If people seek to maximize the probability of achieving their goals, then there are circumstances when maximizing the volatility of outcomes is the optimal approach.

---

[3]M. Friedman and L.J. Savage, "The Utility Analysis of Choices Involving Risk," *Journal of Political Economy* 56, no. 4 (August 1948): 279–304.

The Friedman-Savage puzzle is a paradox in normative economics. And though it is predicted and described by behavioral economics, it is still considered irrational. In the goals-based framework, however, it is not only predicted but is considered *rational*. Here is how the Friedman-Savage puzzle is resolved under this paradigm.

First, we know that individuals have multiple goals. Rather than have one uniform variance-aversion constant, goals-based investors are assumed to have many different tolerances for risk—each informed by the objectives for a goal. However, in all cases, goals-based investors want to maximize the probability of achieving their goals. Gambling, giving up return to maximize variance, is then rational when the return required to accomplish a goal is greater than the maximum return offered by the mean-variance efficient frontier. This can be easily demonstrated more formally.

Let r be the return required to attain our goal, m is the portfolio return, and s is portfolio variance. We know that variance-affinity is experienced when the second derivative of the utility function is positive, and variance-aversion is experienced when the second derivative is negative (variance-indifference is experienced when $u''=0$). Using the logistic cumulative distribution function as our primary input of utility, we are concerned with

$$\frac{d^2}{dr^2}u = \frac{d^2}{dr^2}\left[1 - \frac{1}{1+e^{-\frac{r-m}{s}}}\right],$$

which is

$$u'' = \frac{e^{\frac{m+r}{s}}\left(e^{\frac{r}{s}} - e^{\frac{m}{s}}\right)}{s^2\left(e^{\frac{m}{s}} + e^{\frac{r}{s}}\right)^3}.$$

Since the bottom of the fraction is always positive, $s^2\left(e^{\frac{m}{s}} + e^{\frac{r}{s}}\right)^3 > 0$, as is the coefficient in the numerator, $e^{\frac{m+r}{s}} > 0$, it must be so that $u'' > 0$ only when the term $e^{\frac{r}{s}} - e^{\frac{m}{s}}$ is positive, meaning

$$e^{\frac{r}{s}} > e^{\frac{m}{s}}$$

must be true. Simplifying to isolate r and m:

$$\frac{r}{s} > \frac{m}{s},$$

leading to

$$r > m.$$

Therefore, variance-affinity is present when $r > m$. By contrast, $u'' < 0$ only when

$$e^{\frac{r}{s}} < e^{\frac{m}{s}},$$

yielding

$$\frac{r}{s} < \frac{m}{s},$$

leading to

$$r < m.$$

Therefore, variance-aversion is present when $r < m$. This, of course, is a result echoing the one derived in Chapter 2.

This is also confirmed by a simple inspection of the utility-of-wealth curve for goals-based investors, shown in Figure 13.1. For lower values of wealth, the curve is clearly concave, while it is convex for higher values of wealth. Traditional utility theory tells us that concave utility curves are indicative of variance-affinity and convex utility curves are indicative of variance-aversion. Thus, goals-based investors are variance-averse for higher levels of wealth and variance-affine for lower levels of wealth.

Counter to our training and intuition, the logic and subsequent math clearly demonstrates that, in some circumstances, gambling is entirely rational, and so is paying a small amount to protect a large amount. As it turns out, there is no paradox at all. People are, in fact, behaving rationally by buying both insurance and lottery tickets simultaneously.

Someone should tell my grandparents they were not so irrational after all.

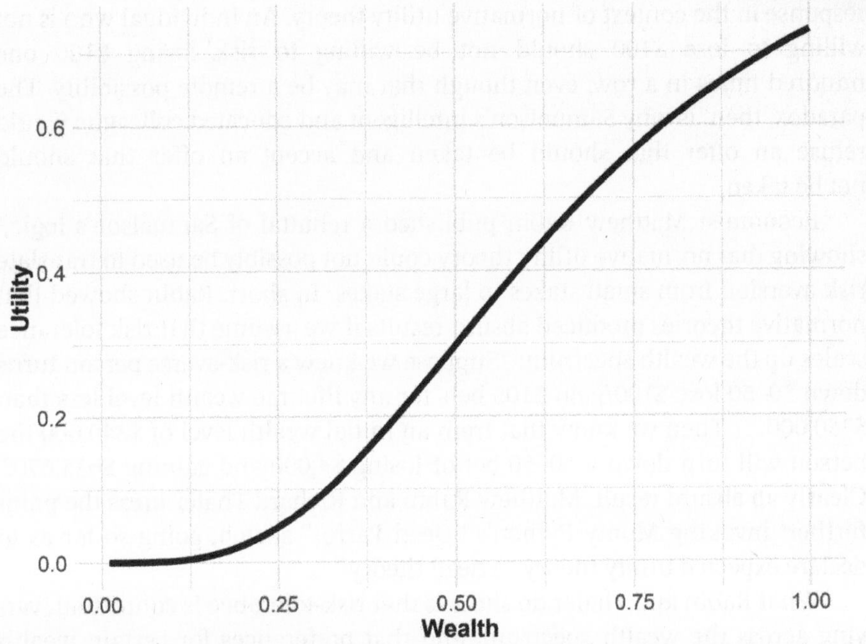

FIGURE 13.1 Goals-Based Utility-of-Wealth Curve
Assuming 1.00 is needed in five years, and the portfolio returns 8% with 14% volatility.

SAMUELSON'S PARADOX

Famed economist Paul Samuelson—author of numerous economics textbooks, and winner of a Nobel Prize—once offered a colleague a bet:[4] one coin flip, heads pays the colleague $200, tails the colleague pays $100. His colleague responded that he would not accept that bet but would accept a game of 100 such coin flips. Samuelson demonstrates how this is an irrational

[4]Whether the offer actually happened or whether it was a foil to launch a discussion is not really known. In either case, the point stands. The more nuanced result Samuelson reached was that the risk-aversion that can be calculated from the refusal of a small-stakes offer would indicate risk-aversion for large-stakes offers, and also refusal of the colleague's counteroffer. Cf. P. Samuelson, "Risk and Uncertainty: A Fallacy of Large Numbers," *Scientia* 98 (1963): 108–113.

response in the context of normative utility theory. An individual who is not willing to lose \$100 should not be willing to risk losing \$100 one hundred times in a row, even though that may be a remote possibility. The paradox, then, is why Samuelson's intelligent and educated colleague would refuse an offer that should be taken and accept an offer that should not be taken.

Economist Matthew Rabin published a rebuttal of Samuelson's logic,[5] showing that normative utility theory could not possibly be used to translate risk aversion from small stakes to large stakes. In short, Rabin showed that normative theories produced absurd results if we assume that risk tolerance scales up the wealth spectrum: "Suppose we knew a risk-averse person turns down 50–50 lose \$100/gain \$105 bets for any lifetime wealth level less than \$350,000. . . Then we know that from an initial wealth level of \$340,000 the person will turn down a 50–50 bet of losing \$4,000 and gaining \$635,670." Clearly an absurd result. Matthew Rabin and Richard Thaler press the point further[6] invoking Monty Python's "Dead Parrot" sketch, going so far as to declare expected utility theory "a dead theory."

What Rabin and Thaler do show is that risk-tolerance is contextual, varying across the wealth spectrum, and that preferences for certain wealth levels cannot reflect preferences for other wealth levels. Of course, this is exactly what goals-based theory predicts, but Rabin and Thaler press their point as a mark against the whole project of normative economics (Thaler, and to some degree Rabin, too, are both in the behavioral camp). That is ground, however, I am not yet ready to cede. Goals-based portfolio theory may offer some relief here, showing that people may not be as irrational as normative theory would have us believe. Let us analyze Samuelson's offer through a goals-based lens.

We can understand the colleague's utility before Samuelson's offer as

$$u(\text{baseline}) = v(A)\phi(w),$$

where $v(A)$ is the value of the goal the colleague wishes to achieve, w is the current wealth dedicated to the goal, and $\phi(\cdot)$ is the probability of

[5]M. Rabin, "Risk Aversion and Expected Utility Theory: A Calibration Theorem," *Econometrica* 68, no. 5 (2000): 1281–1292.

[6]M. Rabin and R. Thaler, "Anomolies: Risk Aversion," *Journal of Economic Perspectives* 15, no. 1 (2001): 219–232.

achievement function, given all the goal variables. For ease of discussion, I have removed the extra variables from our formulation. We can understand Samuelson's offer as

$$u(\text{offer}) = v(A)\left[0.5\phi(w+w^{+}) + 0.5\phi(w-w^{-})\right],$$

where w^{+} is the wealth gained if the colleague wins the coin flip, and w^{-} is the wealth lost if the colleague loses the coin flip.

The colleague did not accept the offer, so we can infer that $u(\text{baseline}) > u(\text{offer})$, or

$$v(A)\phi(w) > v(A)\left[0.5\phi(w+w^{+}) + 0.5\phi(w-w^{-})\right],$$

and this simplifies to an interesting result:

$$\frac{\phi(w+w^{+}) + \phi(w-w^{-})}{2} < \phi(w).$$

In other words, if the amount of probability gained from a win is less than the probability that would be lost in a loss, the colleague should not take the offer. This can be easily seen by restating the above equation to

$$\phi(w+w^{+}) - \phi(w) < \phi(w) - \phi(w-w^{-}).$$

Recall that the goals-based utility of wealth curve is convex for higher levels of wealth and concave for lower. We do not know where the colleague sits on that curve, of course, but there are places where the above inequality is satisfied. In other words, refusal of the offer may be entirely rational, depending on how much wealth the colleague has currently dedicated to the goal. To be fair, Samuelson never argues that it is irrational to turn down the offer. There is nothing revolutionary about this analysis so far.

Assuming 100 coin flips is a negligible increase in time, the colleague's counteroffer is an entirely different game. In fact, the probability of any loss[7] whatsoever is 1/2300. Using these figures, let's analyze the colleague's

[7]We learn this from Rabin and Thaler (2001), who ran the numbers. I won't repeat their work here.

counteroffer in a similar manner. Again, we are concerned with the truthiness of $u(\text{counteroffer}) > u(\text{baseline})$, or

$$v(A)\left[\frac{2299}{2300}\phi(w+w^{+})+\frac{1}{2300}\phi(w-w^{-})\right] > v(A)\phi(w),$$

simplifying to

$$\frac{2299\phi(w+w^{+})+\phi(w-w^{-})}{2300} > \phi(w).$$

Given that the winning probability is weighted 2,299 times more than the losing probability, it would be quite a stretch to deny this offer, no matter how extreme the loss. Suppose, for the sake of discussion, that the offer was such that *any* loss would be catastrophic and result in a zero probability of success, so $\phi(w-w^{-})=0$, then the problem simplifies to:

$$\phi(w+w^{+}) > 1.004369\phi(w).$$

So long as the resultant probability given a win is greater than 1.004369 times the baseline probability, the colleague should accept the counteroffer. That is a move in probability of, say 62.000% to 62.271%. Rabin and Thaler are right to say, "A good lawyer could have you declared legally insane for turning down this gamble."

Note, though, that the resolution of this paradox is not due to some behavioral flaw present in the colleague (and all of us). Rather, the paradox is an artifact of a flawed normative theory. When we look through the lens of goal achievement, the paradox ceases to exist. And, what's more, the colleague acted entirely rationally despite the claim of Samuelson and the intimation of Rabin and Thaler. In the end, whether the colleague should have accepted Samuelson's original offer is dependent on the value of variables that we do not know but rejecting it can be reasonably defended. In almost no circumstance should the colleague reject the counteroffer, however.

INFINITE PAYOFFS, LIMITED COSTS—THE ST. PETERSBURG PARADOX

In a previous chapter, we briefly discussed Daniel Bernoulli's critique of expected value theory. As a counterargument, Bernoulli proposed a gamble: An individual begins with an initial stake of $2 and we flip a coin. The initial $2 bankroll is doubled every time heads comes up, and when tails comes up the game is over and the winnings are the value of the bankroll. What is interesting about this game is that it has an infinite expected value:

$$\sum_{n=1}^{\infty} \Pr\left[\text{Heads}_{\text{i}}\right] \times V_i,$$

where $\sum_{n=1}^{\infty} \Pr\left[\text{Heads}_{\text{i}}\right]$ is the probability of getting heads on the ith coin flip, and V_i is the payoff of that flip. The probability of winning the first flip is $1/2^1$ and the payoff is 2^1. The probability of winning the second flip is $1/2^2$ and the payoff is 2^2. We can generalize the expected value of the gamble as

$$\sum_{n=1}^{\infty} \frac{1}{2^i} \times 2^i.$$

And it becomes clear that the sum is infinity:

$$\frac{1}{2^1} \times 2^1 + \frac{1}{2^2} \times 2^2 + \frac{1}{2^3} \times 2^3 + \cdots = 1 + 1 + 1 + \cdots = \infty.$$

Since the game has an infinite expected value, Bernoulli argued that someone should be willing to pay *any* price to play the game! Obviously, no one would pay an infinite price to play this game, and therein lies the paradox.

The paradox can be solved if individuals do not weight probabilities objectively, as proposed by behavioral economics, but that solution implies that people are not behaving rationally when they pay a limited cost for the game. Since normative economics solves the paradox using the theory of marginal utility—that the utility of wealth grows slower than the raw payoffs, so the benefit reaches an apex—this is no longer considered a paradox. Even so, it is an interesting problem, and I find it a useful foil to further our intuition of goals-based utility theory, hence my desire to include an analysis of the game here. With that, let's explore how goals-based utility theory solves Bernoulli's paradox.

If our individual chooses to play the game, she stands to win 2^n with probability $1/2^n$, and she stands to lose the cost of entry, c, with probability $1-1/2^n$. We are trying to find the maximum cost an individual would incur to play the game, and that means that there is a cost at which the individual is indifferent to the gamble or the status quo. We can infer from that point of indifference the maximum cost she would be willing to incur to play the game. To find that point of indifference, we set her baseline probability of achievement equal to the probability of achievement if she plays the gamble:

$$\phi(w) = \frac{1}{2^n}\phi(w+2^n) + \left[1 - \frac{1}{2^n}\right]\phi(w+c),$$

where $\phi(w+2^n)$ is the probability of achieving her goal if the gamble is won and $\phi(w+c)$ is the probability of achieving her goal if the gamble is lost and the cost of c is incurred.

Okay, we are forced to make some simplifying assumptions here. First and most obvious: no one can flip a coin an infinite number of times. Goals are time-limited, so any real-world analysis of the gamble must include the time it takes to flip coins and calculate winnings—not to mention how long humans are physically able to sit at the gambling table to participate in the game. Obviously, all of those answers are less than infinity, but by how much? Since the game itself is a thought-experiment, and no casino offers the actual game, my purpose is not to provide a completely realistic analysis of the game. Rather, the purpose is to keep the spirit of Bernoulli's thought experiment and put our theory through its paces. In order to do that we have to assume that an infinite number of coin flips is at least possible to witness.

Second, we know that a goals-based investor has a point of wealth satiation, so she will stop playing the game when $2^n = W$, where W is the wealth required to fund her goal. This is helpful because it means we can solve for n, the number of flips our investor needs to accomplish her goal:

$$2^n = W \Rightarrow n \ln 2 = \ln W,$$

$$n = \frac{\ln W}{\ln 2}.$$

By replacing n with the ratio of the log of required wealth to the log of 2, we can keep the equation above limited to the goal-variables and go about solving for the cost variable, but that also means that n, the number of coin flips required to achieve the goal, may not be an integer. Obviously, we cannot flip a coin 6.64 times, but for the sake of this analysis we are going to assume that we can. Again, this is a thought experiment, not an actual gamble demanding exacting accuracy!

With these simplifying assumptions, we can press forward. Leaning on a logistic portfolio distribution (for tractability) we can set $u(\text{baseline}) = u(\text{gamble})$, replace $n = \ln W / \ln 2$ and solve for c:

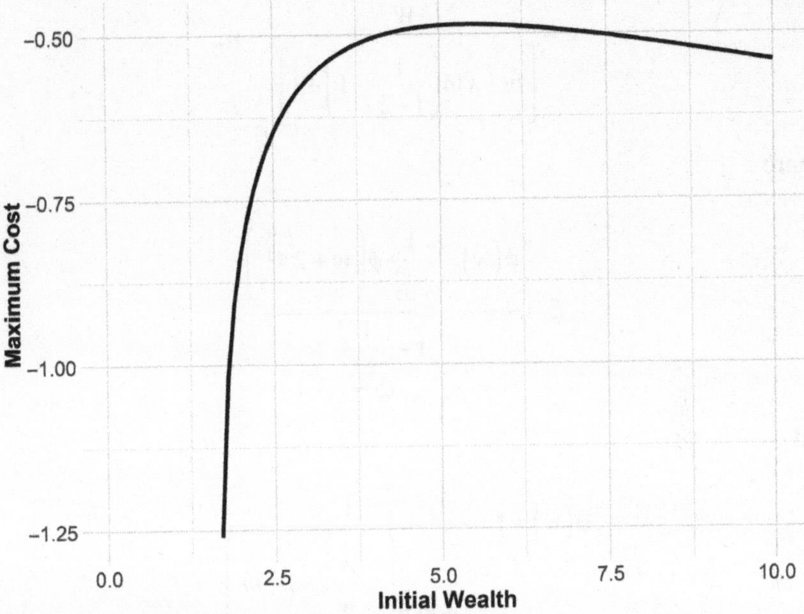

FIGURE 13.2 Willingness to Play the St. Petersburg Game
Where required wealth is 10, distributions are logistic, $m = 0.10, s = 0.13, t = 5$.

$$\phi(w) = \frac{1}{2^{\frac{\ln W}{\ln 2}}}\phi\left(w + 2^{\frac{\ln W}{\ln 2}}\right) + \left[1 - \frac{1}{2^{\frac{\ln W}{\ln 2}}}\right]\phi(w+c).$$

Reorganizing the equation to begin isolating the cost variable yields

$$\frac{\phi(w) - \frac{1}{2^{\frac{\ln W}{\ln 2}}}\phi\left(w + 2^{\frac{\ln W}{\ln 2}}\right)}{1 - \frac{1}{2^{\frac{\ln W}{\ln 2}}}} = 1 - \frac{1}{1 + \exp\left(-\frac{\left(\frac{W}{w+c}\right)^{\frac{1}{t}} - 1 - m}{s}\right)}.$$

Applying some algebra leads to our general-form cost function for a goals-based investor playing the St. Petersburg game, shown in Figure 13.2:

$$c = \frac{W}{\left[m - s\ln\left(\frac{1}{1-\xi} - 1\right) + 1\right]^t} - w,$$

where

$$\xi = \frac{\phi(w) - \frac{1}{2^{\frac{\ln W}{\ln 2}}}\phi\left(w + 2^{\frac{\ln W}{\ln 2}}\right)}{1 - \frac{1}{2^{\frac{\ln W}{\ln 2}}}},$$

and

$$\phi(w) = 1 - \frac{1}{1 + \exp\left(-\frac{\frac{W^{\frac{1}{t}}}{w} - 1 - m}{s}\right)}.$$

As has been the case in our goals-based framework, how much an individual is willing to pay to play the St. Petersburg gamble is dependent, not just on the nature of the game, but also on her goal-variables. I have plotted the individual's willingness to play the gamble given some example goal particulars. Interestingly, the results square with our intuition, at least mostly. When initial wealth is low enough, an individual is willing to spend all of her funds on the gamble, which is consistent with the $r > \mu$ portfolio structure we discussed in previous chapters. Gambling is rational for low-probability goals. As initial wealth grows, willingness to pay drops very rapidly until peaking. After finding its peak, willingness again begins to increase as initial wealth increases, which is not what I would have expected. However, this is reflective of the portfolio's ability to recover the cost of the game through portfolio growth over time—the goal is overfunded, in other words, and some of that overfunding can be dedicated to a gamble, thereby increasing achievement probability.

What this analysis shows, quite clearly, is that a goals-based investor would not pay an infinite amount to play the gamble, resolving the paradox.

Behavioral economics has relied on subjective probability weights to solve the paradox, but that, of course, means that individuals are behaving irrationally with respect to the gamble. By contrast, the goals-based solution is rational (assuming you accept the initial axioms). It would be very interesting to offer the gamble to real people in the real world (ideally for real money) and see if their behavior corresponds to the predictions of goals-based utility theory. Unfortunately, I am not aware of empirical data on the subject, so this must be left for future research.

QUESTIONS OF PROBABILITY, QUESTIONS OF DOUBT

In 1953, as a critique of Von Neumann and Morgenstern's axiom of independence, economist Maurice Allais[8] conducted an experiment. He offered his subjects two sets of choices:

1A:	\$1,000,000 with 100% probability
1B:	\$1,000,000 with 89% probability
	\$5,000,000 with 10% probability
	\$0 with 1% probability

The second choice set:

2A:	\$1,000,000 with 11% probability
	\$0 with 89% probability
2B:	\$5,000,000 with 10% probability
	\$0 with 90% probability

Allais found that people tended to choose choice 1A over 1B and also chose 2B over 2A. Though it is not immediately obvious, this is a contradiction!

From the first choice set we learn that $u(1A) > u(1B)$, or

$$v(\$1{,}000{,}000) > 0.89v(\$1{,}000{,}000) + 0.10v(\$5{,}000{,}000),$$

[8]M. Allais, "Le Comportement de l'Homme Rationnel devant le Risque: Critique des Postulats et Axiomes de l'Ecole Americaine," *Econometrica* 21, no. 4 (1953): 503–546.

which can be simplified to

$$0.11v(\$1{,}000{,}000) > 0.10v(\$5{,}000{,}000).$$

In other words, we learn that an 11% chance of gaining $1,000,000 carries more utility than a 10% chance of gaining $5,000,000. We learn from the second choice set that $u(2A) < u(2B)$, or

$$0.11v(\$1{,}000{,}000) < 0.10v(\$5{,}000{,}000),$$

which directly contradicts the first choice set!

Allais concluded that the axiom of independence cannot be a valid one because it fails to predict "reasonable people choosing between reasonable alternatives." Markowitz rebutted that people choosing the wrong alternative acted irrationally, but that people are irrational does not negate the axiom. So the behavioral-normative split was formed.

Later authors saw in Allais's results a clue: perhaps it is not the axiom of independence people do not intuit; maybe people do not weight probabilities objectively. Allais's paradox can be solved if people feel the move from 99% to 100% more than they feel the move from 10% to 11%. This idea led to numerous papers in behavioral finance, all of them offering a theory as to why people choose seemingly contradictory choices. It was Daniel Kahneman and Amos Tversky's cumulative prospect theory, however, that seems to have been accepted as the answer. Cumulative prospect theory has two basic components. The first component deals with how people value gains in wealth versus losses in wealth. The second component is that people do not weigh probabilities objectively, but rather tend to overweight low probability events and underweight high probability events, as Figure 13.3 demonstrates. This result has been confirmed in experiments by other researchers and is now widely accepted as true.

While I do not suggest that people objectively perceive probabilities always and everywhere, it is worth noting that the method used by researchers to derive these results may be tainted if individuals are processing the experiment through a goals-based lens. To fully understand why, we need to look more closely at the experiment.

When testing for subjective probability weights, it is standard practice to determine the certainty equivalent of an offer. The certainty equivalent is derived by offering the subject a gamble, then finding the certain amount of money that makes her indifferent to the gamble or the sure outcome. For example, suppose I flip a coin. If it lands heads, I pay you $100, if tails you get $0. Now I offer you a choice between that gamble and a sure

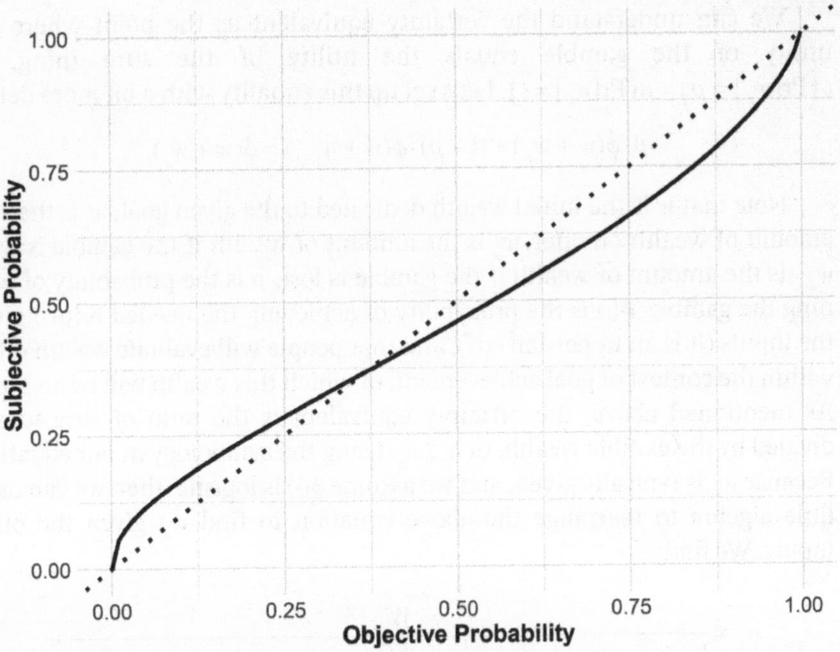

FIGURE 13.3 Standard Probability Weighting Function[9]

amount of money. What amount of certain money makes it so that you are indifferent to the gamble of the certain outcome? That amount of money is your certainty equivalent.

Here is the key to the goals-based critique: to derive how the subject is perceiving the probability of the gamble, we divide the certainty equivalent by the expected wealth offered in the gamble. That ratio is interpreted as the probability that is perceived by the subject. Continuing our coin flip example, suppose you were indifferent to $40 for sure or the $100 for heads/$0 for tails gamble. We would then infer that you perceive the 50% probability of the coin flip as $40 / $100 = 40%—an underweight of 10% points. However, when we look at this experiment through a goals-based lens, we can make a case that the results may not indicate what they have been so far interpreted to indicate. Let's dive into why.

[9]From: D. Prelec, "The Probability Weighting Function," *Econometrica* 66 (1998): 497–527. Prelec's probability weighting function is $w(p) = \exp\left[-(-\ln p)^{\alpha}\right]$, with $0 < \alpha < 1$. In the case of this illustration, $\alpha = 0.70$.

We can understand the certainty equivalent as the point where the utility of the gamble equals the utility of the sure thing, or $u\left(\Pr[w_p]=p\right)=u\left(\Pr[w_s]=1\right)$. Let's set up this equality with a bit more detail:

$$p\cdot\phi(w+w_p)+(1-p)\cdot\phi(w+w_{1-p})=\phi(w+w_s).$$

Note that w is the initial wealth dedicated to the given goal, w_s is the sure amount of wealth on offer, w_p is the amount of wealth if the gamble is won, w_{1-p} is the amount of wealth if the gamble is lost, p is the probability of winning the gamble, $\phi(\cdot)$ is the probability of achieving the needed return given the inputs (it is an upper-tail cdf), and that people will evaluate wealth offers within the context of goal achievement, of which this wealth will be an input. As mentioned above, the certainty equivalent is the ratio of sure wealth divided by the gamble wealth, or w_s/w_p, using the symbology in our equation. Because w_p is typically given, and we assume $\phi(\cdot)$ is logistic, then we can use a little algebra to rearrange the above equation to find w_s, given the other inputs. We find:

$$w_s=\frac{W}{\left[m-s\ln\left(\frac{1}{1-p\cdot\phi(w+w_p)-(1-p)\cdot\phi(w+w_{1-p})}-1\right)+1\right]^t}-w.$$

From here we can play with the inputs to estimate how a goals-based investor might react to the experiment. The results are rather intriguing. The plot shows two types of goals, one aspirational and the other a standard goal. Recall that our technical definition of an aspirational goal is one where the return required to hit the goal is greater than the return offered by the last portfolio on the efficient frontier (or in this case, it is simply greater than the portfolio return assumption). A foundational goal is one in which the return required to attain the goal is less than the maximum portfolio return.

For aspirational goals, we find that the goals-based utility model accurately predicts how individuals will behave in this experiment. The ratio of the certain offer to the gamble offer mirrors the standard probability weighting function from the literature (and may help explain the wide range of results experimenters have logged).[10] For foundational goals, the model

[10]See, for example, A. Tversky and D. Kahneman, "Advances in Prospect Theory: Cumulative Representation of Uncertainty," *Journal of Risk and Uncertainty* 5, no. 4 (1992): 297–323. Also R. Gonzales and G. Wu, "On the Shape of the Probability Weighting Function," *Cognitive Psychology* 38, no. 1 (1999): 129–166.

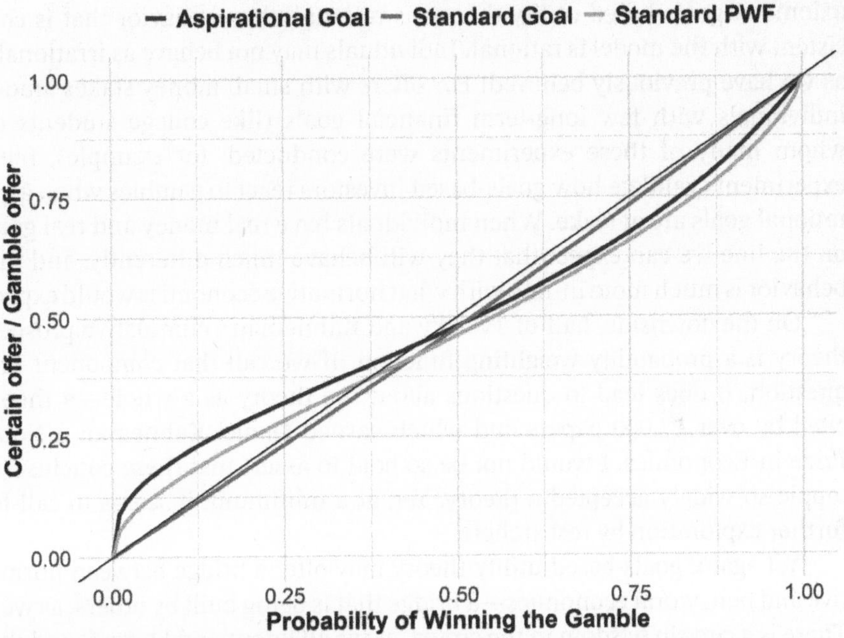

FIGURE 13.4 Goals-Based Utility Prediction of Probability Weighting Experiments and Comparison to Standard Probability Weighting Function

shown in Figure 13.4 returns an interesting result! For foundational goals, individuals will behave in a way *almost* consistent with what normative economics would predict. That is, the amount of certain wealth that makes the individual indifferent to that offer or the gamble will be about equal to the probability of winning the gamble. So, for example, if we offer a goals-based investor a 30% probability of winning $1, we will have to offer a certain $0.29 to make her indifferent to the choices. Normative economics would expect that we would have to offer a certain $0.30—not too different a result.

Again, the point here is not to argue that individuals are weighting probabilities objectively.[11] Rather, this demonstrates the robustness of the goals-based utility model, but, more importantly, calls into question the behavioral-normative divide in economics. Remember, if we accept the

[11]Much to my chagrin, Allais's paradox cannot be solved, even in a goals-based paradigm, unless investors weigh probabilities subjectively. This, of course, has implications for the rest of our goals-based framework, but all of that is beyond the scope of this discussion. Again, it is a wonderful topic for future research!

axioms of goals-based utility theory as rational, then behavior that is consistent with the model is rational. Individuals may not behave as irrationally as we have previously believed! For offers with small money stakes among individuals with few long-term financial goals (like college students on whom many of these experiments were conducted, for example), these experiments validate how goals-based investors react to gambles when aspirational goals are at stake. When individuals have real money and real goals on the line we can expect that they will behave much differently, and that behavior is much more in-line with what normative economics would expect.

On the downside, half of Tversky and Kahneman's cumulative prospect theory is a probability weighting function. If we call that component into question, it does lead to questions about the theory as a whole—a theory cited by over 17,000 papers and which earned Daniel Kahneman a Nobel Prize in Economics. I would not be so bold to assert that these conclusions topple so widely accepted a theory. Yet, at a minimum, it seems to call for further exploration by researchers.

Yet again, goals-based utility theory may offer a bridge between normative and behavioral economics—a bridge that is being built by others, as well. There is a certain wisdom in the crowd, as we all know, and I have found that people generally operate in their own best interest, even if that is via intuition and nonquantitative methods.

IRRATIONAL PEOPLE, IRRATIONAL MARKETS?

As goals-based investors aggregate, it seems clear that they will have an effect on market pricing. People are not isolated and, hard as it may be to remember these days, markets are comprised of real people. If these people were entering markets not for the fun of it but because they had specific objectives, that would carry some interesting consequences for the pricing mechanism. In this section, I would like to explore some interesting outcomes of market pricing if people are behaving in ways consistent with goals-based utility theory.

As we have explored, investors will seek to maximize the probability of attaining a goal. However, when considering something like pricing dynamics, it may be easier to simply analyze a line of indifference—that is, the points at which utility stays the same if we vary the other inputs. We assume that investors enter capital markets attempting to get a probability of goal achievement of *at least* α, but greater than α is obviously preferred.

This treats the probability of goal achievement as a risk-aversion metric, which is essentially what it is. So, we can set up our form like this:

$$v(A)\alpha = v(A)\phi(w, W, t),$$

where α is the minimum probability our investor is willing to accept to achieve the goal, w is the initial amount of wealth dedicated to the goal, W is the amount of wealth required to achieve the goal, and t is the time horizon within which the goal must be accomplished. Using the logistic cumulative distribution function, our equation becomes

$$\alpha = 1 - \frac{1}{1 + \exp\left(-\frac{\left(\frac{W}{w}\right)^{\frac{1}{t}} - 1 - m}{s}\right)}.$$

From here, we can solve for m, or the minimum acceptable return, given some acceptable level of α:

$$m \geq \left(\frac{W}{w}\right)^{\frac{1}{t}} - 1 + s\ln\left(\frac{1}{1-\alpha} - 1\right).$$

In other words, an investor will enter capital markets attempting to get at least m, but willing to take more m if it is offered. Naturally, this minimum acceptable return is driven by all of the goal variables relevant to the investor—how much money she has dedicated to the goal, how long until the goal is to be funded, how volatile the asset is, and the minimum acceptable probability of achievement.

With this rough model in mind, consider Figure 13.5 as representative of a very simple market, where we have three potential investors, A, B, and C. Each has different inputs to their minimum acceptable return equation, hence, as the expected volatility of the asset moves higher (on the horizontal axis), we find that each investor has a shifting minimum level of return—again, this is to maintain their minimum acceptable probability of goal achievement, α. To illustrate the point, let us further suppose that all investors agree on the fundamentals of the security: that it will deliver volatility of s in the future. What we find is that investor A requires the highest return to

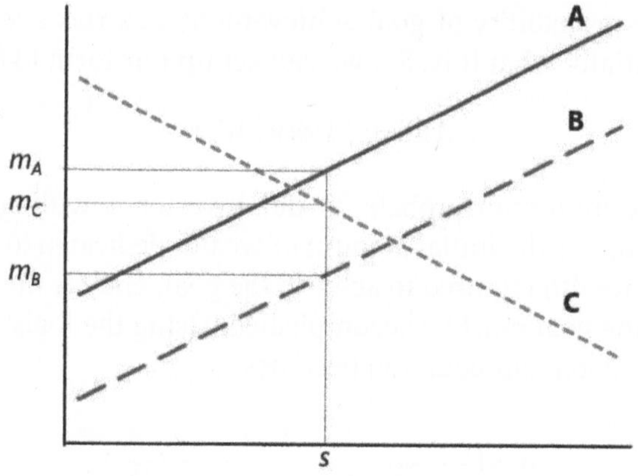

FIGURE 13.5 A Simple "Market" of Goals-Based Investors

invest in this security, represented by m_A. Investor C requires the second-highest return, m_C, and investor B requires the lowest return, m_B.

Pressing this a step further. If we think of price as some function of this minimum acceptable return, perhaps most simply as its inverse, $1 / m$, then we can conclude that *even though every investor in the market may agree on the fundamentals of a security, they are each willing to pay an entirely different price!*

Take the difference between investor A and investor B. Both require a minimum 65% chance of success, and they both need \$1 in 10 years. However, investor B has more current wealth than investor A (\$0.75 vs. \$0.55). This one change means that investor B is willing to pay a higher price (accept a lower return) than investor A for the same security. Again, it is not that A and B disagree on the behavior of the investment—they both agree that it will carry volatility of s. Rather, they simply have different *needs*, and this leads to disparate pricing.

Investor C is, of course, an oddity. C is willing to accept lower returns for *higher* volatility, counter to traditional theories of risk. Investor C, however, is acting perfectly rationally for an aspirational investor, as we have discussed. Investor C has a mere \$0.22 dedicated to a \$1.00 goal needed in 12 years (a required return of 13.4%). Because investor C has a minimum probability of achievement of 35%, this leads to a willingness to accept lower returns for higher volatility (of course, she would be willing to accept a higher return, were it offered).

If, then, all investors agreed that this portfolio were to yield s volatility in the coming period, we should find that investor B will pay the highest price for it. Investors A and C will sell to B until B's liquidity is exhausted. Recall from above that investor B has $0.75 of liquidity dedicated to the goal, which is more than either investor A or investor C individually, but it is not more than A and C taken together. Even so, we should expect investor B to dominate the pricing in our simple market since she has the most liquidity. Once B's liquidity is exhausted, we would see the investment's price drop to the price investor C is willing to pay, and investor A will sell to investor C until investor A has no inventory (or C's liquidity is exhausted).

An interesting wrinkle: why would any investor sell in this simple market? If A sells to B, for example, that would leave A with no investment at all, and with a lower probability of goal achievement than if she held *some* investment. It is here that the simplicity of the illustration breaks down. In truth, every investor would be running this process for every investment in the marketplace and selling one investment very likely means purchasing another with that new liquidity. What's more, almost never will investors exactly agree on the fundamentals of a security, so not only are investors bidding their needs in to the price, but also their view of the fundamentals. In other words, if there is no alternative to the existing investment, then the existing investment will not be sold unless the price is even higher—a dynamic market veterans know all too well.

My ultimate point here is not to build a complete and accurate model of market pricing dynamics. Rather, my point here is that markets price *more* than just security fundamentals, they price investor needs, too. For example, if you give investors more cash today, they become willing to pay a higher price *for the exact same fundamentals*. This could be why the global coordinated quantitative easing program seen through 2020 and 2021 has lifted the valuation metrics of markets (expanded P/E ratios, for example). Investments may be overpriced from an historical fundamentals perspective, but not necessarily from a liquidity perspective. By printing cash and pushing it into the hands of investors, prices rose even without a shift in business fundamentals—much to the consternation of value investors. Of course, we should expect the opposite to be true. As excess cash gets drained from the pockets of investors, they become less willing to pay higher prices and—all else equal—valuation metrics should shrink.

It cannot be enough, then, to simply analyze the fundamentals of a given security or portfolio. The marketplace of that security's investors must also be considered. Though we cannot expect to know every goals-based variable for every investor, we should be able to make some broad-brush assumptions. We should expect to find some securities dominated by aspirational-type investors, variance-seeking and likely quite active. For other securities, we should find an investment marketplace dominated by long-term, variance-averse investors who are seeking steady returns given their already-stable financial positions. In both cases, we could do well to model the effects of changing security fundamentals, as well as changing *investor* variables, at least to the extent we can estimate them.

In his book *Fractal Market Analysis*, Edgar Peters comes to a very similar model of the marketplace:

> *Take a typical day trader who has in investment horizon of five minutes and is currently long in the market. The average five-minute price change in 1992 was –0.000284%, with a standard deviation of 0.05976%. If, for technical reasons, a six standard deviation drop occurred for a five-minute horizon, or 0.359 percent, our day trader could be wiped out if the fall continued. However, an institutional trader—a pension fund for example—with a weekly trading horizon, would probably consider that drop a buying opportunity because weekly returns over the past ten years have averaged 0.22 percent with a standard deviation of 2.37 percent. In addition, the technical drop has not changed the outlook of the weekly trader, who looks at either longer technical or fundamental information. Thus, the day trader's six-sigma event is a 0.15-sigma event to the weekly trader, or no big deal. The weekly trader steps in, buys, and creates liquidity. . . .*
>
> *Thus, the source of liquidity is investors with different investment horizons, different information sets, and consequently, different concepts of "fair price."*[12]

It is this last point that I have attempted to demonstrate in this section. Every investor has a different "fair price." In fact, an investor may not even agree with herself on "fair price" across her accounts. For one goal, *x* may well be fair, but for another goal *x* may be far too low a price!

[12]Edgar Peters, *Fractal Market Analysis: Applying Chaos Theory to Investment and Economics* (New York: John Wiley & Sons, 1994), 42–43.

Peters makes another profound and important point:

> *If all information had the same impact on all investors, there would be no liquidity. When they received information, all investors would be executing the same trade, trying to get the same price.*

It is *because* fair price is dependent on so many individual variables that we see the volume of shares traded that we do! If fair price were readily agreed on in perfectly rational markets, trading would cease and markets would not be so liquid.

Indeed, the marketplace of goals-based investors looks very fractal, supporting many of Peters's arguments. Within the marketplace, you have tens of thousands of individual security markets. These security markets have groups of individuals, each with similar characteristics, pushing this way and that (think of retired individuals who are trading with those nearing retirement, those who are in their early 40s, and those who just started saving). Each demography has its own general fair price, based on their shared variables. But within each demographic group, you also have sub demographics, and still further subdivisions of *those* groups. Each of those subgroups has its own approximation of fair price. Finally, we have the individual, who is herself divided with respect to pricing across each account, as each goal will have a separate fair price for a security. All of that sounds quite fractal to me.

Goals-based portfolio theory, then, may better explain some pricing anomalies, as well as offer market practitioners some insight on how large-scale forces might influence prices in the aggregate. While it is beyond the scope of this discussion, goals-based portfolio theory may yield interesting fruit in not just macroeconomic theory, but also market microstructure theory. There is plenty of work yet to be done.

CHAPTER 14

The Future Structure of Wealth Management Firms

"Standing against the march of history might be a better solution,
but only until history marches all over those who have resisted its progress."

—*Jean LP Brunel*

Jean Brunel once quipped that goals-based investing really does change everything.[1] Now that we have covered the nuts-and-bolts of goals-based portfolio theory, it should be clear how right he was! The whole approach of goals-based investing changes both the structure and nature of client interactions, as well as the actual management of the investment portfolio. As should now be obvious, the math is fundamentally different for goals-based investors. Another keen observation made by Brunel is that goals-based investing blurs the line between financial planner and investment manager.[2]

---

[1]J. Brunel, *Goals-Based Wealth Management* (Hoboken, NJ: John Wiley & Sons, 2015).

[2]J. Brunel, "Extending the Goals-Based Framework to Comprise Both Investment and Financial Planning," *Journal of Wealth Management*, 24, no. 4 (2020): 1–16. DOI: https://doi.org/10.3905/jwm.2019.1.096.

Investment portfolios must be informed by goals, and goals, in turn, are influenced by the choice of investments.

Unfortunately, the current structure of wealth management firms is not conducive to delivering true goals-based solutions. While financial planning has now long been part of most wealth management practices, to execute the plan, firms build model portfolios—large boxes that can only ever approximate client needs. Of course, to date this has been the only way to scale a practice. It is not possible to run thousands of different portfolios, each with a separate objective and investment universe without a considerable investment of man-hours. Goals-based portfolio theory brings a need for better plan implementation. Those differences between account objectives and the differences between clients, though ignored by monolithic model portfolios, are fundamental to the proper execution of a goals-based plan.

Therefore, we need to update the structure and skill set of the wealth management firm.

To best understand the needed changes, we need to first understand the client experience. Goals-based investing puts the client at the absolute center of everything we do, so to properly understand the changes needed it is best to first understand our center of gravity. Let's walk through the client experience from the point of first contact to the accomplishment of a goal.

A prospective client comes to the firm. Clients, of course, do not come to an advisor looking for goals; they have plenty of those. Clients come to the advisor looking for ways to accomplish their goals. The first meeting, in addition to the usual rapport-building, should be focused on understanding the panoply of goals: their relative importance, time horizons, funding requirements, and all else that has been discussed in this book so far. A clear understanding of the client's current financial picture is also important. *As a general rule, investment recommendations have no place being discussed in a first meeting.* Certainly prospective clients will want some understanding of the firm's opinions of markets and investment solutions offering, and some brief discussion on the firm's points of difference is all sensible. But there is no way for an advisor to properly know what investment solutions are needed by the client without first doing the work of financial planning. Investments, in a goals-based framework, are simply tools to get a job done. How can we reach for the correct tool when we do not yet know what job needs doing?

After the initial discussion, the advisor takes the client's data and builds a financial plan. Of course, the nature of the client and the listed goals will determine how detailed this financial plan needs to be (I am not fond of the 127-page financial plan, simpler is better in my view). Much of the plan is calculating the relative value of goals, calculating the allocation of current wealth and future savings across goals, the determination of optimal investment allocations for each subaccount, the determination of taxes on the various account types, and so on. The role of the financial planner is to map the plan of attack—it is, perhaps, the most important role in the firm. Errors at this stage will compound into later stages, becoming magnified and possibly catastrophic to the client. Financial planning done well is of paramount importance.

Our prospective client is called back for a second meeting in which the financial plan is presented and discussed. Central focus should be on the achievement probabilities of goals, and discussion of the investment strategy and market philosophy is now warranted. A discussion of the biggest risks threatening the plan should also be discussed, and this is much more than investment risk. If the plan is fragile with respect to the client's human capital inputs, or to potential inheritance, these points need to be discussed. Risk allayment may be warranted, but only if it increases achievement probability, rather than decreasing it.

Assuming the client agrees to proceed, the plan is implemented by the investment strategy team.

Proper plan monitoring is important, too. Currently, most firms only report investment performance relative to some benchmark. But a benchmark is not our client's objective! Rather, we have some return that must be achieved to progress toward a goal. It would be considerably more sensible to report progress toward the goal, relative to what was originally forecast. Are we ahead of schedule or behind? If behind, why are we behind? Was this a forecasting error at the financial planning stage (i.e. we overestimated what was possible), was it a bad but transient market environment, or was it simply a poor job by the investment management team? Understanding what is wrong (and how to correct it) begins with proper, goals-based, reporting, and goals-based reporting is different from the current industry standard.

As mentioned, goals-based reporting represents a move away from a focus on reporting performance relative to a benchmark and a move toward reporting performance relative to the client's goals. This is certainly more complicated, as it requires the reporting system to track the holdings and performance of each goal's subaccount, even if those subaccounts are aggregated in practice. It also requires a reporting system to track the projected funding of each goal for each client at any given time, perhaps with some margins of error, and that means synthesizing disparate pieces of information from the client's financial plan and the firm's investment view. How much liberty a firm should have in the presentation of such information is an open question, a question on which regulators will, no doubt, form an opinion.

None of this to say that reporting benchmarks carry no utility. Benchmarking is important as it easily shows the market opportunity of a given period. Given the client's personal restrictions, expecting something other than the opportunity set offered by the marketplace is unreasonable, and that should always be part of the conversation. Similarly, benchmarking can help asset managers identify sources of weakness. If progress toward a goal was hampered by a poor opportunity set (i.e. a bad market), some conversation around protecting hard-won gains is reasonable, but perhaps not urgent. If, however, progress toward a goal was hampered by poor choices amidst a good opportunity set, the conversation (and solution) is much more pressing. In both cases, clients should be engaged in an honest discussion that is tailored to their level of sophistication—hence the need for more than simple performance-relative-to-a-benchmark reports.

Finally, if we have done our job correctly, our client attains her goal!

Now, I laughably oversimplified a step a few paragraphs ago. When I said, "The plan is implemented by the investment strategy team," I skipped quite a lot. From the perspective of the client, other than the nature of the conversation and the nature of ongoing reports, there is little difference between the current service model and the goals-based service model. Sorry to say that this is where the similarities end. Everything about the *execution* of a goals-based approach is different. Pretty much everything behind the advisor-client interaction has to change in the wealth management firm of the future.

First, firms will need a two-part technology solution to execute thousands of individual client plans at scale. Part A of the technology solution will be a firm-level algorithm that houses the firm's view and philosophy of markets. If the firm, for example, believes value stocks and fundamental analysis are best for clients, the firm-level algorithm will be responsible for intaking market data and building capital market expectations across the firm's investment universe. The automated component of this is important (though possibly not the only solution), because it is likely that each client—and possibly each client account—has a separate investment universe. Some accounts will benefit from dividend payments, while more tax sensitive accounts might avoid such forced taxable events, just to name one example. The point is, the firm's capital market expectations will need to be more granular than stocks, bonds, and commodities. Capital market expectations will need to include enough to enable the level of customization demanded by the goals-based approach, likely a focus less on specific securities and more a focus on the rules that define the expectations of any security. The chief investment officer will be mainly responsible for overseeing the firm's master algorithm, though the role of "chief communicator" will maintain its importance.

ESG constraints are another aspect of the investment universe for which me must account. Every client has an individualized portfolio of ESG constraints. Up to now, the industry has focused on defining these constraints for clients, then "selling" investors on the value of that particular view. I see the future as clients defining it for themselves, and investment advisors implementing that customization. Ethical/ESG/impact mandates are as unique as the individuals who value them. What may be important to me may not be to a client, and vice versa.

This is one of the most exciting aspects of goals-based investment tools, especially when implemented at the individual level rather than the model portfolio level. When we, as an industry, build and give individuals the tools to achieve both their financial goals and ethical goals through capital markets, then security prices will reflect not just all fundamental economic information about a company but all ethical information about a company as well. This could be capitalism's greatest moment. That will be when we can look at market prices and agree that they are an accurate mirror of who we are as a society. We may not like everything we see in the mirror, of course, but we could at least agree that it is an accurate reflection. But such a world only appears with individualized customization, and, likely more difficult, ecumenicity toward client ethical views that may challenge our own.

Such portfolio customization requires investment teams to maintain coverage on a wide range of securities. It seems unlikely to me that an investment team of reasonable size could maintain a database of all possible investment solutions by hand, and an investment universe that is too small would not deliver the level of customization that would be required across a whole book of accounts. Therefore, I see investment teams of the future focused on building the rules and technology systems that themselves build capital market expectations for thousands of possible investments, which is a significant shift in thinking.

Part B of this technology solution will be the account-level algorithms. These algorithms will interface with the firm-wide algo and implement each account's financial plan. They will, of course, take account of the tax consequences of trades, dividends, interest payments, along with the client's ethical constraints and financial goals. While at first they may not interface with markets directly, it is likely that they will come to fully trade accounts—minute by minute aligning the firm's market view and the client's financial plan with ongoing market developments.

Clearly, the maintenance of these systems will be the joint effort of investment and technology teams. Investment teams will be responsible for developing the firm's market philosophy and particular view, while the technology team will be responsible for designing and maintaining these systems. This means a team of coders, IT, and system architects—unfamiliar territory for investment advisors!

The role of the portfolio manager will evolve, as will the needed skill set. The PM role will become about translating the financial plan into code for the firm's systems to execute—overseeing the client-level algorithms to which she is assigned. While I could see PMs themselves coding the algorithms using common components, more than likely the technology team will build modular systems with specialized graphical interfaces, allowing PMs to focus on constructing and translating the investment policy statement rather than on the nuts and bolts of the code. Keeping PMs away from the code base of the firm has the added advantages of reducing the risk of incorrect implementation as well as reducing the risk of fraud. However, such a system comes with the cost of added development time and increased monetary costs.

The role of the compliance team will have to shift, as well. With tens of thousands of lines of code running considerable sums of money, compliance teams will need to ensure that the architects of these systems (the technology and investment teams) are not burying millisecond frauds amongst legitimate code. It will also fall to compliance teams to answer regulators' questions. No doubt that will be a significant undertaking—especially as this structure will be just as new to regulators as it is to practitioners. All of this in addition to the already traditional role compliance teams play in overseeing advisors.

Regulators will need to adapt, as well. The expectation that every trade can be reviewed and explained may be too much. The focus will need to shift toward actual client experience with the firm's technology (i.e. is it doing what we said it would do?). There is also the move away from risk-tolerance questionnaires (which are entirely superfluous in the goals-based framework), and the needs of $r > \mu$ portfolios. Exactly how regulators will feel about those dramatic shifts remains to be seen. Likely the first focus for regulators will be ensuring there are no frauds built into the firm's code base. Two to three lines of code are all it would take to create a front-running scheme in an inattentive firm's algorithms. Finding malicious code amongst tens of thousands of lines is a problem yet to be solved.

Finally, a technology team will need to keep this whole system friction-free. At the scale of a firm, the ongoing and growing computing needs—in

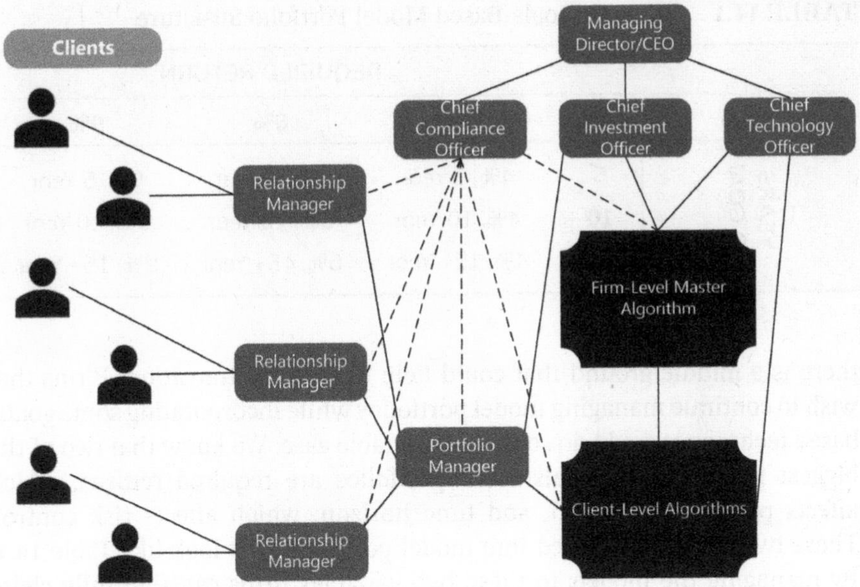

FIGURE 14.1 Possible Future Org Chart

addition to the traditional IT service—will need to grow and develop. Not to mention, a firm will need to keep pace with the ongoing shifts in enterprise-level technology architecture. It also seems likely that the technology team will aid the compliance team in finding and protecting the code base from fraud. Much research in this field is needed (does this field even exist yet?). Indeed, it is my strong belief that we are entering an age when Nobel laureates in economics will be computer scientists by trade.

Behind the client-advisor interaction the wealth management firm of the future will need to look more like a technology firm than a traditional wealth management shop, as Figure 14.1 demonstrates. The transition to this adjusted set up is likely to take decades, but Luddite firms are sure to be left behind. Not only will clients come to expect a fully customized solution, but it is also how firms will stave-off the "feepocalypse" that has long been foretold. I believe that people will pay for legitimately better solutions. In the end, the theory, execution, skill sets, and firm structure should all coalesce around one objective: delivering the best solution to the client. With a dogged focus on that, firms will do no less than thrive.

Of course, many firms will be loath to implement such changes. The cost alone could be considerable. Technologists do not come cheap and the prospect of retooling the skill set of an entire firm is daunting, to be sure. But

TABLE 14.1 Example Goals-Based Model Portfolio Structure

		REQUIRED RETURN		
		4%	6%	9%
YEARS TO GOAL	5	4%, 5 Year	6%, 5 Year	9%, 5 Year
	10	4%, 10 Year	6%, 10 Year	9%, 10 Year
	15+	4%, 15+ Year	6%, 15+ Year	9%, 15+ Year

there is a middle ground that could help to ease the transition. Firms that wish to continue managing model portfolios while incorporating some goals-based techniques could do so with reasonable ease. We know that two of the biggest influences on goals-based portfolios are required returns, which affects portfolio allocation, and time horizon, which affects risk control. These two can be combined into model portfolios that look like Table 14.1. By managing the models to these two variables firms can rightfully claim they are incorporating goals-based concerns, and clients can rest assured that their portfolio is, at a minimum, managed with allocations and risk controls that maximize the probability of achieving their financial goals.

In this approach, the firm builds capital market expectations and, rather than infuse individual client portfolios with those expectations, the firm simply optimizes asset allocations based on a representative goal. The 6%, 10-year portfolio, for example, would be optimized to deliver a 6% annualized return over a period of 10 years. The practitioner would need to update the client's model assignment each year to ensure the goal the allocation remains appropriate—what begins as a 10-year goal becomes a 7-year goal after 3 years have passed. The other advantage to this approach is that the portfolios could be blended to solve for those years that are not represented (the 6%, 10-year portfolio could be blended with the 6%, 5-year portfolio to yield a 6%, 7-year portfolio, for example).[3]

Clearly, this comes with a considerable loss of customization, both with regards to impact/ESG concerns as well as with regard to taxes. A

[3]Blending goals-based portfolios like this brings up a whole separate theoretical issue, one that I do not wish to tackle here. In short, the portfolios can be blended horizontally or vertically, but not diagonally, though the validity of this will vary greatly with the firm's view of markets and methods for risk control. Firms interested in the approach can experiment themselves and find the best way to blend goals-based model portfolios.

"representative client" would have to serve to estimate tax impacts of portfolio decisions, which is certainly not ideal. This also leaves open the question of whether highly appreciated transferred-in positions should be sold or blended. Even with these questions, clients would still be better served by this middle ground than by the existing low-variance to high-variance model structure that carries no goals-based concerns whatsoever.

Why not simply use a glide-path fund? The central reason is that they are not allocated with any regard whatsoever to a required return. Rather than assume some goal needs to be accomplished, they simply grow more conservative in the allocation over time—whether that is in the best interest of the client's goal or not. That is, to me, like buying a smaller horse as you get older so that it doesn't hurt as much when it kicks. While that may be safer day-to-day, a smaller horse also does considerably less work. For investors who need to accomplish goals, a portfolio that delivers less and less return as time passes is likely to make it harder to achieve goals, not easier.[4] Glide-path portfolios are built on a *psychological* sense of safety, rather than a rational sense of goal achievement. To my mind, then, they have no real place in a goals-based portfolio.

Most firms will need to change *something* about their current approach. Technology, skill sets, organizational charts, asset allocation engines, even marketing should shift to align with a goals-based methodology. In my view, firms that fail to make this transition will be swept away by those who do. Clients intuitively understand when an approach is better for them, even if they may not understand all the technicalities of why. Even absent full customization, there are some basic changes to the model portfolio structure that would better serve clients. It is my genuine belief that people will pay for real value. Goals-based investing is about delivering real value to real people in the real world. For their own sake, firms would do well to get on board sooner rather than later!

Those that do not are very likely to be left behind.

[4]This intuition was backed up by a rigorous quantitative analysis, showing that as investors withdraw funds through retirement, they may need to grow more aggressive in their portfolio allocations rather than less. See S. R. Das, D. Ostrov, A. Casanova, A. Radhakrishnan, and D. Srivastav, "Combining Investment and Tax Strategies for Optimizing Lifetime Solvency under Uncertain Returns and Mortality," *Journal of Risk and Financial Management* 14, no. 285 (2021): 1–25. DOI: `https://doi.org/10.3390/jrfm14070285`.

Some Final Thoughts

As I hope you will now agree, goals-based investing really is different. It is much, much more than a marketing buzzword. Dare I say it has become its own branch of portfolio theory.

The central point of goals-based investing is to align the math with what it is investors are actually trying to achieve. Modern portfolio theory, when invented, did not have the benefits of modern computing power. Thus, simplifying assumptions had to be made to make the framework manageable. Markowitz himself discussed these necessary shortcuts once, saying that as long as portfolio returns did not fall "too far" into the extremes "too often," then the management of portfolio mean and variance was an appropriate proxy.[1] However, with modern computing power, we might as well discard the simplifying assumptions (some of which are so absurd as to be laughable) and build the model again.

It is simply not possible for investors, of any stripe, to leverage a portfolio without limit or cost. Most investors are also bound in their ability to sell securities short, by both account type and regulation. These two assumptions, central to modern portfolio theory, have been widely critiqued, of course, but continue to persist. My estimation is that they persist because there has been no realistic alternative. Goals-based portfolio theory may well be that alternative—dispensing with many of the absurd assumptions and focusing on how real investors can achieve real goals using real markets.

That is not to say that goals-based portfolio theory does not make its own simplifying assumptions. The use of a return distribution, even if not Gaussian, is itself a simplifying assumption. Furthermore, many investor goals are not so easily quantified. Indeed, we must always remember that the map is not reality. Practitioner intuition, insight, and wisdom, properly cultivated, are worth the fees they earn in the marketplace. No one should blindly follow a model into oblivion. That said, all else equal, better models generally

[1]H. Markowitz, "Portfolio Theory: As I Still See It," *Annual Review of Financial Economics* 2 (2010): 1–23.

produce better results. The idea of this book is not to replace practitioner insight, but to augment it with better tools. Attentive craftsmen can build finer products with finer tools; it is the objective of this book to present finer tools to attentive craftsmen.

Contrary to the traditional approach in the financial industry, which has largely focused on building products and convincing investors to buy those products, goals-based investing starts with the investor. The investor is at the center of everything that comes next. Understanding, first and foremost, an investor's needs, wants, wishes, and dreams, as well as her financial picture, human capital, ESG and impact objectives, and tax situation, is central to goals-based investing. Only once we are armed with a detailed understanding of the investor can we enter financial markets looking for the tools to help accomplish those objectives. After all, that is what investments are: they are simply tools to get a job done. Giving our investors the best screwdriver in the world does nothing for them if they need a hammer.

Goals-based portfolio theory, then, is really about better understanding *people*. Understand real people in the real world, and that effort will surely pay dividends in more places than just investing. I have seen the dynamics described here present in negotiations around the sale of small businesses, for example. While the buyer often (rightly) focuses on the fundamentals of the business—a conversation centered around the numbers—the seller is more concerned with maintaining her lifestyle and achieving her goals post-sale. Representatives of the buyer would do well to begin negotiations with an understanding of what it is the owner wants to accomplish by selling the business. At least then the buyer could understand if a fair deal, based on the numbers, is an acceptable deal to the seller.

Understanding the broader opportunity set offered by capital markets is equally important. If investments are tools to accomplish objectives, we cannot accomplish anything if we have no toolbox to draw from. A clear and accurate view of capital markets is a perquisite to operation in the goals-based paradigm, but that comes as no surprise to anyone in the industry. The challenge, especially for firms attempting to deliver these solutions at scale, is to marry the two. On the one hand, emotional intelligence is required to interact with clients and understand their goals. On the other hand, acute quantitative skills are required to develop and maintain a repeatable investment process that actually delivers value to clients. This marriage of skill sets is no small feat. Doing it right is very, very difficult. No doubt this is why wealth management commands such high pay, and why, one could argue, the industry's recent vacation from their value-add has created downward fee pressure across the industry.

Goals-based solutions require, as mentioned, a deep understanding of the individual. Also, goals-based solutions require hyper-customized portfolio management. At the moment, this capability does not exist in the industry—a distinct market opportunity for our technology partners. The quantitative work can barely be done by hand for one portfolio, much less a whole book of portfolios. Our only hope of scale is through the leverage of technology.

In addition to the data management load the goals-based approach presents, the calculation of multiperiod portfolio optimization is a technology feat all its own. Once multiperiod capital market expectations are built, incorporating them into a portfolio optimization structure involves sampling multiple portfolio distributions—all of which are in flux across various weight trials—and returning a final, "averaged" distribution. While the computational burden is heavy, the results are worth it. Goals-based investors, especially those nearing a funding requirement, stand to garner significant benefits from their portfolio manager—assuming these forecasts are accurate enough, of course.

The goals-based framework can be further applied to portfolio hedges. All of the research on portfolio hedging of which I am aware has focused on pricing, the market component (the "big world"). Yet, insights derived from the goals-based framework demonstrate that the big world is only half the picture. Yes, the probability of a bad year is an important input into the fair-value cost to hedge calculation. But equally important are the investor's goal variables—how much money is available now, how much is needed, and in how many years. As much as the market view, the individual informs the calculation of hedging costs. What's more, each individual may not agree on fair values across her panoply of goals! Each goal will have a different fair value cost to hedge, even given the same market view, an echo of the results of our "market of goals-based investors" thought experiment from Chapter 13.

We find a similar result when we consider a marketplace of investors who interact with capital markets attempting to attain some minimum probability of goal achievement. Each investor has a different fair-value price, even though all investors may agree on the fundamentals of a security! This difference in pricing has nothing at all to do with behavioral biases; rather, in a goals-based context all of these investors are behaving perfectly rationally from the perspective of their goal achievement. A surprising result to traditional economics, but not to practitioners. As most practitioners well know, a security's price action is heavily influenced by the types of investors who trade it. Rather than lean on heuristics and ad hoc explanations, goals-based portfolio theory offers to help resolve some of these apparent conflicts between normative and behavioral economics.

Other apparent paradoxes can be resolved using the lens of goals-based investing, as well. The simultaneous purchase of lottery tickets and insurance is one telling example. As we have seen, investors may be variance-averse for goals lower on the Maslow-Brunel pyramid, but variance-seeking for more aspirational goals higher up the pyramid. Insurance purchases are perfectly rational for goals where extreme losses destroy needs like shelter, food, or other basic expenses. Lottery tickets, by contrast, are perfectly rational when the traditional investment space does not offer solutions with sufficient return to attain an objective. In that case, increasing the dispersion of outcomes is the rational approach. Again, this comes contrary to traditional portfolio theory.

And it comes with some serious questions. Namely, what is prudent investing when the objective is to increase the volatility of outcomes, rather than decrease it? I admit to being at a loss for a clear answer here. We explored some preliminary ideas, but my intent was more to prompt conversation than to offer definitive answers. A whole lot of work needs to be done before practitioners should feel comfortable building and maintaining portfolio objectives of high volatility and low potential return. At the moment, I consider that aspect of goals-based portfolio theory firmly theoretical. Even so, I cannot deny the conclusions of the logic and math. My genuine hope is that a theory for high-variance portfolio management gets worked out in the near future, though I suspect the answer is already lurking among practitioners and investors. I have come to respect the folk wisdom of markets, even more so with the development of a theory vindicating a considerable chunk of investor behavior previously considered irrational.

Taxes, a thorn in the side of investors, prompted much of the early research on the topic of investing by real people in the real world. Indeed, we can partly thank the burden of taxes for the development of these ideas. When it comes to taxes, we find that they are but one cost among several, including commissions, bid-ask spreads, and other costs of ownership (like internal fund fees and trading costs). They should be taken into account, and models that fail to do so are blatantly deficient. Unfortunately, taxes are as personalized as everything else about an individual—each client will have a different tax situation and legacy tax status for their portfolio, all of which must be considered to do a proper job. Transaction costs will heavily influence portfolio implementation, and that means implementation must be individuated, even if capital market expectations are common across accounts. Again, this is an argument for our technology partners to build solutions that can marry the myriad individual client needs with the firm's philosophy of markets.

Naturally, reporting all of this in a meaningful way to a client is no small feat. Here I see ample room for improvement. So many metrics in common use today have little to no meaning to goals-based investors. They are a foreign language. They are nigh meaningless. Replacing those metrics—as meaningful though they may be to a practitioner—with metrics that are valuable to a client seems a perfectly reasonable project. Not easy, of course. Reporting progress toward individuated client goals requires a heavy computational burden across the level of a firm. Even so, the marketing opportunity alone is enormous. Placing portfolio gains and losses in the context of goal achievement probability is an effective way to change the conversation with clients. When clients are unaware of exactly how losses affect portfolio achievement, they tend to feel that *all* losses are too much. By presenting portfolio movements, especially losses, alongside the change in achievement probability, over time our clients can feel more secure in their ability to achieve their goals, and, by extension, more confidence in our skill as portfolio managers.

Of course, many of the greatest risks to long-term wealth have nothing at all to do with portfolio losses; they have to do with more human risks. How families structure, manage, and pass down businesses is a concern, not just for them, but for all employees in the business. Everyone operating in society has a stake as well, as family businesses make up some 45 percent of the US economy. Getting transitions across generations right is a very big topic. Among the most pressing risks are how the business should be operated, family dynamics, proper governance, and training subsequent generations on how to be effective shareholders. Very often, these are the greatest risks to wealth, by far. Unfortunately, these are also the most difficult to get right, and the least quantifiable. There is no equation for the management of family dynamics and effective shareholding. More than anything, these subjects require family members who are engaged, responsible, and intellectually humble, not to mention advisors who are perceptive and respectfully honest.

Investors often seek to offset other risks, as well. Very specific risks, such as the risk of car accidents, the risks of medical care, and the risks of losing a family home, all call for insurance. In addition to these very specific risks, people are willing to pay to offset much less specific risks, like "not outliving my money." Fuzzier risks are a challenge to insurance companies, portfolio managers, and investors alike. Exactly which risks are investors wanting to offset? Little research has been done, and considerably more is needed, on how individuals and families should approach the problem of purchasing the various types of insurance products in the marketplace. It would behoove the industry to move away from clever marketing schemes and toward real solutions directed at real people. Not only would this result in better outcomes for real people, but there is even the potential for customizable insurance products and individuated pricing—both a potential boon to the insurance industry!

In the end, there is plenty of work to do to upgrade our own skill sets and firm structures. The wealth management firm (or family office) of the future will likely look nothing like it looks today. Though robo-advisors may have a different opinion, it is my belief that people want to interact with other people. The client-advisor relationship is likely to maintain its central importance. Everything behind the advisor, however, is likely to look more like a technology company than a traditional wealth management firm. The maintenance and execution of tens of thousands of individual mandates can only be done with the help of technology. Roles, then, must adapt and change. The portfolio manager will need to translate an investor's needs into code. That code must marry with the firm's philosophy of and outlook on markets. Compliance teams will have to be equipped to monitor and report on this new structure, and C-level executives will be responsible for building and maintaining the systems—both human and silicon—that make the whole thing possible. While it is a removal of the human touch, and perhaps some of the art, the end result is a service that firms can be proud to sell, and which clients should buy. While the "feepocalypse" has been a long-time coming, I do believe this is the remedy.

Sadly, much of this is still in its infancy. Nothing brings out the procrastinating tendencies like spending money on new people, infrastructure, and technology. Wealth management, like much of the financial industry, is slow to change. I admit, it can be tough to justify large capital expenditures when existing clients seem perfectly happy with the way things are. But they are not happy. The firm that capitalizes on that just-under-the-surface unhappiness stands to gain a significant advantage over their Luddite counterparts. Goals-based investing, despite its benefits to the end-user, has been slow on the uptake across the financial industry, but *there is gold in them thar hills*!

Likely, some of that sluggishness is from regulators, who are themselves firmly entrenched in traditional portfolio theory. Despite the demonstrable futility of risk-tolerance questionnaires, for example, US regulators insist on their use. An advisor who does not properly understand a client's risk tolerance is an advisor operating illegally. For goals-based investors, risk-tolerance questionnaires are superfluous—it is a meaningless variable. But more intuitively, they make little sense. Imagine if you went to your physician because of some ailment that plagues you. Your physician runs a battery of tests, and then describes the problem to you with extreme detail. It is clear you need to undergo a procedure, "but," your physician says, "I cannot give you the procedure." "Why??" you retort incredulously—this is a very serious condition, after all. "Because," she responds, "the pain tolerance questionnaire you filled out at intake indicates you do not have the pain tolerance for it."

As absurd as this sounds, regulators apply the same logic, daily, to firms and their clients (and many firms happily apply this logic to their clients). Investors seek out professionals to help them achieve their goals. While their psychological preference for portfolio volatility should be part of the conversation, it certainly should not be *the* conversation. Besides, the whole conversation is flawed anyway, at least in my view. Investors perceive portfolio volatility in relation to its effect on goal achievement. By adjusting the portfolio math to account for this, the practitioner will have already changed the conversation around a client's tolerance for volatility. In some cases, as we have discussed, volatility is a good thing, and a client will seek it out! At any rate, it is clear that firms are not the only institutions in need of change; regulators are in need of an overhaul in thinking, as well.

As we come to the end of our intellectual journey together, I want to leave you with some resources to keep walking on, should you so choose. There are many wonderful resources on these topics—many of which I am myself indebted to.

An understanding of goals-based portfolio theory is incomplete without having read Brunel's book *Goals-Based Wealth Management*. It is now widely cited, and his framework for client interaction and shifting the firm structure is important to any practitioner looking to apply these ideas. I would also direct interested readers to the work, both past and ongoing, of Sanjiv Das, the William & Janice Terry Professor of Finance at Santa Clara University. His personal website is a compendium of very valuable goals-based publications—many of them open-sourced: `srdas.github.io`. Though much of the goals-based literature is spread across numerous outlets, the *Journal of Wealth Management* is a wonderful collection-point for much of the practitioner-oriented research. For active advisors and researchers, the journal is a great resource for staying up-to-date with the latest research. Not to be too self-serving, but I also maintain a personal blog with many resources and ongoing updates. I have also included several "how-tos" on the site specifically aimed at practitioners who are looking to implement the ideas of goals-based portfolio theory, and I include many other things I find interesting: `www.franklinparker.com`. And as I mentioned at the top of the book, the companion website, with code examples and some other interesting tidbits, is housed at `www.franklinparker.com/gbpt-book/`. Obviously, I would recommend reading many of the papers and books cited in previous chapters.

For investors interested in modeling the non-Gaussian nature of capital market returns, Jondeau, Poon, and Rockinger's *Financial Modeling Under Non-Gaussian Distributions,* is about as deep a dive as anyone might want, though Edgar Peters's *Fractal Market Analysis* may be a better choice for most practitioners. Impact investing is a big topic, and I am certainly no expert on it. However, the *Journal of Impact and ESG Investing* is a burgeoning resource for practitioners interested in building their knowledge. For a deeper understanding of fragility analysis, and even investment management for aspirational portfolios, Taleb's technical works are good, as is his book *Statistical Consequences of Fat Tails* (part of his ongoing "technical incerto" series). Taleb's *Dynamic Hedging* is a classic text on portfolio hedging, and Vineer Bhansali's *Tail Risk Hedging* is highly recommended for goals-based practitioners.

For folks generally interested in the financial planning business more broadly, Michael Kitces maintains a well-run site dedicated to the industry: `www.kitces.com`, and the *Journal of Financial Planning* covers a wide range of topics dedicated to planning and investment management. For a survey on methods for the construction of capital market expectations, Ilmanen's *Expected Returns* is a classic text and highly recommended. Of course, the CFA Institute's resources are among the best in the industry; the CFA Institute's blog, *Enterprising Investor*, the past and ongoing publications from the *Financial Analysts Journal*, and the various publications from the CFA Institute Research Foundation are all very good. For readers interested in deepening their knowledge, there are plenty of resources out there to do so!

In the final analysis, goals-based portfolio theory could be the way forward for an industry struggling to define its value. For clients, as well, struggling with the mismatch between their intuitions and results, and subconsciously struggling with the traditional portfolio theory which currently drives investment decisions. It is good theory, coupled with good practice, that promises to push both forward. While ample technology will be needed to implement at scale, there is plenty of room for a more artful touch.

I am genuinely excited about what is to come. With more practitioners than ever, there are bound to be new problems that need solving, problems for which traditional theory is stale or silent. Coupled with the unparalleled distribution of knowledge, most of it now free to the dedicated learner, I am confident that the next phase of investment orthodoxy will not be handed down from ivory towers but shared among those of us daily in the trenches, each finding and sharing answers to the everyday problems that we all face. Some of these solutions will be jury-rigged constructs, ugly yet viable, but there is a wisdom in such battle-tested solutions. Some of these solutions will be a complete rethink of how investors should operate. In all cases, though, what sticks should be what is best for our clients and the achievement of their goals.

Let's take these next steps together.

Index

Page numbers followed by *f* and *t* refer to figures and tables, respectively.

Y

Z